By Jean Guitton

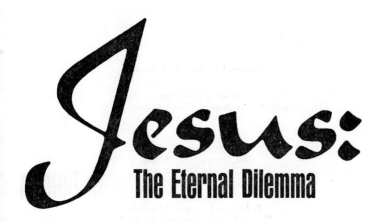

Jesus:
The Eternal Dilemma

alba house · DIVISION OF THE SOCIETY OF ST. PAUL STATEN ISLAND, N.Y. 10314

Translated by Donald M. Antoine

Original title: *Jésus*,
published by Bernard Grasset Editeur, Paris.

Nihil Obstat:
Gall Higgins, O.F.M. Cap.
Censor librorum

Imprimatur:
✠ Terence J. Cooke, D.D., V.G.
New York, N.Y. November 26, 1967

Library of Congress Catalog Card Number: 68-15384

The nihil obstat and imprimatur are official declarations that a book or pamphlet is
free of doctrinal or moral error. No implication is contained therein that those
who have granted the nihil obstat and imprimatur agree with the contents,
opinions or statements expressed.

Edited, designed, printed and bound in the U.S.A. by the Pauline Fathers and
Brothers of the Society of St. Paul at Staten Island, N.Y.

16297

Contents

Part Four: The Two Unknowns, Resurrection and Divinity

end

Preface

THIS book, which treats of an eternal subject, should be like no other. I have not written it simply to add one more scholarly, polemical or mystical book to countless others written about Jesus. I wanted only to arrange my impressions in an orderly way on a subject I have continually reflected upon during the last forty years. In Descartes' time this work would have been called a meditation of the existence of Jesus and, particularly, on the difficulties we in the second half of the twentieth century after Jesus find in believing in him.

Today, when a man absorbed in philosophy and religion has passed middle age, he is probably not going to be learning anything more that is really essential. I believe that it is valid to ask such a man, "What do you think about Jesus? Justify your beliefs in a language I can understand and in a way that does not presuppose your faith."

Saint Peter's First Epistle insists that Christians be always prepared to answer calmly and reverently whoever asks them to clarify their faith. This obligation is still more general, for he who has hope must show why he hopes to everyone who asks him to.

I wrote this book to still the voice of my conscience. And in this book I describe to the educated people of my times what I think about Jesus.

Anatole France was quite right in telling a friend that Jesus was not all he was said to be. We tuck such first gnawing questionings in the back of our minds to deal with them privately. It is better to keep quiet about them in public. It is more sensible to forbid such disturbing questioning, and people should stop arguing with each other since, after all, the most brilliant intellects are at loggerheads over these questions, and it appears unlikely that this diversity of opinion will ever be resolved. Offend no one — this is the rule for good social living. Between believers and unbelievers stands the unwritten law of secrecy and reserve which is best not to break.

Nevertheless, I have never considered it worthy of the human intellect that it should remain silent over the essential questions. A society is truly civilized when it can discuss its most profound questions "calmly and reverently" without rousing any hard feelings.

The question whether Jesus is a mythical being or an historical figure, whether he is truly risen, has confronted every generation since the Gospels were first written. Perhaps no previous generation has so persistently asked these questions to the extent we have. We see this today in the differences between Bultmann and Karl Barth. Tomorrow, surely, because of mass education programs, the well-educated will not be the only ones to raise doubts or make flat denials. The average man will begin with doubt. [1] But I am confident that each critic, in this field as in so many others, will set the foundation stones in place upon which a sturdier conviction will eventually evolve after the difficulties have been cleared away and more refinements made. As Newman said, the uneducated "have never had the temptation to doubt, and

1. Last month, a priest told the life of Jesus to some children in a village in the heart of France. One of them stood up and said, "We know these are only children's stories." This goes to show just how universal the problem we raise in this book is.

never the opportunity to be certain." And long before him, Saint Gregory the Great said, "The long period of Thomas' doubt has been more helpful to me than the instantaneous faith of Mary Magdalen."

*

I have compiled this work for the man who is courageous enough to believe that he can think — and think for himself. Because another's reflections cannot substitute for your own, what can you rely on when you are thinking, but your own reflections?

I have written this book in the first person: Stendhal maintained that this was the shortest way of being thorough.

The one speaking is, from the second part on, an open and free spirit who has not yet solidified his own opinions. He is a man who wishes to make a precise account of everything, to see the pros and cons, and he is careful not to reach any hasty conclusions. He uses common sense in the domain of religion, and it is a calm and refreshing thing. A thoughtful and open-minded man like this makes a methodical inquiry, for he is careful to note those digressions and crossroads which must come before any final decisions.

In keeping with the tradition of the seventeenth-century French authors, I have desired that the order in which the thoughts are set down be enlightening. I follow the path I think most reasonable and, having no disdain for solutions I believe must be rejected, make them as understandable as I can, while preserving their plausibility. I should have taken Lacordaire's phrase for a motto: "I do not seek to convince my opponent of error, but to become one with him in a higher truth."

This is opposed to Montaigne, who made light of inconsistent studies and now and then plied his hand at them without any reasonable outcome. Nor is it Pascal's method. At least not in his famous "Wager" where he calculates the odds, basing them on the notion that the infinite enters into the reckoning of the possible in either winning or losing, and that the finite is then made short work of. I do not want to solve my problems by giving alternatives and, rising above investigation, playing with your hopes and fears as you stand before the nothingness of eternity. Above all, I am raising a problem which will necessarily interest a mind that is willing to resolve the unknowns of historical algebra — a mind which cannot maintain one position without having impartially examined the revealing problem beforehand. I am surprised how difficult it is to arouse curiosity on this point — curiosity is a strong drive, but such a frivolous one.

✿

And now, reader, you are about to begin this book. Accept it as it is written. Know that I have taken great pains to remove from these pages all technical and overly abstract language, needless references, and anything which smacks of one particular school or controversy. I have had to delete several sections so that this book could be read straight off, meditatively, in several days of undisturbed privacy.

I have tried to make myself as clear as possible; I kept silent about what I did not know, separating what I did know from what I did not know and what I know from what I believe. I have enriched my exposition with personal experience, and I always maintain a dialogue with my characters, thereby combining various literary devices, like the Gospels of which I speak, so that the narrative, the dialogue and the teaching are but one message.

Part One

Jesus Today

CHAPTER I

Attack on the Incarnation

HAS anyone ever clearly and reverently raised what I call the "problem of Jesus"? Could anyone have done so before now?

Consider the last twenty centuries of history. The Fathers of the Church, the medieval theologians and the seventeenth-century spiritualist philosophers all thought this problem was solved by faith, guidance, tradition and Christian civilization. Biblical criticism in the eighteenth century was practically non-existent. No one ever raised objections against the central point of Jesus by examining the most important texts upon which the faith establishes her divine premises. Pascal, who had so many presentiments, was much more interested in the *mystery* of Jesus as the Church depicts and gives testimony of him, than in the *problem* of Jesus. Newman's thinking has greatly appealed to me, but he leaves the question of the Christian origins unanswered. He preferred to study the Church's development beginning with the end of the first century when its seeds had begun to take root. He spoke only incidentally of the development of the Jewish people. Yet he implied the period between the two developments, continually pondered over it, but never discussed it critically.

We must wait until the end of the nineteenth century and the diffusion of the themes of German exegesis into public education before we come upon Christian thinkers compelled to examine the foundations of our religion by working with the positive network of facts, texts and history as their opponents did. The great debates at the turn of this century, in the era of modernism, were stopped by the Church's solemn condemnations. The general public believed that this question was far too complex for their untrained minds to solve, and they felt that it was a quarrel between the scholars and theologians. Most people believed it surpassed their competence particularly with regard to those issues which even the authorities could not settle. There is no lack of written evidence. But the individual's difficulty in forming an opinion on this matter resulted in each man going his own way, the believer to live his faith, the unbeliever to further his doubts about the historicity of the evangelical Jesus. And silence once again fell over this primordial question.

However, this is the point where revelation augments reason and where eternity is impregnated into history. If doubt were cast upon this vital link, if it were destroyed or abolished, then all the rest of the religion would crumble to pieces. Where would theology, faith and the sacraments be if there were no Resurrection, if divinity were but a myth? Nothing would have any meaning.

The attempts of certain modern writers, like Bultmann, to preserve the essence of the faith by protecting its mysteries, can satisfy religious souls — but with difficulty. It is amazing what little time Christians actually do set aside to ask this basic question about Jesus in relation to the time spent in devising soaring structures of reasoning built upon this cornerstone! I have observed that the loss of faith usually begins when the shadow of doubt falls over the historical character of the Gospels. When a man loses his childhood certitude on this matter, his convictions begin to founder on all the rest. The autobiographies of Renan, Loisy, and the more recent one of Alfaric, illustrate the law which dictates that everything depending only on one point, crumbles if that point fails.

But how can we achieve a personal, solid and reasonable conviction? There is very little time for it in our fast-paced living. A critical study of the origins of the faith is a difficult and discouraging one. The vast bulk of prerequisite knowledge is enormously varied and difficult to acquire. The specialists, who in the sciences form a body unified by competence, here seem so divided among themselves that there are as many sciences as there are distinct convictions.

Shall we ever find out, then? Does not the future hold surprises of its own? The discoveries along the Dead Sea give the impression that the sands are hiding texts that will force us to re-think Christianity. Then, what is the point of trying to arrive at some kind of opinion? Tomorrow may cast aspersions upon it because of discoveries unforeseeable today. Historical science accumulates documents and compounds its technical skills. At the same time it diminishes that peace of mind essential to inquiry. It takes back with one hand what it offers with the other, while our anxiety mounts. We are in danger of making our age look like those times of rapid change when the survival of some biological species was dubious.

*

What, then, is inevitably going on in those few minds that do think about these basic problems?

The cautious entrust themselves into the hands of the technicians. They feel it is better to leave the problem of Jesus to qualified historians, as though it were really a question of a Pythagoras or a Tutankhamen. Their views are those of an impartial and unbiased man moulded by scientific discipline, indifferent to possible solutions, isolated from all preliminary faith.

We cannot censure this recourse to scholarship, nor even the holding off of this study for a better-informed future. When we consider the human person in his confinement in time, his obligation to make a decision without sufficient study, this attitude becomes quite inhuman. In *all* other branches of historical research, the virtue of waiting and trusting in the experts is the reasonable thing to do. But our problem does not permit us to wait for better conditions: no one waits for a better water pump while a fire rages about him. The disproportion between a lifetime (especially when you consider the very few hours given to reflection) and the time a specialist needs in which to gather some bits of obscure data has become so vast that no one, not even a truly patient man, can hope to bridge it.

It is more common today for people to think that the faith should be free from inquiry into its historical foundations. They expect such an attitude will help give the faith greater certitude and strength and will not enfeeble it.

I see a profound law at work here: when the mind meets with apparently insurmountable difficulties, it looks for a way to overcome them, and the best solution is the one nearest at hand which solves the problem by placing itself above it. In the same way that mystics once looked for short-cuts, I have noticed the tendency today for some religious minds to try to find quick security in a certitude which rises above problems and contradictions. They stand aloof from all the controversies and critical examinations they do not feel qual- ified to handle. I recognize that same yearning we saw in Pascal's "Wager" — the desire to reach out for a practical and immediate assurance without having to climb the tortuous path of reflection. We find ourselves basking in the peace and quiet of Fénelon.

We may excuse our epoch for being enamored by "short- cuts." Why look for Christ in the past through which he blazed like a quick meteor flash? Why seek him in events that time makes so remote? Is it not better to find him outside these questionable and vague horizons — to discover him in the only actual and present moment? Why be so careful to unearth what has been over and done with for

twenty centuries? Let them be! Let the Protestant be satisfied
with the vivid impressions that so often overwhelm the devout
reader of the Gospels. Let the Catholic be satisfied with the
"sacred history" which the Church's teaching reveals, and let
him not try to verify what is impossible to prove anyway.

*

I have also observed that the awareness of the singular
and the historical is disappearing today. Generally speaking,
one may say that Jesus is less interesting than Christ, and
Christ even less than humanity.

A certain rhythm recurs throughout the ages in the
development of thinking. Sometimes we advance from the
particular to the universal, and then we swing back from the
universal to the particular. And sometimes Christian thinking
moves from Jesus to Christ, as in the early days of the Faith,
and then it comes round from Christ to the humanity of
Jesus. Now, it seems to me, as I write, that the upcoming
generation consider Jesus Christ less a particular man who
died under Pontius Pilate than the representative of the
whole of humanity. Even the mystics seem more attracted
by the Mystical Body of Christ than by Christ the individual
present in this man, and still less by Jesus of Nazareth as he
was in himself during his sojourn in his time.

I have taken the following testimony to illustrate what I
mean. It comes from an investigation which appeared in the
review *Christus,* concerning the state of mind of several
young men: "I only find Christ where he lived. When I read
the Gospel, the actual mass of men caught up in their suffering
is made present to me. And then Christ becomes for me the
men I live with." I have also observed the desire to depict
Christ not as a man but as humanity, meaning by humanity
the total man comes forth in time and is vaguely present all
around us, especially in the world of work, *as an already visible
Pleroma.* This Christ-Humanity, lacking a face, definite

features, and with no ties to past history, is appealing. This tendency seems to pass for the highest form of adoration. It also appears to bring several of Saint Paul's views together. But there is a world of difference. Saint Paul referred to the historical Christ whom a people still remembered seeing alive. He summed up humanity around this singular being he had *seen,* whose living eye-witnesses he knew. But today, when the historical visage of Jesus is obliterated by distance and critical doubt, there remains only the vast humanity, the great unimaginable moving being. We are in danger of making Christ vanish into today's humanity, and that in turn into the humanity of the future. [1]

We are no longer clear about what the source means. And that immediately affects the significance of the final end: the end of time is conceived as a great annihilation and not as a definite judgment and the return of him who is the focal point of history and its judge.

Surely this is why historical research of Jesus or the Church's origins, which generations prior to World War I had been so caught up with, attract little attention today.

Because we are living in a period of profound change and are living through the end of an *era* and an *age,* not through

---

1. The inquirer in **Christus** asked, "Christ our friend, on whose shoulders we were asked to find repose, is placed for a much more interior Christ and becomes life and the principle of life. But a parallel evolution is only possible gradually in each soul, through grace, and often at the price of a painful purification. If one passes prematurely from one stage to the other, does not one risk losing the substance for the shadow and, forsaking the living person of Christ, risk becoming attached merely to Christian ideals which are indeed excellent in themselves, but which are empty of the one who was their force and who made their defense possible?"

It is strange to see that same problem in the mystical writers of our own day which had disturbed Saint Teresa of Avila and Saint Ignatius Loyala: to what extent ought the mystical soul be devoted to Jesus' humanity? This question recurs again and again to the Catholic mystic who is distinguished from the other mystics who lose their souls in God without the human person intervening mid-way.

the end of a century or an epoch as our fathers before us, we can appreciate that the range of historical experience must be diffused over immensely long periods. It is a Christian attitude to examine all of history and not just a limited part of it: the Sacred Books of the Jewish faith imply this broader outlook. This perspective was developed to a high degree in the first centuries of the Christian world by meditation on the work of Jesus. Saint Augustine portrayed this expansive vision when he wrote the *City of God* at the final collapse of the ancient world. In our own times, for similar reasons, Christians are deeply attracted by large-scale universal studies on time from its origins and on through crises and new thresholds. We see it in the comparative and global history of all human activity and all civilizations in such writers as Toynbee. Again, we see it in the reconstruction of the evolution of life in which humanity plays a sublime role, as in the writings of Bergson, Edouard Le Roy and Father Teilhard de Chardin. It would seem that the religion of Jesus could have a clearer title to authenticity if it were part of the vital movement in the history of the entire human species whose élan is being reconstructed.

Although we behold time on an infinitely grander scale, and though it is much more difficult and uncertain to ascertain how it was in the beginning and what course creation is taking, yet, through the study of the genesis and emergence of life, the history of humanity as part of the evolution of the species, the glotting-out of macro-evolutions, the re-thinking of the future they promise, many Christians of our times are reaching out for what they see as a more verifiable and scientific general hypothesis than the explanation offered them in ancient texts about Jesus. These views on the origin of life draw many people closer to Christ. They come to see how he coexists in a special way in time. They recognize the face of Jesus diffused across the whole screen of evolution.

Our epoch is the first to see — and we owe it to science — that the theory of an abrupt end to historical time is not a

ridiculous assumption. Until now man knew he was mortal;
but he dies only as an individual and hoped for survival in
humanity. Now mankind is learning that it too is mortal,
indeed that it is liable to die a sudden death. Such a prospect
leads people to read the Gospels in a new and realistic light,
if it is true that one better understands a book by getting the
feeling of those circumstances which prompted its writing.
But thinking oriented towards the end of things, towards the
coming of the last days or towards a great future upheaval,
disregards the return to the past.

Though we think more about such things today, our minds
still falter before the supreme questions: God, Jesus, the life
to come. We are inclined to file all these questions between
brackets to pick them up later on. This kind of suspension
is characteristic of our age. It is worse than doubt. We can
escape doubt or at least put up with it as we do pain. But
whatever we file away in the back of our minds remains
with us always.

Our epoch is correct to investigate the relationship, the
development and the fusion of all beings into a fuller unity.
Because we do search we are more naturally attuned to the
state of mind of the first-century Christians than was ever
before possible. The first-generation Christians were keenly
aware of the sense of community. They believed that with
the final gathering of all men, time would come to an end, as
though time were but an instrument of communication among
all creatures and that it had to end as soon as humanity has
been fulfilled after Christ had come, and the Gospel had
been preached. Today, as then, we look ahead, not behind,
and ours is a global perspective.

But the first Christians possessed the Source in their hearts:
while waiting for the End, they awaited the return of the
Source. It is different with us. We speak a great deal about
history, but we have blurred the meaning of the singular
historical act.

There is much talk now of a return to primitive Church — Bible-reading, especially Saint Paul is held in great esteem. But both the entire Church of the early days and Saint Paul's message are secretly enriched by their attestation to the Resurrection as a tangible experience witnessed and not as something revealed. Catholic theologians, to follow a writer like Bultmann where he has seen correctly, insist that the character of the Resurrection is a mystery founded on faith. If we do not stress the essential fact which is that the believer considers the Resurrection primarily as a miracle and a supernatural act, we are left to suppose that we may put this divine act between brackets. If so, then the union between faith and witnessed fact, the principle upon which Apostolic testimony rests, would be jeopardized. I believe an attack is now being launched against the notion of *testimony*, and it corresponds to the attack on the very notion of *fact*. Both spring from the same stock. It is also an attack, and for the same profound reasons, on the notion of *Incarnation* understood in its historical sense: God becoming man, God entering into history. They would have the Author of Life independent of a real historic resurrection. They would like to give undivided attention to the redemption and ignore the historical reality of the Incarnation.

We owe this tendency in part to the world-wide influence of Karl Marx and Hegel. For Hegel (who today is replacing Aristotle as the teacher's teacher) there can exist no contingent fact outside us, and of course there can be no testimony of this non-existent fact. Ideas alone have being within us and outside us. They are the texture and tissue of development, and their dialectic is discovering the law of sequence and generation. Idea and knowledge are but one single thing which is the true God in the act of becoming. For a Marxist there can be no room for individual acts and testimonies handed down by individuals; there are only collective situations, movements of thought expressing mass movements.

The message is distinct from the individual and must be kept separate from him. A Christian cannot have it this way. But we can understand how a man who really believes in Christianity and who lives in the intellectual atmosphere of our times, may be reluctant to assent to the oneness of the spirit in himself and to think that this Christian doctrine is so contrary to the spirit of the age.

There is more than one way to come to believe in Jesus. There are many ways to the message of Christianity, but only one way to define its essence, structure and basic relationships. The essential relationship which tells us that Christianity is neither a myth nor a philosophy, nor even a pure theology, is the relationship between fact and idea in the unity of a real historical person which we can attain only through history and testimony.

We always come back to this point: the real Jesus, the risen Jesus — author of life because he truly rose from the dead. I wanted to write these words, which some would like to forget, in an intellectual light and show how I finally arrived at them.

❋

I have mentioned the confusion besetting an educated man who wants to give a complete account of all the hypotheses when he runs into the vastness of what he has to learn. To be fair, we must get into the proper perspective and stress the advantages which we have today over all past generations.

More than ever before, since that privileged generation which heard his very words, I believe that an educated and prudent man can attain reasonable conviction by himself and can often go so far as to put himself in the position of the first witnesses. As Albert Schweitzer noted in his classical work,[2] after more than a century of relentless investigations, we now have on hand certain elements of fact, critical texts

2. The Quest of the Historical Jesus, Macmillan, 1948.

and permanent data on the Problem of Jesus. Of course we shall eventually correct our errors in the light of our new knowledge. But, the essential facts pro and con are now clear to us by our sifting of the certain from the doubtful. We cannot say as much for Pascal, Spinoza and Richard Simon who had only rudimentary and often inexact data to go by. Even in the nineteenth century, Hegel and Strauss mixed even more uncertain data with the dialectic to shape a philosophy of history before all the facts were in.

Due to the work of so many exegetes of all persuasions, we now possess a network of convergent conclusions accepted by prudent scholars. We have a solid and refractory bulk of information upon which we can work. When the emotions are held in check, discussions are both possible and rewarding. And the era of dialog on the forbidden has finally arrived.

The abstract and dialectic forces which lead one to accept a too-premature synthesis are ebbing and I believe I can see a return towards that kind of knowledge which demands a greater sounding out of individual things. Because of this we shall be able to proceed quite as much from Jesus to Christ as from Christ to Jesus. This is what I meant when I gave this book the humblest title possible: JESUS.

I shaped my thinking during the first half of the twentieth century and it bears the stamp of the times. However, this is a logical work: it is a Logic of Testimony which, I believe, is offered for the first time. The logician's desire is a timeless one, and I hope that this work will still hold its truth-values in the future generations when our incidental conclusions will have been reshaped in a way I cannot now foresee, while the framework of the problem remains intact. I have tried to avoid the ever-present ephemeral aspects by discerning that which is eternal in the mind's puzzlement over these problems in their difficulties and in their solutions. I have desired especially to point out the unswerving dividing line between the zones of the clear and the obscure.

Because the thoughts I am about to share with my readers come from the circumstances of my own life, and since it is my wish to be absolutely honest, I shall begin our study by describing the personal influences and encounters that inspired them.

Jesus is so bound up with existence that books cannot teach us enough about him, and mental isolation is ruinous. It is good to meet people who have dedicated their lives to this examination. It is good to set down their findings and to mull them over in oneself silently.

CHAPTER II

Several Encounters in the Course of My Life

> *For I did not think that I could get*
> *so much profit from the contents of*
> *books as from the utterances of a*
> *living and abiding voice* — PAPIAS [1]

I ENJOY reading this fragment from Papias which Eusebius of Caesarea has preserved for us. It is one of the oldest documents in ecclesiastical tradition. Papias, living at the beginning of the second century of the Christian era, tells how he used to visit and question the apostles or others who knew them for, as he said, nothing was more profitable than coming in contact with the "living and abiding voice."

I know what he meant. Time steadily separates us from the historical presence upon which we base our lives and effaces its memory. We must hold on to it, if even by a single thread. From my youth, I have longed for a concrete presence to support the faith of my childhood. But, in the twentieth century after Jesus, such a contact is out of the question. *Lives of Jesus* of historical depictions have never appealed to me, and the sight of the land of Jesus would only have served to make him more remote, for I imagined it a drab wasteland.

---

1. **The Apostolic Fathers,** J. B. Lightfoot, Macmillan and Company, Ltd., London (1912).

My temperament was such that I could never attain Jesus through reproductions which I ignored, but only by a genuine critical scrutiny, for I sought to determine what was certain, probable, doubtful or legendary in my heritage. I was like the Theophilus to whom Luke dedicated his *Gospel* and the *Acts of the Apostles*. I wanted to know "the *strength* and *certainty* of the teaching in which I had been instructed." I also admired Spinoza's thought on demonstrations being expressions for the mind.

When I was old enough, my parents let me go to Paris. I cherished the secret hope that at Paris I would have the good fortune to meet those professors of rational religion who had studied the problem of Jesus — an already basic problem for me — with all the advantages of modern knowledge and that discretion for which the University has given me a life-long taste. The masters would then be for me what they had been who, in the days of Polycarp or John the Elder, had *heard* the apostles. "Of course," I said to myself, "I don't know enough and haven't the necessary diligence or spare time to take part in their work, so I will have to make up for these shortcomings and learn by synoptical comparison. I should choose my guides in the different Schools. Then," I thought, "I can take stock of their secret postulates with, perhaps, more of an insight than they themselves had, for these men are always unaware of their own implications. I could become familiar with their methods and see to what extent they confuse facts with mere wishful thinking."

My approach was terribly presumptuous for so young a man. But my early schooling, my living with classmates of different persuasions, the fact that my teachers had no solid religious background (none of them were Catholic), perhaps also my innate compulsion to look behind masks, had all conspired to accustom me to distinguish, even then, between matter and form, between the sound and the meaning behind the sound, between the facts and their interpretation, in all that I heard. My mother trained me to make such distinctions by showing me how to analyse the day's events every evening.

In the world of 1920, I soon became aware that the Process of Jesus — that distress in men's minds which endures to the very end — was one of its finest moments.

M. Loisy completed his tenure at the Collège de France, supported by M. Guignebert, a professor at the Sorbonne. I took in their courses furtively. It was not so much the substance of their teaching that struck me, but that tone, that accent of assurance which teaches more than words can ever, because it allows of a direct communication between one mind and another. I can still hear the accents of absolute certitude, here fine and subtle, there gross — almost vulgar — in naïve simplicity. It was the tone of superiority, at once callous and exuberant, of a contained but visible emotion which sporadically flashed out probably because of their former suffering. Loisy explained Saint Mark's Gospel and, when he had finished, Saint Mark lay in a heap of rubble. Guignebert made Saint Paul out to be a braggart and a combiner.

I expected to find these university professors steeped in the spirit of impartiality. But I saw them somewhat haughty and aloof. I was shocked to discover that the scientific mood of the Latin Quarter, in exegetical matters, seemed impregnated with the tone of polemics and hard feelings, as though it replaced faith by another kind of faith less naïve but more corrosive, as though it were impossible for criticism to remain purely critical, that is, gentle and respectful towards its object, impassible and equally open to two solutions even as it examines a third. I have never forgotten my impression of the partiality I saw among the supposedly impartial. At times I wonder whether the human intellect is capable of putting a belief (or disbelief) aside to dispassionately examine the data of experience, letting this data direct the mind even where it may not wish to venture.

About this time I met M. Pouget, whom I have since

tried to portray. [2] He at least was a patient man. He raised
questions and took them in hand every morning. He was
deeply curious, not bothered over fine points, and continually
strove for a positive certitude. He had the slow and regal
sound judgment of one sprung from peasant stock. Most of
all, he showed me that a believer must think in terms of the
whole, that he must use his intellect as a plow always, and
every so often as a cross. Criticism must become a tool, the
chief tool, the swing-plow that turns up the ground and
casts aside the appearances of two sides in order to make the
ground once more productive.

It was, above all, a question of closely examining the
Gospels by comparing one with the other and avoiding, right
from the outset, the mistake of taking them for *inspired*,
unerring or even truthful. These were precisely the issues at
stake. Nor could you begin your examination with a preconceived doubt, accusing them of interpolation, or assume that
everything of value is legendary because it is significant.

M. Pouget's whole intellectual formation was of a scientific
nature. He was eager for concrete, tangible historical knowledge. He believed in the existence of a *given subject*,
not of course an immediately obvious one, but one that is
substantial, penetrable, refractory in the beginning, and
ultimately knowable if you but have the necessary scholarship
and patience. The first given subject was *nature* and *history;*
the second was in the history of Israel and the Church of
which the Gospel was the favored axis. His humble and
noble life was an excellent commentary on the Gospel. It was
difficult to believe that the *logia* of the Gospel could have been
mythical when you saw this blind man living them.

M. Loisy also came from peasant stock, a line of cautious
people. Criticism was for him what the newest self-binding

---

2. Jean Guitton, Abbé Pouget Discourses, Helicon Press, Baltimore
(1959).

combine harvester is to the modern peasant — a tool he looks at and examines to find out what it can do. Whenever I visited him, whether in his apartment in the Rue des Ecoles, or at his little country house in Montier-en-Der, I always found a secularized priest staying out of the Church, yet living in the midst of the memories of his clerical youth. But as soon as you began discussing any technical problem about believing in Jesus, his face would flush. That was his sorespot. He would not admit you had touched it. I discerned that his thinking about Jesus Christ ran in two directions. Being the product of his times, he divided Jesus Christ into a Jesus seen from the viewpoint of the faith alone — a Jesus about whom you may affirm everything because he has no bearing on history — and an historical Nazarene who is being more and more reduced to size. I believe that at the end of his life he affirmed nothing except that Jesus had once lived and met an unfortunate end after stirring up the people. Loisy had transformed the Jesus of the Christian faith into Humanity through a gradual and profound metamorphosis that is so frequent today (we see it in Auguste Comte, Jaurès, many lay mystics and some Marxists). Loisy's Jesus had, as it were, come the full circuit, stripped of divine glory and even of his human personality to become identified with Humanity. The last time I saw him, he gave me the impression that he believed in nothing but humanity. He recited the *Credo* with the word *humanity* inserted where we put *Jesus Christ*.

In 1939, on the eve of the war, I received one of his books in which he gave an ironical treatment to the several essays I had sent him. He called me *Serapion,* after the bishop of Thmuis, and he cut me to pieces as though I were a sacred text, treating me precisely as he had M. P. L. Couchoud the year before — although for different reasons.

One would expect that in an age when scholars are concerned with the same problem, they would come to know and visit each other. They do greet each other and are courteous,

but modesty, indifference, and the fear of contradiction have
so dried them up that there is scarcely any real communication
among them.

In 1934, I found Bergson reading that little red book
which Loisy, the indefatigable critic, had dedicated to the
Two Sources. Bergson was so cautious that he never told
anyone what he thought about Jesus except in strict confidence.
He would say that nothing Jesus claimed to be surprised him.
He had no use for immature scholars, and exegesis was not
really his field. He never expressed himself in those areas
in which he believed he was scientifically incompetent.
Bergson would have been the first to admit that his opinions
about Jesus were those of any ordinary man. It was a
refreshing sight to see a mind of his calibre ennoble common
sense.

I spoke to him of Loisy and he told me how astonished he
was that this priest was so "unmystical," and he attributed it
to the exaggerated intellectual formation of the clergy around
1880. He believed that the receptive soul had no need for
undue instruction or problematics. The soul did not even
have to know whether Jesus existed historically to grasp the
unequalled source of divine humility in the *Gospels*.

Bergson's contact with the psychologists and sociologists
at the turn of the century showed him just how many postulates
and logical developments go to make up the conclusions of
the so-called positive sciences when they are applied to human
affairs. Because he learned how much science fabricates and
draws out pseudo-facts from conditional assumptions, Bergson
defied M. Loisy's conclusions. I thought that in this respect
he was like those who had read the *Gospels* and based their
lives on them. Unable to prove them, and not daring to say
that *criticism* is mistaken, they cannot help but suppose that
the critics deny them out of some secret necessity and not
solely in the name of science. Bergson would readily assert
that one cannot prove the impossibility of a fact, and that
science — thanks to the expansion of our knowledge — advances

by assimilating certain facts thought "impossible," unthinkable, as we are coming to see with wave mechanics and relativity. He never entered into the area of historical research, which was not his field. But he thought that in the area of experience he should discover the same difficulty as in the domains he had already studied — the separation of the operation of the knowing mind and the nature of the given subject. Unfounded presuppositions were to be avoided as well as those observations we prematurely call *positive* which correspond to our own desire because they are products of it. Bergson longed for an exegesis freed from postulates and symbols — one that criticizes its methods and procedures, one that tries to discern the reality behind the methods.

Several days after I heard Bergson tell how Loisy criticized his *Two Sources of Morality and Religion,* I visited M. Loisy in his retreat at Montier-en-Der. Loisy and he did not speak the same language and were unable to communicate with each other. I have often been struck by the abyss between them, but never so much as on the day I saw the two destinies of Bergson and Loisy cross each other's path from opposite directions — on the one hand that of the priest entrenched in the certitude of his initial error; on the other hand that of the Israelite reared in the Jewish faith, who later grew indifferent to this faith out of respect for science and who was only gradually coming to recognize the Jesus of Catholicism as the fulfillment of Judaism. I recalled that it was in October, the same month Renan left the seminary in 1845 because of *Devenir* and that Newman was converted from Anglicanism to Catholicism because of his *Essay on Development.* How true it is that people and what they think differ so widely. But I did not consider the four choices on the same level. It seemed to me that in 1845 Renan was still inexperienced and that Loisy in 1935 was possessed by his experience without having it under control, while, as I see it, Newman and Bergson lived in a more interior and real world.

Ten days after my visit to Montier-en-Der, I set out for
Jerusalem to see and listen to the Father Lagrange, then
quite an old man. His ninetieth birthday was celebrated with
good cause, for he had dedicated his whole life to the problem
of Jesus, approaching it with something of a landowner's way
of comparing every detail of the Gospels with the details of
the earth, of history and of tradition. He never used dem-
onstration, and he was more humanistic than critical, more
theological than philosophical. He gathered the little verified
facts, the judicious remarks with the unmatchable advantage
given on the very spot by existence and the contact of earth
and flesh. The net result of his fifty years of work together
with his companions was that he had no historical objection
to the truth of the Gospels. He *upheld* this truth in spite of
the contradictions, even because of them, for according to
Heraclitus, "invisible harmony is higher than the visible."
This held true particularly with (profane) *history* "except for
miracles." "I wanted to prove Jesus," he told me, "as one
proves motion by walking."

He was in the twilight of his life and had no regret or
bitterness, but contemplated the 46 tomes of his review, the
32 volumes of his collection, or rather neglected them (for they
were stacked behind his desk) to continue writing in his tiny
script without ever erasing. He rarely walked out in the close-
packed city so full of opposites, with men from every nation
rubbing shoulders in indifference and in suppressed hatred.
He showed me the way of the Passion and the sharp angles
of this minuscule area. We sometimes climbed a tower from
which we could see the entire highly ambiguous city which
blinds and gives sight. Or we went up the Mount of Olives,
the strategic spot from which Jesus beheld against the sky
the temple of the monotheism that overwhelmed it, and on
the other side, towards Bethany, the unchanging horizon, the
aridity, the absolute poverty of the land. The only beauty
I saw in these places came from the light and its effusion.

Father Lagrange did not seem aware of it. He doubtless thought the study of texts alone permitted one to see the true light. "Let's get back; we've work to do," he would say.

In those days, I knew M. Paul Louis Couchoud, philosopher, doctor, exegete, analyst, careful observer of everything. I read his works with great curiosity, for his unprecedented paradox intrigued me: Jesus is the greatest being in all of history and today he still is the greatest man on the face of the earth, but he did not exist *in the historical sense of the word*: he was not born, did not suffer under Pontius Pilate. All that is a mystical fabrication.

At first I did not take these strange things seriously. Later, I understood that in problems of this nature where the infinite is at stake, there are terminal hypotheses (atheism is one), impossible excesses, in which the intellect is driven into a corner. In thought, as in love, excess is a language that can conceal doubt. And every so often we accept an opinion, a choice, a belief, not by inclination, but rather because we think — at least at that moment in our lives — all other solutions except that one are impossible.

Later, M. Couchoud told me how he had known and loved Anatole France. Lacking the faith and seeing Renan's prejudice, Anatole France freed himself from everything.

To Anatole France, who was so much like Montaigne, M. Couchoud was a Pascal: a Nietzsche. He resolved his skeptical remarks to their ultimate conclusions. After he lost the faith "which is not within our power," he said, quoting Pascal, and "which alone would have permitted him to take the Gospel texts as they were without having to risk choosing one over the other," unable to bear up under Loisy's pruning sheers which finally reduced Jesus to merely a poor man whose very existence was in question — he preferred to admit that this minimum of existence ought in turn to be nullified and that Jesus-God-and-Man had existed only for the faith. Saying this much, he had no intention of diminishing belief

in Jesus.   In his opinion, Jesus was actually believed to be
God in the beginning.   For us God was dead, a lamb sacrificed.
He was as a living and timeless being mystically sacrificed in
a kind of eternal mass.   To satisfy people enamored with
"history" — an inferior kind of knowledge — the God-Jesus
was clothed with an anecdotal humanity, with a likely enough
biography.   I perceived a quest for security in views of this
nature.   By concluding to the historical non-existence of Jesus,
Doctor Couchoud believed he had vested Jesus with a superexistence which could not fall victim to doubt. [3]

*

The one thing that struck me in his arguments was that
before I realized it I had come to the conclusion that there
were ultimately only three possible stands to take on Jesus:
Renan's, Hegel's and the believer's that is to say one which
makes of the faith an undue prolongment of an authentic

---

3. One day he let me read over his shoulder a letter Claudel wrote
him on April 24, 1951: "Dear Sir, I enjoyed reading **Le Dieu Jésus** which
you sent me. You have shown how, in turn, Renan, Loisy and Guignebert watered down the historical figure of the Redeemer until nothing
was left. Someone simply had to come along and burn away what remained of this redoubtable, scandalous and untenable reality. You have
been this audacious and intrepid individual. As P. Monachanin said,
you have carried out the 'ultimate hypothesis.' I almost envy you
while I congratulate you. . . .

"Unless I am badly mistaken, Jesus is a spiritual reality for you. That
is too much. You sketched him out in a negative way as did Mallarmé
who preferred the terms 'silence' and 'abstraction' to signify the positive. You are improving upon the Good Lord. Your imaginary incarnation
is much more difficult to swallow than the real Incarnation. A truly
heroical effort is called for. A kind of grace!

"How much simpler it would have been for you to cry out like the
centurion when he had pierced Christ's body with a lance: 'He was
truly the Son of God.'

"Don't bother to answer me. I wanted only to tell you that I have not
been unaware of the Christian stirring which is coming to the surface
in a new and hopeless assertion."

history — that of a sacred history taken from the faith alone —
that of a true but supernatural history.

I wanted to explain to my satisfaction how knowledgeable
and sagacious minds could be "mythological," and I pondered
over the relationship of history to the faith. I perceived that
even among believers there are attitudes not unlike those of
unbelievers. Saint Paul, who had *seen* Jesus only at that
moment on the road to Damascus, was not interested in
details about the historical Christ (the historical problem once
settled by corroborative harmony among the Twelve, the
Three and Peter), he seems not to have regretted never
"knowing him according to the flesh." He was content with
— as was the unknown disciple who wrote the *Epistle to the
Hebrews* — Christ "who was yesterday, who is today and
forever." The same might be said for the author of the
Apocalypse, whoever he may have been.

I thought there might be a certain kind of people afraid
to see with the eyes of the flesh and who are more at ease
directly contemplating his essence without first beginning
with his existence. Or rather who, having known the Existent
during his sojourn on earth, prefer to look for him further
ahead in time or in the beyond, not among the dead but
among the eternally living, as the Angel of the Resurrection
declared. But when such people are Christians, they assume
this history and refer back to it.

Doctor Couchoud carried out his indifference to the
historical element to an unheard of and desperate degree.
We cannot say with any certainty today how strictly he
maintains his thesis of the non-existence of Jesus which he has
reduced to the idea that Jesus was not properly a man at all,
that one can never fully know whether Jesus is God, and
that there cannot strictly be a "history of God." Pascal would
say: "The Incarnation is an impenetrable mystery, and yet,
one can understand the reality and meaning of the Gospels
only through the Incarnation."

This insupportable doctrine, this line of thought which I

consider absurd, did at least help me awaken to the paradox inherent in our faith — that paradox whose razor edge the sheer force of habitual belief has dulled immeasurably: the eternity, the consubstantiality of Jesus of Nazareth with God, although Jesus gave himself up to time and to history, being really *made temporal*, truly the son of man.   Again, the problem whether Jesus is God is not one we can put safely between brackets as though it were sufficient to give an account of the facts and consider Jesus the "first of the mystics." The famous question: "And you, who do you say you are? . . . (what is your SELF?)" remains the primary, ultimate and fundamental question.   The answer: "Jesus is the Messiah," in addition to the fact that it does not mean very much to us today, also lacks the ability to face up to the mystery and the equilibrium of the Gospel.   Moreover, between the thesis of the critics according to which Jesus is a man whom the imagination has *deified* and that of the mythologists according to which Jesus is a God whom fabrication has made into a man and *historified,* it is the latter which struck me as the more religious.   It conforms to the essential movement which proceeds from God to man (God made man).   Today it is very possible to encounter deeply religious persons who cling wholeheartedly to Christianity, so long as it has no relationship with authenticated truths and that it be as a revealed myth.

André Maurois wrote in a confession of "his faith": "The only difference between Alain and an Orthodox Catholic was that Alain was indifferent to the historical truth of religion, and this idea alone was a scandal to him: 'What matters,' said Alain, 'is not whether Jesus said something or other on such and such a day, but that it is true.'   That was his stumbling block, and it is mine as well.   It does not mean we refuse to believe in miracles or in testimonies.   Our faith is beyond these things."

There is a strange similarity on this point between the "simple man" and the *"intelligenzia,"* between a "modernist" and an *"intégriste"* — both diametrically opposed to anyone who would try to discern in biblical tradition through historical (psychological, sociological) methods the *point of insertion* of the divine and its human expression through the human zones of language and mentalities. It is much easier to maintain the slipshod position which accepts everything with equal faith or equal indifference. People taking this over-simplified position can have certainty without making a distinction between the Old Testament miracles and those of the New Testament, between the story of Adam and Eve and that of Jesus and Mary, between the Tree of Paradise and the Tree of the Cross. Because they would encounter such difficult problems as the setting up of boundaries and the distinguishing among various levels of acceptance, they prefer to accept revelation in a lump sum, taking it for a true discourse, a sacred writing based, for Catholics, on divine authority and the Church's authority, and for Protestants on interior feeling, and for unbelievers on the power of mystical illusion and primitive mentalities. Always, it is more or less understood that the question *whether it actually happened* is an unseemly one.

It is wrong for me to intimate that these problems are exclusively those of our times. Every age is alike where the enigma of Christ is concerned. Names change, ideas are clothed in different terms, but the essential difficulty remains. Its source lies in the discrepancy between Christ's complex being and our Western tendency to dissociate.

The human mind, such as Greek education has shaped it (and perhaps as it actually is in itself, or at least in its inclinations) feels ill at ease with the mystery of the God-Man. It may interpret the fact allegorically — a nice meaningful myth. Or it may dissociate: on one side there will be God in his eternal life, on the other the Man-Jesus — but with no real and intimate relationship between the two. Or again, applying to nature and history what the Catholic faith professes of the unique human nature of Jesus, it may see in the universe and in humanity an emanation, a mode, a moment of the

Divine Being, an eternal and necessary incarnation. [4] At the heart of the matter we find that child of pantheism sometimes called idealism which crops up time and again. Marxism presupposes it. They maintain it is not possible, except as a religious story or logical construction, to believe, as Christians do, that the Eternal has chosen a particular point in humanity and history, a place, a time, a race, a mother, a human nature to become intimately and unconfusedly united to it.

The further I advanced the more I became aware of this tragic conflict between the general atttitude among the learned and the essential given subject of Christian testimony. I came to see that the position of the Council of Chalcedon is a typical and often recurring one. The Nestorian solution especially — which separates the Divine *Logos* from the *Nazarene* in whom it dwells as though in a temple — is the most secretly alluring one for the Western mind. I found it among the modernists who divide Jesus into a Jesus of the faith and a Jesus of history. In Bultmann I saw its latest form, a very subtle but identical one.

Christianity's essential problem is to determine the relationship between faith and history. I have often noted the many differences between the position and solution of these problems that the Protestant and the Catholic Schools take. Contrary to the Catholics, who do not resign themselves to compromise and whose logical minds cannot admit that contradictions exist on the same plane, Protestant thinkers are more at ease with an essential distinction between the planes of faith and history. Even if Jesus had not risen according to historical truth, that would not have prevented him from being truly risen for the faith alone. In this sense the Protestant mentality is less vulnerable to radical criticism. If science demonstrates that Christ is not what the faith says he is, then the faith

---

4. For a further development of these views I refer to my work on **L'existence temporelle**, ch. VI.

would not be hurt. A Latin Catholic who doubts the historical reality, abandons his belief in Jesus. And yet it has often happened that a devout Protestant, placed in the same situation, keeps his faith, his preaching ministry and even his teaching position on a theological faculty where he is responsible for training men to the ministry.

I can understand this, since Protestant theological faculties for over a century now have constructed a choice environment for critical investigations on Jesus. They welcomed all the methods of critical science without fearing to disrupt their consciences or to slacken that enthusiasm which is the driving force behind all research. New systems and views have arisen since then. But as I observe them from a distance I do not see the structure of the problem change.

I have seen the School of Dibelius growing up. It is called by one of those untranslatable German words the *Formgeschichte*: "history of forms," "criticism of forms." It is an unpretentious method of describing appearances, and it is related to Husserl's phenomenology because it developed from it after those epochs which hoped for too much. They abstract from the Gospel content and retain only its literary *form*: anecdote, miracle tale, dialogue, parable. La Fontaine could be taken apart like that, but it is not worth the trouble to dissect the *Fables*. But a dissection of the Gospels makes it easier for one to depict an orally transmitted common tradition. Thanks to this dissection they are able to catch a glimpse of the *living Gospel* that preceded the written Gospel, just as narratives come before *stories*. The "narratives" and the "sayings" of the Gospel were told over and over within these living communities, in worship, preaching, in matters of conscience. They bear the mark of this early usage. Thus, throughout the written Gospels one may divine the life of the first communities. This is what the *Gospels* and the *Acts* and the *Epistles* reveal.

The nineteenth century (which only ended with the First World War) enjoyed seeing individuals in action. It was still an individualistic age like Voltaire's, and romantic like Hugo's. It was also enthusiastic about Saint Paul, the man of great plans, whom they looked upon as the second creator of Christianity. After the war of 1914-1918, mankind entered into a more collective phase, and it shows up in exegesis. When they read the *Epistles,* they were interested in the traces of the Church's life — hymns, religious symbols — which were like the traces of their way of life. They no longer studied the *Gospels* as pure documents related one to the other progenitively (as Claudel springs from Rimbaud, or Valéry from Mallarmé). Rather than attempt the restoration of the primary textual source which no one had ever seen, they came to realize that the true primary source was not a dead text, but a community. They understood the Church's earliest activity and, as they say, catechesis, sometimes *kerygma,* a word meaning "proclamation" rather than "preaching": the first apostles were properly *heralds.*

These investigations raise the primordial question without answering it. The *Formgeschichte* draws attention to the emergence of evangelical teaching in the earliest Christian community. But how is this community of the "poor of Jerusalem," or for that matter the little groups which emigrated into Asia Minor and Greece, related to the mysterious primitive *Origin,* to the change which sets these times apart?

How are all the forms of language, preaching, teaching, symbolism, worship, related to the center from which they emanate? The grammarian, the stylist, may study the words I use without speaking about me. The time will come when it will be better to know whether I lived and what I wanted to say. The question raised now more than ever before is how to distinguish cause from effect. Did the *community* create the *event,* or did the *event* create the *community?* And if there were a reciprocal action between the *event* and the *community,* what was its first term?

Bultmann is the guiding light for the present.   Hellenist, humanist, theologian, exegete, he is the only one to offer a complete system of the problems which have occupied his whole life, the only one who does not side-step the ultimate questions, who above all discerns the latent philosophical positions in the exegeses.

Bultmann notes that revelation takes on a positive language and is expressed through mental frames of reference.   When you make this observation, which I have often done, [5] you cannot fail to see that the spirit must be liberated from its old vocabulary and reclothed with expressions that conform to new mentalities.   The same message would then be more accesssible to a world which no longer recognizes it as new. And, if we think that Christ's message must continue throughout time — especially since we may be living just in the dawn of time — we must admit that the continuation of Christianity is closely bound up with the problem of distinguishing the archaic and the up-to-date in its expressions. A time of crisis, such as we are certainly living in, helps us to realize how necessary it is to discover which is which.

But can one *isolate the spirit?*   Can one retransmit the spirit in different forms on its own authority?   Above all, is it possible, right now, through an intellectual operation and, so to speak, a surgical operation, to distinguish between the spirit and its expression without being arbitrary about it?

The danger involved in divesting the spirit of the clothing it took at the time of its evangelical emergence is indeed a formidable one.   We risk plucking out the wheat with the weeds.   And, what is more, we risk making the new clothing still less well fitting than the old.   Why should German philosophy as expressed by Heidegger be more suited for expressing a timeless revelation?   I prefer cosmogonical or eschatological images — the image of heaven and hell imagined

---

5. See the Introduction to my book **Le Temps et l'Eternité chez Plotin et Saint Augustin.**

as place to which one ascends or descends, the image of the approaching end of time — because these images correct their shortcomings while it is obvious that they are but images. Bultmann's concepts ultimately destroy the historical value of the Resurrection and at length reduce the Christian faith to the soul's awareness of its justification by the cross. The Resurrection is never just the supreme significance given to Jesus' death and to the judgment by which God strips the cross of its power. It cannot be historical; for as Jaspers wrote, " a corpse cannot come back to life." We can understand why Karl Barth would reproach Bultmann for stripping the faith of its content. [6]

A rigorous thinker will see in this a new example of the dissociation of reality from existence, of history from mystery. As I see it, it takes the heart out of Christianity which, before too long, only Catholicism will preserve, for it alone has the courage to maintain the foundations at whatever cost. "They have taken the Lord away, and I know not where they put him."

*

A different kind of problem has arisen in the last few years. In general, our changing views of the Bible and the Origins springs from an improvement, or at least a change, in the methods of analysis. From behind their desks scholars decide to adopt some point of view; or, by reading the works of their predecessors and comparing and contrasting them, they come upon a new and promising approach. The renewal would be much different if these men began with an incontrovertible fact and not a theory, I mean a fact such as the

---

6. In his work **Dogmatics** (Westminster, 1960), H. Diem concludes with these words: "Bultmann's interpretation of the notion of **Kerygma** (preaching), which is not, as far as I am concerned, that of the New Testament, depicts it as being the object of its theology, not the history of Jesus, but merely the personal interpretation of the believer, which no longer has any bearing upon the historical aspect of this history."

discovery of a fifth gospel or some Jewish or pagan inscriptions about *Chrestus* and his earliest followers. Then it would be a question of fact and not of hypothesis. The Dead Sea Scrolls are "facts" of this nature: datable texts prior to Jesus' coming. They give us a hitherto unknown text which sheds an oblique light upon the Scriptures and takes away from them that regal exclusiveness of canonization, a light that casts shadows upon everything else except the text conforming to the faith of a particular group.

These documents show us that there were other "movements" before the "Movement" of Jesus — movements which in some respects are comparable to his. Then, it is up to the mind to discern the originality of the Origin. We can define more precisely the point at which Jesus offers us something that is essentially new: what an advantage for a doctrine called from the very outset Good *News*.

*

I have pursued these investigations off and on throughout my life which has been primarily concerned with philosophical investigations on the meaning of time.

Everything in the life of the mind is inter-related. Only, you have to live quite awhile before you come to know how they are related. Between the two areas of my research there were two objects of equal importance, a relationship which has become more and more meaningful to me. I became increasingly aware that historical methods alone could never resolve the problem of historical truth: not because these methods ignore philosophy, but rather because they contain a latent philosophy which is neither made explicit nor criticized.

An historian of religion has a built-in conception of nature and law; also of movement, of occurrence, of duration and development. And increasingly: of the relationship of time and eternity. On the other hand, texts and dogmas, affirmations and denials and reflection always refer back to them. Kierkegaard quotes Lessing: "Contingent historical truths can never prove rational and necessary truths." He asks, "Can one take an eternal certitude from history? Is it possible to find at the starting point an interest other than historic? Can one base eternal happiness on historical information?"

In this book I shall restrict myself to occasionally point out the metaphysical aspect of these problems.

※

I shall only tell some of the lessons I have drawn from this experience. Not that I think them original, but rather because I think my reader has also discovered them if he is sufficiently mature, and, if he is still young, he will come across them some day.

I was convinced, as I mentioned before, that somewhere in the midst of the "problem of Jesus" there was a *teacher* who would guide me along the right path if I but sat at his feet. His teaching, based upon a lifetime of research, would dispel all my uncertainty. Life has taught me that he could never exist because there will *always* be things clear and obscure; that no man, however enlightened he might be, could ever act as a substitute for myself. When I had acquired the sufficient knowledge and experience, I would eventually have to come to a decision. I wanted to make this decision by reducing the uncertain as far as I could, "by a long series of many considerations" as Descartes said, by an increasing growth in certitude, by seeing how absurd the other solutions are. I wanted to face and assess every conflicting solution. I had not the least idea that my adversary was contemptible, all the more so because he thinks the adverse is a part of himself. I had too often met great minds that were hurt by their doubts about Jesus. I had seen them trying to fight off their doubts by either seeing in them the mind's inability to fathom religious problems, or the price that has to be paid for some offense against the light. I also knew that every method is good so long as it remains a method — and that every appearance is a true one so long as it is recognized as appearance.

If the dialectical method, which has won over a great many people, has any value, it lies in the fact that it accustoms one to ascend the difficult trail that leads upwards from appearance to truth. It involves phases and changes of opinion which lead one to a more comprehensive truth.

I promised myself that I would calmly envisage the possibility, even the plausibility, of the solution I rejected.

I believed my initial faith would be of some intellectual advantage. Faith is an act which implies that it has mastery over possible doubt, that it is a guide in uncertainty, while disbelief claims to be absolutely sure. The believer admits that if some basic principle were put in a questioning light, he would have to revise his position ("If Christ has not risen from the dead," said Saint Paul, "your faith is in vain."). We rarely hear a non-believing critic repeat Renan's profound observation: "If miracles are real, my book is a pack of errors."

*

I thought that after a century of critical examination, we could distinguish, like statistician or characterologists, a few basic explanations from among the various hypotheses. Péguy said: "May every type of thought be realized in its accuracy and in its fullness; may every type of thought be realized in its most beautiful expression; may every type of thought be harvested in due season in its highest and most perfect maturation."

Now, if we look back over the history of the last one hundred and fifty years, we see the same themes recurring. New systems change but do not alter the few *choices* we have got. The men who began the critical examination of the Origins in the middle of the last century could wait for future discoveries which were to make at least one of the explanations (orthodoxy in particular) scientifically untenable. This did not happen. Only the frontiers were realigned. Therefore, I believe Strauss' book, the *Life of Jesus,* is still current and, in my estimation, more so than Renan's. It would seem that the further one advances, the less renovation there is. Granting that new papyri may be unearthed, that new allocations may be brought forward (making multiple that which was thought to be one, discerning many sources where only one was evident before) — none of these changes will modify the essential relief.

When I tried to make a list of the various solutions, as Albert Schweitzer once did, I was surprised to see that they were few indeed. I even began to think that there were not, *that there could never be more than,* three: two which deny, one which affirms.

The men I had seen thinking about the problem of Jesus were led to each of the three original models.

It is this which I shall set down in the form of a meditation, for I believe that an analysis of this kind is useful not only for studying Christianity, but also for sketching out the progress of the human mind.

Part Two

The Eternal Dilemma

CHAPTER III

The Historical Jesus,
or
The First Approach

WITHOUT depending on outside sources, I wish to give an exact account of what I think about Jesus. I want to bring the whole of my intellect into play to the best of my ability and retrace the steps of an honest, sincere and unprejudiced mind which, once it has digested the works of the critics and the apologists of the faith, will try to weigh both sides and choose according to its conscience. It is a difficult but rewarding task. It is pushing me ahead to complete this *mémoire* which will be as clear and as timely as possible: I am concerned with the quest for truth, not a reputation for scholarship. I shall let several of my friends read this text so I can learn, understand and thoroughly examine their objections.

My starting point? It is hard to find one. I want to proceed from the known to the unknown, to first determine the undeniable — that which all men can admit. It is difficult because I cannot easily detach myself from this subject that has become so much a part of me, yet I must in order to forget what I know, or rather what I believe I know or what I believe I believe.

I shall try to find the incontestable element that only a fool could reject. Then I shall see whether I can go on from there.

The Starting Point

The two gentle syllables of the name JESUS have inspired the lives and deaths of countless people. They have deep meaning for me also. I cannot prevent this name — sacred to my race and to my land — from directly evoking an individual, his deeds and his words, which have been handed down to us and recounted and embedded in the computation of my Western world. They carry me back to events that are actual or fictitious (I do not know which). But when all is said and done, these events are quite recent when you consider that this planet's age is measured in millions of years. A living species last about twenty million years. A direct word-of-mouth chain of about sixty persons is enough for a deed or a thought of Jesus to be handed down to us today. He is recent, he is very close to us and well-rooted in the three Jewish, Greek and Roman histories. If he is a legendary character, at least he is one that has been protected with chronologies and is well-established in recorded history.

One of the first questions I raise, as do simple people, is where to find the very texts which were written about Jesus. They tell me about four narratives called Gospels. But can I see these manuscripts, touch them, read them? How old are they? Can I be certain that they are not the work of a forger?

I am told that in London, the Vatican and Leningrad, there are Gospel manuscripts dating from the fourth century which I could see beneath their protective glass cases. I am told that Virgil, Lucretius and several Greek and Latin actors are known to us only through copies that are much older — and yet this does not prevent us from believing their authenticity. They point to still older papyrus fragments such as the *Egerton Papyri* which I have this moment before my eyes. They are torn and shredded, but I can still read the well-written Greek characters that date from the middle of the second century. There are some that are still older.

I am absolutely certain that Jesus was not invented by a wandering monk. I would like to point out that very little time had elapsed between the event — whether actual or supposed — and the recording of this event by the written word which, if the worst came to the worst, one may find in the halls of Egypt. Thirty years? Perhaps less. It is an incontrovertible fact that about the year 40 of the Christian era a group of Jews lived within the confines of the Roman Empire and that they believed in a certain *Jesus*, in a certain *Chrestos*.

The whole problem is to find out just who this *Chrestos*, this *Jesus* was, who has become the object of so much propaganda and inquiry. Now, twenty centuries after his appearance on earth, I would like to determine his authenticity and historicity.

Indifference of the Moderns and the Problem of Competence

Most people I come into contact with are not at all interested in the problem which has taken hold of me. It is meaningless to many of my contemporaries. If a disciple should come to tell them of Jesus, they would treat his message with indifference — an ancient question long since resolved and evaluated. Their indifference is largely due to the fact that they associate Jesus with apparently outworn traditions. Above all, they link him to the powers that threaten their freedom or which seem all too human. Should they read any of the Gospels, they would be out of their element: its terms, doctrines and aspirations do not correspond to their vocabulary and horizons. Miracles, particularly, have become incomprehensible to them, for they are contrary to what reason and science demand. They are unrelated to their world and seem no different than the stuff dreams and fiction are made of. Here is how I'd translate this confused impression of my neighbors: "It doesn't interest me or concern me. None of it ever happened because it's all impossible."

Why consult an expert in this field? Besides, where can you find such a man? The qualifications are so at variance. Prudence cautions us not to tamper with the insoluble.

When Jesus is seen as a mysterious being whom you could meet beyond the grave, you should be forgiven for disregarding his message that is presented in such a sibylline way, that is presented on completely different terms than the modern mind demands from reality. If the message is real, we must admit that it bears no resemblance to the teachings of science or even to that part of history people study to get their degrees.

On a more cultured level, an educated man who is aware of the difficulty by having read all the books published on the problem of Jesus confesses his ignorance and impotence. For example, one of the greatest historians, Lucien Febvre, wrote in a book review about some meditations on Jesus that he could not understand: "There is a peripheral assemblage of inconsistent facts and data circumscribing a void just-inhabited by a barely tangible shadow." Our most technical investigations conclude to an instinctive judgment. Jesus: a shadowy void, a singular abyss.

I am just beginning my investigation and am too hopeful and courageous to follow the opinion of either the majority or the élite. I shall not give in without a struggle.

I have an inquisitive mind that is eager to penetrate the obscure, and I am, like the biblical Solomon, enthralled by enigmas.

The enigma of Jesus touches upon the problem of the meaning of our existence and ought to intrigue us more than any other enigma. Are we unwanted in this world? Why transmit the seeds of this so short life? Is suicide punishable? Is there an after-life, and if so, what kind? . . . These questions are being raised more today than in the past and science will never answer them. Reason alone will not solve them. Is it wrong to think that there will never be a positive glimmer of light in this dark night, a jarring something, a penetration, an abrupt communication, perhaps even a secret message confided to a select few?   I am speaking vaguely and am convinced that many people are secretly hoping (perhaps superstitiously) for some definite information, for a convincing experience.   If they ever learned that this mystery were actually experienced somewhere, even in the smallest degree, they would spare no effort to learn of it.

Now, except for the *event of Jesus,* I do not see any instance in the past where one can discover even the very least experience of the mystery of being, of the mystery which lurks behind me.   But if people could recognize this experience somewhere, they would rush upon it like starved animals after scraps of food!   Universities and banks fight to lay hold of a few square centimeters of tattered papyrus upon which they can decypher three half-effaced words of an unknown Gospel, of some information about an unknown prophet or master similar to Jesus.   Such sorry lacunae are paid for more dearly than the finest pieces of art.   I think that if a man were not checked by the fear of being laughed at by another man, like himself in this respect, he would confess his deep interest in the problem.

All the more so because a man of the Western world breathes the oxygen of Christendom.   He knows that if his way of life and thinking differ from others, it is ultimately because of Jesus, or at least because of the jolt provoked by the Idea of Jesus.

The Gospel may relate events that are rather obscure for me, a modern man, but its atmosphere is my atmosphere; it is my hidden source.   It is precisely this disparity between the difficulty of believing it and the necessity of living it which irritates me and excites me to investigate it.   The Gospel excites me — these are painful words: yet, I recognize in myself the repercussions of the text which becomes clearer the more I read and compare other books.   I feel myself being almost compelled to set my mind to the problem.   And, as I have decided, I ask help from no one. It is my method and my joy to work alone with my intellect. I see no other way to arrive at a real conviction.

Someone is bound to say that I am not really competent. But who is *competent?* This is not the realm of pure science where the findings of researchers are compiled into a body of knowledge. There must still come a moment of uncertainty in which the incompetent in exegesis, in the history of religions, makes a decision that is not based entirely upon his competence. Might he not already have made a hidden decision at the outset by his omissions and silences, by the way he describes and classifies texts and primary data? How shall we decide what qualifications the problem of Jesus necessitates? They are so varied: Celsus and Origin, Porphyry and Saint Augustine... and on a lesser plane, Spinoza and Pascal, Renan and Newman, — and today, Loisy and Lagrange, Bultmann and Barth....

In a problem of universal magnitude in which there is always the shadow of uncertainty even in the light of some clarification, a problem whose final solution will directly influence human conduct, one in which every undue attention to detail may throw out of focus the whole picture which one must always keep before himself, I would say that anyone who is to solve this problem must have the following qualifications: he must be well grounded and skilled in the ancient Greek and Semitic tongues; he must be an historian of religions, a specialist in the Old Testament; he must be particularly skilled in the study of the New Testament; he must also be a psychologist, a psychiatrist, and a sociologist when necessity demands; he must understand the religious soul. These conditions are already difficult to fulfill, but they are just the beginning. The competent man would have to be able to stand back and criticize his certitudes and his doubts; he must put each truth in its place and he must put the part in the whole and the moment in evolution: he would have to be a philosopher, if philosophy can teach him all that. There are more requirements: I would want him to be religious, a doer of good, he must have the same loftiness of spirit and the same relationship to the infinite as those he must describe and judge, approve or condemn.... I know that competency is difficult to define, that it is highly complex and cannot be fully realized. Impossible. And that consoles me.

Attitude of the Scientific Mind towards Miracles

Obviously, my first obstacle is the question of, and the account of, miracles.

What am I going to do? Must I decide that there are no miracles — and terminate my research then and there? I cannot. I leave its credence, probability and feasibility to the miracle, at least in the sense of an event that cannot be reconciled to the rules which until then dictated what was possible. The history of the sciences teaches us that the human mind must sometimes acknowledge the reality of facts previously judged improbable.

I understand the objection well. The Gospel is not a body of recorded data, testimonies and verifications, bearing on one fact alone that was judged impossible by an earlier science, as was the suspension of mercury in Toricelli's tube in Pascal's time. This little fact could be reproduced and verified indefinitely. Roentgen's accidental discovery of the florescence of X-rays in 1895 may have looked like a miracle. But anyone who desired to could reproduce it thousands of times. And that involved everybody's consent.

There is nothing like that in the Gospels. We are not concerned with a single little fact that will happen again and again under the same conditions. The Gospel is a test comprised chiefly of miracle accounts.

Now, if nothing is more difficult for me to accept, and more impossible, than a genuine miracle, nothing is also simpler to invent, to write about and to transmit than a miracle narrative.

Prudence and reason dictate the economy of explanations. If we can explain lightning by electricity, we do not have to disprove the existence of the god Jupiter. I say: "When you are looking for a cause, you must not assume the unnecessary." To suppose more than the necessary is to be superstitious.

Sometimes people believe they see things 'going on.' Even in our age of incredulity, the press occasionally writes articles on strange sightings. The most notable of these are the flying saucers which so many people say or thought they saw in the sky. Their sightings have led to many theories, especially the plurality of worlds. Doubtless they saw only a change in the air and light, one of the sudden corona, aurora or halo phenomena that the heavens experience from time to time. Some thought the atmospheric disturbances were traceable to atomic explosions which may have upset the balance of our now highly ionized atmosphere. I do not know. But the imagination takes advantage of, and feeds upon, the unusual. And since these apparitions seem to have improbable, spontaneous, capricious, almost voluntary trajectories, it is tempting to speculate that intelligent beings controlled them. Where did they come from, if not another world? Some people have also seen statues weep. It is surely the same phenomena: a real situation, bizarre, inexplicable, poorly observed in an aura of dread or desire calling for a preternatural explanation. Note that they are never entirely at fault. The possibility of rational creatures existing in another corner of the universe is a plausible one and cannot be disproven. The idea that an unseen power behind the universe is concerned over the troubles of mankind, just as a woman weeps over her children, is beautiful and profound. But the relationship of the first idea to flying saucers and the second to wooden statues must, if genuine, be minutely examined and proven at great length. We know that the mechanism of illusion is thrown into motion by surprise. The inventive imagination turns a little truth into fact, into an unverifiable belief. A shadow at night suggests a possible ambush or assault; a garbled sound makes one ready to scream for help. All things considered, it is the duty of a work of art which, with poor means, evokes our unconscious ideals of beauty.

When I see something extraordinary, my imagination first tries to find a normal explanation for it. I know that eye-witnesses can be sincerely mistaken. They can, by means of an admixture of obstinacy and loyalty, stick to their first assertion which we cannot make them change, yet we wait forever for an exact and impartial observation renewed on an event which has broken the order of the laws. We may even doubt that there will ever be an observation made about such a breach of the law: for in the face of what appears to be an exception to the laws, a learned man will suspend judgment and will appeal to a future science that is better informed about the secrets of the universe. Let no one speak here of inde-terminacy. The indeterminacy of the trajectory of a real or virtual particle of matter bears no resemblance to a miracle. And if one calls the indeterminate act a "miracle" out of care-lessness, we must state that these countless little "miracles" in every instant of the cosmos drop from sight and balance each other out in their multiplicity and produce a stable order of things: which is precisely the opposite of a miracle. Miracles are rare. They are also singular by essence. If they occur in calculable cycles — like the coming of spring — miracles would be indistinguishable in appearance from nat-ural facts.

That does not mean that a breaking away from deter-minism is *by rights* impossible in my opinion. I want to keep my mind open and free to every possibility.

How the Mind Rejects a Verification from Appearance

What would I do, then, if I actually saw something, if I were forced to witness an obviously paranormal phenomenon?

I believe I would first of all *deny* it and call it an *appearance*.

I remember being invited to a friend's home in the English countryside. He lived in a manor house that was, of course, haunted. At dinner we spoke lightly of the *ghost*, refuting its existence with that attitude of "after all, why not?" which lends so much charm to English conversation. In the middle of the night, with my own eyes I saw that *ghost* come out of a trap door and walk across my room. I recalled my logical processes. I could not deny the evidence of my senses: it was really a human being — a boy wearing a hideous Chinese mask over his head and moaning balefully. But, finding security in the *impossibility of such a thing*, I rejected the solid evidence of my senses as being imaginary. Even had the ghost struck me, I would have denied it and considered it "purely imaginary," "unreal," a "phantom." It is in the same way that my power of sight, as La Fontaine said, straightens out a stick that looks bent when plunged into water. You cannot deny the "bend," but I call it a *"correct misinterpretation,"* this is, an appearance. The causes of the illusory appearance remain to be seen.

Each one of us can study in himself the sovereign operation of the mind which is not afraid to reject a "fact" as illusory for the sake of mere principle, however obvious, however well-observed and verified it may be. It is impossible. Therefore, no matter how convincing the proofs, the experience or even the evidence, it is certainly the product of imagination. *It cannot be: therefore, it is not.* I find that the operation by which one subordinates the obvious proves the power of thought which never lets itself be constrained. We must be confident that it has the advantage over experience.

I realize that some will object: in most cases, thinking yields to experience, testimony to fact, and the mind finds afterwards that it was right in doing so. Reasoning which denies experience is the reasoning of Don Quixote; nonsense, a fool's logic. I see in advance the extreme difficulty in deciding which is more advisable: to give in to it or to deny it.

That does not prevent me from denying things about Jesus at first either out of prudence or excessive caution. The stakes are too high not to have a go at all the solutions which reduce, and that in the interest of both reason and faith. Faith must not shield the beliefs of a bad conscience: it must be strong enough to temporarily assume grounds for doubt.

I am returning to the problem which I left somewhat in suspension, the problem of determining the immediate, incontrovertible given.

Emergence and Origin

Where shall I begin? I think that in every question of source and beginning we must distinguish between *emergence* and *origin*.

Emergence is the moment when what existed *beforehand* comes to the surface and becomes the object of discussion. We call it the moment of birth. But birth is not the true origin or the actual beginning which arises in a very real secrecy.

The history of mankind knows the emergences and not the generally unseen origins. We must proceed from emergence to origin.

We have no direct knowledge of Jesus, only a collection of texts written by his followers, gathered together, selected, preserved, venerated and defended by a society, the Church, which is united to Jesus as its founder and which, having existed in time, is still visible. The Church is the *emergence*. The Church gives us the Gospel which tells of the *origin*. Or, as we say, Scripture is a part, an aspect of Tradition. The Church is prior to it, instigates it, inherits it and carries it to others.

I must start with the Church and, reducing my argument to the minimum, say that in the Jewish religion I first encounter a group of the faithful who, instead of waiting for the Messiah, think that he has already come and ascribe to the very recent past an event which the other Jews ascribe to the future.

Msgr. Duchesne, who had an acute historical mind and who was very moderate in speech, once expressed it this way:

"How and in what circumstances did the movement begin which was to result in the foundation of a Church in the religious world of Palestine? All our information points to, as a starting point, a group of people living in Jerusalem at the end of the Emperor Tiberius' reign (30-37). These first of the faithful bore witness to the name and doctrine of Jesus of Nazareth, recently executed by the order of the Procurator Pilate at the instigation of the Jewish leaders. Many of them knew him when he was alive: they all knew he had been crucified and believed he had risen from the dead and that a certain group of them had enjoyed his presence after his resurrection. They believed he was the promised and long-awaited Messiah, the one sent by God, the Son of God, who would set up a reign of justice in the world and win a staggering victory over evil. He promised to found a kingdom, the kingdom of God, from which evil would be excluded and to which all who followed him would belong. True, his execution delayed the fulfillment of the promise; but it would not hinder its realization. This they gleaned from the Lord's triumph over death. He was presently seated at the right hand of God his Father from whence he would come to manifest his glory and found his kingdom.

While awaiting it, his followers kept busy by spreading the good news, the Gospel, and by forming the body of the elect. They lived in a spiritual union: a single faith, a single expectation bound them closely together. Their leaders were twelve men who, in the past few years had lived intimately with Jesus, received their instructions which they spread abroad in his name and found themselves bearing witness to his miracles. In spite of their intimacy with the Lord, they forsook him in his hour of need and they found it hard to acknowledge his Resurrection. Now their conviction was so strong that no contradiction or proof could shake it. They were not long in verifying it.

The first group of the faithful remained rooted in the Jewish spirit. There was scarcely any difference between them and the pious Jews. The religious people of their nation believed and practiced all that they believed in, hoped for, or practiced. The faithful went with them to the Temple and, like them, they observed the ordinary Mosaic observances. Only one thing distinguished them from the rest: the Messiah was not an indefinite future event. They had found him, for he had come and had revealed himself: they were secure in the hope of seeing him soon."

The existence of the first disciples of a *certain Jesus,* the "poor of Jerusalem" whom Paul persecuted, Paul's conversion to this *certain Jesus,* his missionary voyages, the rapid expansion of the movement that had its beginnings in this *certain Jesus* — these are the foundation stones. We must proceed from one particular man called Jesus to a positive Jesus. No one would think of writing the history of Napoleon, Caesar or Socrates in this indirect style and optical reflection. I must proceed from the emergence to the origin, and the Gospel text affords me the guiding lines.

But the Gospel, which appears from a single growth, from a single fabric like the seamless garment in the Passion narrative, must be divided into two parts if one is to remain faithful to the position I adopted a little while back on fact and appearance.

An Attempt to Distinguish between the Historical and the Mythical

I am going to examine this strange mixture of *anecdote* and *wonder* which at first glance comprises the Gospel texts.

I hope to distinguish between what actually happened and what has been superadded by whatever it is that makes fables come to be.

It is not easy to make a division, for it is always difficult to set up boundary lines. Where does the water end and the dry land begin? The sea foam only knows. There are no well-defined shorelines or hairlines in human events. And who will be able to judge whether something is impossible? The technical world is filled with one-time impossibilities. Look at the steam engine, the heavier-than-air-flying-machine, television. And science is built upon a network of ideas once believed incompatible and contradictory. I remember hearing Bergson say, in his gentle way that was spiced with a touch of irony, that he did not know an *a priori* method which could prove the impossibility of facts. And yet, we always can. *If we have a fact,* then any attempt to dispute it by reasoning from its impossibility not only becomes disgraceful: it actually rationalizes itself away to nothing. What then, will afford us a correct and sure way to distinguish the solid and the certain in the Gospel accounts where the points of union are blurred and the boundaries nonexistent?

I am not unduly disturbed over the questions I raise because it is not my place, here, to be concerned with the subtle distinction between what is possible, probable and improbable. That is the historian's concern when he explains ancient things and interprets the intentions of the characters in history or the probable outcomes of such and such an event. Why did Napoleon decide to attack Russia or execute the duc d'Enghien? We can build up a whole series of possible reasons, choosing some, rejecting others, without being at all certain of any of them. Or we can argue endlessly whether Socrates was really what Plato made him out to be, whether Homer is one man or many. There just is no geometrical rule to help us decide among several equally possible hypotheses.

That is not the case here: the distinguishing mark is not a flexible and sinuous rule of the probable, but rather it is the rule of the possible and the impossible. On this one point the historian of Jesus has the advantage over this historian of Caesar or Alexander. He knows beforehand that certain things are not because they are impossible. It is quite easy to spot what rings falsely. No critic has ever had such a simple task.

For two thousand years critics have applied this rule to Christianity: Pilate or Herod as well? In any case, King Agrippa and the Counsul Sergius in the *Acts of the Apostles;* Celsus and Porphyry, Spinoza and Bayle, Voltaire and Diderot, Hegel, Strauss, Taine and Renan, Loisy, Goguel, Jaspers, Bultmann. It is the infallible rule which defines the two realms that are equally respectable and equally sources of the life of the spirit, but only one of which has the right to be called true: the domain of *reason* and the domain of the *heart*.

My rule will be easy to apply, as easy as it is necessary. If I should state that everthing is true, if I accepted all of it without any distinguishing among them, I would be a believer and there would be no problem. If I rejected everything, I would be more than a skeptic, I would be a kind of nihilist. But I am neither for the *fullness* of the simple faith of the simple, nor for the *vacuum* of negation. I am a moderate man, appreciating the possible and the impossible; I am an historian and a psychologist. I believe I understand what is likely and probable. I take the valid middle-ground between the excess of affirmation which is blind faith and the excess of negation which is not even science.

I am going to work between these two extremes and seek out the true causes of unnatural events, the hidden incentives of the faith. I shall take pleasure in learning more clearly what truly happened than they who lived those events and who believed themselves to be the true witnesses.

There are always two ways of seeing things: the way of

the simple man who believes that the sun is a not too-distant
great red ball in the sky and who, if necessary, will say so.
Then there is the way of the astronomer who looks at the sun
in the proper perspective, who does not deny the sincerity of
the simple man, but who knows that his belief is drawn only
from appearance. I do not deny what the simple man sees,
but I reject the way he describes it.

So too in the Gospel. Everything which is affirmed as
contrary to "the laws of nature" I am going to consider
illusory for the time being. The Resurrection, for example.
And in return, whatever prepares, supports or protracts the
Gospel's unnatural affirmation I shall consider as possible.
I do not say that this is historical. At least I shall not condemn
it for higher motives before my examination. If it is certified,
if it tallies with the contexts, if it is explicable by motives or
variables drawn from man, if it is part of a plausible development, why reject it? Christianity did not begin from zero.
It had to start from something which resembles what the
faith implies, except for miracles. If I find in myself the
model for everything in the Gospel which touches upon
human nature, then why reject the testimonies, especially
when they are so numerous, so corroborative and complex,
when they are rich in minor details that could not have been
made up and have actually been verified? I said that my
rule would oblige me to reject at least in substance all that
concerns the apparitions of a man who came back from the
dead. But why should I reject the account of his death, the
circumstances of his trial, execution and burial? Now, the
date of his death seems a bit questionable because it is so
symbolical. Jesus died on the day of the Passover. This is a
nameless miracle: but why not? Why should there not be,
at least once, one of those coincidences which originate faith
in a providence?

I am delighted because I see clearly the separation of the
two levels of experience which I have since encountered in

modern philosophy: that which proceeds from the object; that which only exists in the thinking subject. A completely different series of motives, reasons and causes correspond to the *objective* and the *subjective*.

The Objective and the Subjective

I explain those events I retain as probable by causes drawn from circumstances, environment, the state of the society, or by the variables taken from human nature: devotion to an exceptional man, love and fear, resentment, hatred, the desire to share his faith, and so forth ... or again by those powerful experiences which are at the source of mystical movements. We see religions — great or small, successes or failures — come into being before our eyes at every moment: Marxism is one of them. When the necessary transpositions have been made, the same causes can be applied to the Christian origins.

Now, I am faced with an element that I reject at once on principle because it is miraculous.

Of course, if worst came to worst, I can still keep that element and try to find a probable explanation for it. For example, I may say that Jesus had prepared the wine jugs (his wedding gift) at Cana, or that on the day of the multiplication of the loaves, he had taken enough bread along secretly to divide with the poor people.

Venturini or Paulus, attempting to write a *natural history of Jesus,* proffered explanations like these. It shows irresponsibility, and one is amazed that such otherwise moderate men were led in this direction. Voltaire almost fell into this error.

These explanations err in that they seek an objective reason for miracles. They are so appealing that they can still attract a man as judicious as Proudhon. Renan fully realized that one must seek a subjective reason for belief. Miracles were defined after the manner of Goethe as the darling child of faith.

I may attribute them to many causes: perceptual illusions, the abnormal constitution of some subjects given to hallucinations, deleria and mass-hysteria;

Or to the weakmindedness of fools, to cheap selfish motives, to the faith's unconscious need to invent proof; to the urge to enlarge upon the facts that is evident even among the mystics;

Or to the presence of earlier religious themes, types, archtypes, ideas or prodigies;

Or perhaps to the power of the World-Soul slowly developing throughout history and giving rise, at certain moments, to a new Idea, a new feeling, a faith. Whoever has read Hegel knows what I mean.

In short, I can apply all the resources of modern technology to the reduction of this inassimilable miraculous element: psycho-pathology, sociology of religions, psychoanalysis, the dialectic of history.... There is no end to the list. It is curious to note that, with each new method discovered in the recent past of analyzing the human mind, one can immediately draw applications that explain away the extraordinary element of the Gospel by reducing it to a natural process.

We are beginning to see possible explanations which will be refined in the next few years. Who can say whether the technique of combinations developing under the name of cybernetics will not eventually become the geometry of change able to reduce the improbable to the probable. This geometry of change was Pascal's dream.

Since, in the case of Jesus, the intellect is concerned with "naturalization," it is possible that these various explanations, although independent of one another, will develop further and will combine with each other — the uncertainty of one being supplemented by the uncertainty of the other. Our certitudes often come from interchanges of this nature.

Numerous histories of Jesus are compiled by this method of sorting, and they will continue to be compiled long after

I have become dust.   Albert Schweitzer catalogued them in his
classical work *The Quest of the Historical Jesus,* a critical
study of the progress from Reimar to Wrede.   The names of
the exegetes are unimportant to me.   The essential thing is
the type of thought which existed prior to the momentary
light who brought it to the world's attention.   Besides, a
famous man has given us this type of selective criticism and
has perfected it so well that he managed to conceal its
weaknesses by giving it his very soul.   One only knows, loves
and describes oneself best.   The true way to restore a subject
or fill in some of the gaps is to transfuse oneself in it.   That
is what Renan has done.

The following is an example, from Renan on the Resurrection, of what I call a selective critical explanation:

"Anyone of perspicacity could have told already, that
Saturday night, that Jesus would return to life.   The little
Christian community worked a miracle that day; through
the intense love it bore him, it raised up Jesus again in
its heart.   It resolved that Jesus would not die.   The love
of these passionate souls was truly stronger than death;
and as passion is nothing if not communicative, lighting
kindred sentiment like a torch and so propagating itself
indefinitely, at that hour Jesus, in a sense, had already
risen.   All that remained was for some trifling material
fact to give grounds for belief that his body was no longer
here below, and the dogma of the resurrection would be
founded for ever.

The cities of the East are mute after sunset, so indoors
there would have been very deep silence: every little
noise could be interpreted in the sense of universal expectation.   And expectation normally creates its object.   In
those decisive hours, a breath of wind, the creaking of a
window, any chance murmur may determine the belief of
whole peoples for centuries.   The breath of air is felt,
sounds are thought to be heard.   Some declare that they

have distinctly heard the word *schalom,* 'happiness' or 'peace'."

Forty years later, Loisy, a critic as formidable as Renan, used the same selective method: one can never avoid the logic of one's principles.

Loisy started with the idea that there *had* to be, although no one had ever seen it (but it is necessary to explain the genesis of faith in Jesus), a natural gospel with no miracles, which was its first condition. He re-wrote it; that is easy enough. And he explained the origin like this:

> "Jesus taught and worked miracles.
>
> "He did these things almost in spite of himself. From the time of his first stay at Capharnaum, they brought him the sick to heal. His distinct popularity frightened him; he was afraid lest his wonder-working would cause him to be taken for the preacher of the kingdom, and he fled from Capharnaum. A useless precaution. Once the movement had started, it could not be stopped. Jesus wanted to preach and convert, he had to heal people. Perhaps they even went so far as to attribute the resurrection of the dead to him, at least that of the young girl they begged him to heal who was dead when they brought him to her. Was he right to refuse the relief that God wrought through his hands? He worked especially well with those sick people believed to be diabolically possessed, the unfortunates afflicted with nervous disorders, brain fever and mental derangement. He spoke to them with authority, commanding the devils to go out of them, and those troubled and uneasy souls returned to normal, at least for a while."

Actually, Loisy is only reiterating Tacitus, Celsus, Porphyry and the Jews of every age. It is the same idea that Voltaire popularized — the position of the eternal skeptic. Jesus was a man hard to understand. He was condemned (whether

rightly or wrongly who knows?) and then exalted by fanat-
icism. Renan only a slight variation on the eternal theme
which Mohammed had proposed long before: Jesus is a
great prophet, perhaps the finest of men.

The selective method has one primary advantage over the
others: through it we can write a history of Jesus. "One
cannot," said Renan, "write the biography of an Aeon or a
God. But, thanks to the critical spirit, we are able to reconstruct the life of Jesus, just as can that of any ordinary man."

A Critique of Criticism

I have applied a method of dissociation to Jesus. From
the standpoint of critical reasoning it is the most honest, the
only really scientific one, and the only one worthy of "reason"
as we have come to understand reason in the last two hundred
years.

I realize the difficulties. It is the nature of every critical
process to be applied to itself as well. You doubt, but why
stop only half-way? If doubt is permissible, you may doubt
whether you are doubting; you may especially doubt your
reasons for doubting. If you admit that it is valid to criticize,
then why not criticize the criticism? The worst superstition is
one that goes unrecognized.

Now, when I think deeply about the selective method which
I have called a critical method, I see that it leads me to a
paradox. It is difficult to confine, it tends to dissolve the
object of its study into thin air. It renders almost totally
incomprehensible the history of Jesus that it reconstructs.
I am confused about it and had better get straightened out
right now.

I have no knowledge about Jesus from outside history; the
unbelievers and politicians of his day do not mention him,
and the documents we possess about Jesus came from the
faithful who already believed in him. I should have been on

my guard against this sacred history and not have used it in
the first place to extract plausible, rational and profane
history by a critical distillation. I took the chance. Without
the aid of faith, I used those texts conceived in the faith;
I sought to look into "the Christian testimony" and find out
what those people really saw.

I accomplished what I had anticipated, but I must ponder
over the strangeness of it. I learned that none of the primitive
"witnesses," who are my only warrantors and sources, would
accept the narrative I put together from those events. What
is more, if those witnesses ever read my account, they would
liken me to the false-witnesses whom they abhorred, for my
system does not only teach something different to what they
say happened, but it teaches the absolute contrary to that
upon which they focused the strength of their witnessing act.
The written Gospel which epitomized the *Kerygma,* the
earliest preaching, was redacted precisely to show that Jesus
was the Messiah, that Jesus had performed miracles and,
ultimately, that Jesus was God. This was his core, his essence, his single purpose, his very reason for being. The
remaining assertions were secondary. Now, out of loyalty
to what I call reason, criticism, understanding, I, from my
retreat fully stocked with secondary information and having
no direct experience at all of what happened, reject these
contemporary testimonies.

We must go a step further. By a strange contradiction,
after I examined and rejected what the authors of those
narratives believed to be essential, I placed myself in full
accord with those very authors whom I repudiate (and whom
I accuse of being fabricators or visionaries, incapable of understanding the events). Here, I say, I am in wholehearted
agreement with them when they describe for me the places,
times, circumstances, the faces, the anecdotes and the words
spoken and the individuals — because, this time, I find that
these things all correspond to my idea of what is possible.

The Tendency of the Critical Hypothesis

Am I being consistent with myself in my double attitude about a single text and a single affirmation? Would it not be more fitting if I were much more skeptical towards those "witnesses" caught red-handed? Why should I be so mistrustful about what is in their mind, and in fact actually is the essence of their testimony (*that for which* they would die), and why should I be so trustful about the extras, the details and the accidentals of the same testimony? If someone tells me he saw a ghost in a red cloak, I will not tell him that the ghost does not exist, but he really did see a red cloak.

"Be logical," my objector would insist, "carry out your distrust to its logical conclusions. Don't pick and choose. Reject the whole thing, or rather, keep it within the unverifiable realm of faith."

A story is told about Anatole France — a man of little certitude but of great spirit — that illustrates the difficulty of the hypercritical historians. M. Couchoud accompanied France to Loisy's conferences and he describes him making sketches in the margins of the notes he took on the course. One illustration depicts Loisy astride the limb of a tree and chopping the trunk with an axe while saying, "I'll leave just enough to hold me up." Long ago, in the same skeptical vein, a phrase of Renan had inspired him to write his short story 'The Procurator of Judaea' in which we see a Pilate who has forgotten all about the Jesus incident. And France parodied Renan in the following manner explaining an Arabic text to the College de France:

"*Under the Caliph Harun-al-Rashid, a merchant of Bagdad. . . .* Gentlemen, we are standing on firm historical ground here; Harun-al-Rashid is a caliph whose time in history is well-known to us. Bagdad is a city that we know, and several sound texts certify that there were many merchants in Bagdad. . . . *He ate a date and tossed the pit up in the air. . . . The pit struck a genie.* Gentlemen, we are confronted with a supernatural fact which cannot be accepted. Let's throw it out and see how we can explain it away."

The consequence of the method of separation is that, if one does not accept the whole at least in substance, one is quickly led to the necessity of rejecting practically everything. This fact soon became evident in the critical school of the Renan style, especially among the French who cannot think for very long on two planes (which German thinkers do not find repugnant) by admitting that the Jesus of faith can remain "true," while the Jesus of history contradicts it.

Descent from the Highest to the Lowest

I would like to find out just what remains of Jesus after one has scoured away everything the narratives attribute to him which surpass the powers that one concedes to nature. May we *demythologize* Jesus and keep him in a normal human stature? Are we not at once forced to make him tumble from the highest category to the lowest, being unable to place him somewhere in between? The news accounts we heard of "de-stalinization" exemplify the law behind those processes that topple former idols: there is no middle ground. The god of yesterday "stripped of his godhead" is no longer even a good Russian, but a monster.

When a being is endowed with superior qualities, either inspired or holy, and is then stripped of these qualities, he does not drop back to normal size. Instead, the most degrading qualities are heaped upon his head. If you love someone wholly and absolutely, and you begin to question your beloved's fidelity, your love turns into hatred. When a being conceived as superexistent is deprived of his superexistence, he does not merely become existent, but plunges into a kind of non-existence.

The Gospel presents Jesus as more than a man, a superman, and ultimately equal to God, God Himself. Destroy this attribute and you will not end up with a man, but with something less than a man, a sub-man, a wretched thing, ultimately a doubtful being, and the human mind begins to rebound between his abnormality and non-existence.

By granting that the origin of Jesus' religion may be pure illusion, indefinite perception or hallucinations of hearing and touch, then no matter how carefully chosen the words, one is essentially attributing an origin to the source of the religion that is no different than that of the meanest of superstitions. The Jesus thus obtained belongs to the most doubtful zones of existence. He ultimately becomes the object about which one knows nothing and about which one suspects everything. [1]

And this metamorphosis extends to the idea one has of the origin of Christianity, in spite of the verbal veneration which is required out of decency.

It then becomes increasingly difficult to explain how this poor carpenter from an unknown village, this prophet having attracted a few brave provincials to himself, who died shortly after his betrayal, could be the origin of a religion that in a short time unsettled the most solid religious institutions there were.

---

1. Towards the end of his life Loisy had this to say about Jesus:

"He was an itinerant preacher-exorcist, the prophet of a unique oracle. . . . His message, if he had one, was rejected. . . . Through an act of religious illumination he resolved to bring the message of the Kingdom to Jerusalem. . . . His presence at Jerusalem provoked an uproar. He was arrested, summarily judged by the Roman official under circumstances we know nothing about."

Guignebert said this:

"This prophet who had, at least, awakened a sympathetic curiosity from among the laborers of Galilee, was one of the more or less trustworthy pretenders which Israel saw turning up every now and then. His downfall was absolute. . . . He was betrayed. In all likelihood, and by the rules of logic, his name and work should have perished like those of so many others who in Israel thought they were somebody.

Problems of the Same Nature Raised
by the Disproportion Between Cause and Effect

If our minds are deeply disturbed by the disproportion
between effect and cause in the problem of Jesus, rest assured
that this is not the only instance of it. There are similar cases
every time, it seems, that a spiritual element is inserted into
the universe.

I am thinking particularly of the story of Joan of Arc. It
sheds some light on the story of Jesus. If Joan were not an
exceptional personality in connection with historical sources,
than her episode is a lamentable commonplace. Her case is a
psychiatric one. She was not even an average decent girl;
she was mentally deranged. It remains, then, to explain how
it happened that other maidens and visionaries of the same
period, Catherine de la Rochelle, Colette de Corbie, Pierrone
de Bretagne, Marie de Maillé, Marie Robine, Catherine Sauve,
the Dame des Armoises, Jeanne la Férone ... lived their lives
without much influence, while Joan alone has posed the
problem of her origins to the science of her age and our own.

It is also the same problem raised by the origin, the
emergence of man:

Among the hominids, how many the parallel branches
which are candidates for hominization, for becoming like
our rational species! A creature that does not differ from
the others in appearance except for a few cubic centimeters
of grey matter crosses the threshold alone. It alone has
received that indefinable seed. Yet, it is like all the others in
outward appearance.

We can say as much for the messiahs who came before and
after Jesus. History knows little or nothing about them, for
history is cruel and effaces the memory of those who run
aground. The discoveries along the Dead Sea bear much
food for thought on this point. The sands or caves will perhaps

someday reveal other "servants of Yahweh," other "Teachers of Righteousness," perhaps other victims of Justice or Idea, perhaps another one sent to the cross.   Then it will be asked why the other teachers or messiahs have no posterity.

The Cult of Jesus from the Beginning

We must include one other topic for reflection. I oppose to return to it at length later on, for I think it is the focal point of every deep study of Christianity: how is the worship which Jesus received right from the outset to be explained?

I believe it is difficult to avoid the fact that Jesus' followers, as we know them through history, recognized him as being something more than a "god" in the pagan superstitious sense of the word by which they understood a plurality of gods, of one god among a host of others.   He was the final master in heaven and on earth, *Lord* in the fullest sense of *Kyrios* as the word was used among the Jews, the Romans and the Greeks, that is, one endowed with supreme power.   "Every knee must bend," said Saint Paul in one of his Epistles, "in heaven and on earth and in hell before this name which is above every other name."   I intend to reflect upon this rather strange aspect of Jesus.   Let it suffice for the time being to note that Jesus is equivalent to God for Paul and for everyone to whom he wrote, even though they never saw him.   Paul produced no personal teaching on this point.   He simply elucidated the common belief of the Christians through his power of expression and characteristic logic.   One may say that while reading him the divinity of Jesus shows up more clearly than his existence in the form of a slave which Saint Paul supposes, but scarcely stresses.

Now that I have brought up this essential factor, I shall return to the thinking of the critical type of mind which, basing itself on the Gospel texts and the postulate of "natural reason," reconstructs the true history of Jesus and the origins of the Christian religion.

They encounter many problems.

Had Jesus received similar divine honors in a Greek environment at Antioch or Ephesus — among people always ready to take in one more god — we would ignore the whole question. Could we conceive as a possibility that Jesus had been on probation in the Hellenistic world as a neophyte god for future divinization and that this Jesus-made-God had been retransmitted to the first Jewish disciples who only knew him as Jesus the man? Could we, over a gradual, lengthy and progressive span of time, perceive any process whatever of the human divinization of Jesus?

Nothing of the kind is evident. Jesus appeared immediately and without any genesis as one equal to Yahweh at least by his offices. To explain how a creature of flesh could be considered equal to God alone in the Jewish world is almost unthinkable — especially if it is asserted that the real Jesus was a practically non-existent man.

Renan foresaw this problem and thought he resolved it by magnifying Jesus, intimating that divinization was the end result. But, since the Jews understood divinity as an inaccessible transcendence, the distance between the greatest prophets and Yahweh was infinite. One cannot reconcile Jesus to the divine identity by exalting him. It goes without saying that when Jesus has been reduced to the condition of a village nabi or to an unsuccessful agitator, — the impossibility of a sudden leap is still more astounding.

Thus, the more one tries to bring Jesus down to the level of the ordinary, the more difficult one makes it to conceive the sudden passage from acknowledgment of his questionable existence to the notion of his divine superexistence.

We are secretly led to an entirely new, very different and even contrary approach which is to reverse the order of the factors and attack the problem from the opposite direction. If we know practically nothing about the man Jesus (or if this man is practically nothing), then why delay over this enigmatical human history? Starting from the man leads nowhere. Then, why not begin with the God-made-man and proceed from the faith to faith?

CHAPTER IV

The Mythical Jesus
or
The Second Approach

I HAVE made it a rule to pursue and refine the negative solutions, to look for their origins and deduce their consequences — and that with more logic, consistency and particularly with more transparency than they who ordinarily support them.

The moment has arrived to be more faithful to this rule than ever before. I feel that we have seen an end to what I call the Critical School. Will it revive in the future in a more scholarly and human form? Today, Renan's *Life of Jesus* is unbearably commonplace. We wonder how our fathers found it so appealing, just as before Renan's time the idea of *Myth* prevailed over that of *History*, even the "natural history" of Jesus. I believe I know why. The critical position is the first one considers. It is so unstable that it soon develops into a different view which I think I recognize and shall have to describe.

In order to explain Jesus I had to reduce him. But the more I reduced Jesus the man, Jesus the phenomenon, the wider I made the gap between Jesus and Christ, between the wretched Jesus and the Idea of a God-made-Man. As I have said, chronology proved useless because it left me with neither sufficient time nor the necessary links to casually explain the emerging development of Jesus into God. The more I diminished the man, the first phenomenon, the more

I ennobled and sublimated the faith in the mystery of this
man and phenomenon — that is to say the *Idea* people had
of him from the outset.

Then, why not consider the Idea-made-into-faith first of
all? Is this not the *immediate given subject* I am looking for?

I do not regret the fact that I just now tried to act like
the scholars and historians, that I wanted to determine a first
historical event from which the faith took its origin. But
this event and person are almost dissolved to nothingness by
the analysis I made of them. And I find myself standing
before an abyss of uncertainty.

Reversing the Approach

I propose to reverse the direction of my research like Copernicus and Kant did. Beginning with the fact and proceeding
to the idea has not helped me. Nor has starting from the
event and going to the faith been very successful. Let me
begin from the Idea.

There is enormous advantage to this approach. I am not
compelled to admit the historicity of Jesus in the usual sense
of the word. This approach permits me to retain his religion,
if it is true that religion consists in beliefs. Perhaps I shall be
able to keep what is essential to Christianity and still remain
faithful to disbelief.

I know that ever since Hegel's time the method I am
suggesting has enjoyed great popularity in German thinking.
The German genius, though it collects all kinds of little
insignificant facts with unflagging patience, is not very concerned with what are properly called facts, I mean those
singular and contingent events within the human scope.
Rather, it quickly moves beyond them by likening them to
concepts, to the favored moments of a dialectic whose
philosophical spirit describes the law. Hegel was not interested in Napoleon as Napoleon, although he had seen him at
Iena in 1806, but only as the moment when, after the Reign

of Terror had repudiated and disrupted everything, the cycle of history righted itself to beget a new synthesis. In short, the German genius neglects fact: it rises up from a scholarly dust to the final dialectical synthesis which consumes all of history and assumes event in Idea.

Today, we have numerous examples of this method of interpreting history: it works wonderfully well in the Marxist ideology which, while based on experience, directly forgets this experience in order to replace facts with laws, syntheses and necessities.

Alain admired, like Auguste Comte, the idea of the Virgin Mary, the Infant God, the bread of life, as richly meaningful; yet, he was not concerned with their truth.

The Mythical Explanation

At least forty years ago (but in our accelerated history forty years are quite a lot), the notion of myth passed through its purgator. Sociologists viewed myths as products of a primitive and infantile mentality. M. Levy-Bruhl's scholarly work taught that this mentality was meaningless to the civilized and scientific adult mentality. Towards the end of his life he altered his position, pointing out that the world of art and religion lived on myths, that perhaps they drew elements of a higher truth from it which are inaccessible to our ordinary means of inquiry.

This is a return to the idea of several German romantics like Herder. It could be called a return to Plotinus and Plato and to everyone who interpreted myths as symbols of higher truths too lofty for our intellects to grasp. Such people as Mircea Eliade and Bultmann have given myths a new stature by transforming them into a helpful means in which to express the substance of the spiritual life.

The way I understand him, Bultmann is not far removed from Plato's inspiration on myths. Plato saw myths as the framework in which the questions of the beginning and the

end of time could be raised, for the timeless science of the
Greeks could not cope with them, and yet they interest and
concern man. Bultmann seems to think that the Gospel, by
assuming the absolute reality of time and space, by confusing
heaven and earth, by causing time and eternity to overlap,
presents mythically certain inexpressible realities to which the
faith adheres. Thus, the descent into hell, the ascent into
heaven, and in a more general way (but here the passage
enters upon the infinite), the union of divinity and humanity
in an historical Jesus, survival after death: so many images
endowed with deep religious value, containing even a divine
revelation — provided one does not charge them with historical meaning.

Amiel said that Hegel's system found its fulcrum in the
ambiguity of the word *Aushebung* which signifies both
putting an end to and *fulfilling*. It has been pointed out that
Entmythologisierung, demythologization, a word Bultmann
coined, signifies at once *cancellation* and *reinterpretation* —
the act of reclothing the Gospels in a new interpretation after
the evangelical myth has been done away with. I have no
objection to this "doing away with," so long as they do not
mean by it "fulfillment," and so long as "repudiation" does not
mean "superaffirmation." I am not criticizing anyone who
rejects evangelical truth, but I mistrust those who pretend they
still retain it once they have rejected it — who take away the
substance and still want to keep its flavor. I cannot imagine
that a rational mind rooted in Western Culture could possibly
reconcile itself to this confusion. I understand the meaning
of the word *mystery* when it signifies a truth beyond our
conceptual framework, a reality incomprehensible to us, and
yet true. I understand the meaning of the word *myth* when
it means a story invented to bring across a truth. We see
this in allegories, moral lessons, fables, or purely imaginative
stories as legends. I know that a myth may contain some
gold nuggets of poetry and truths in certain particulars. But
the attitude of the one who created the myths has nothing

to do with the attitude of the one who certifies them. The former invents, the latter discovers. One assumes, the other verifies. I cannot make heads or tails out of the illicit concept of *true myth*. One should at least be mindful of one's language.

Sketch of a Marxist Jesus

Having said this much, and provided one does not make religious interpretations from mythical conceptions, I now enter into the height, width and depth of the mythical hypothesis. I shall try to imagine what the mythical explanation of Jesus would be like in a Marxist world that has absorbed the Christian mystical doctrine. I shall not make a servile attempt. I endow my fervent Marxist with the highest possible intelligence and take it for granted that he has been brought up on Feuerback, has read Bultmann, is respectful toward Jesus and has Saint Paul's Epistles in his hands.

I can hear him say that humanity has always tended to project itself on a kind of screen so that it could worship itself. I hear him say also that the idea of the divinity of all men was latent in the mind of humanity, that it waited only for an occasion to appear; that mankind never perceives its divinity in times of happiness but only in those times of suffering when the multitude of man feels humbled and suffers hopelessly, when it thinks itself a slave. It protests. It wants to escape. And, in this alienation, it becomes aware that it is able to swathe itself in divine values. Let there be a slave put to death somewhere in the Roman world and the time is ripe for humanity to divinize itself in him.

Example of a Mythical Explanation:
the Multiplication of Loaves

Now, let us see how mythical thinking interprets a Gospel narrative. To begin with, let us take the multiplication of

the loaves. The "critic" maintains there indeed was some
food for that great crowd, but that the bread was already
there and that the unforeseen appearance of the bread was
transformed into a miracle. The problem of the reality of
the event is eliminated right away for the "mythologist."
He will only have to find similar accounts of this story and
show how a story, like a work of art, begets others in imitation of it. Strauss hunted them out in the Old Testament and
found the mannah and quail of Moses, or Eliah's multiplication
of the oil and meal as a favor to the widow of Sarepta. We
may look elsewhere. But it is essential to begin with a literary
type. The older the type, the better, because, too far removed
from any testimony, it is seen more easily as a timeless Idea.
The Idea of the multiplication of food is in itself quite
beautiful and profound: words are the multiplication of
singular thoughts, every discourse is the multiplication of the
bread of truth. Or we may say that the latent Idea of multiplication was at first incarnate in the eucharistic cult where,
at every "breaking of bread," the division and the multiplication of Christ himself, the Word of God, is realized and
participated in. Saint John's Gospel has no trouble passing
from material bread to Spiritual bread. But we must travel
the opposite direction. We had the Idea of heavenly bread
first: it was the substance of the faith. And the anecdotal
and fabulous account of the material multiplication of the
loaves came from this Idea, and is only the mythical image
of a theme or great mystery.

The Paschal Lamb

Also, the primary Idea at the heart of the faith is that
of the Paschal Lamb, the substitution of a voluntary, divine,
holy, human victim for the animals slaughtered in the Temple.
It is "the new alliance by the blood of Jesus." Now, how
are we to explain that Jesus died precisely as Saint John's
Gospel says, at the very moment the Temple's High Priest

was slaughtering the Passover lambs? It implies in him a superhuman knowledge, a divine power over time. To die at the very moment of the Passover rite, he could have anticipated the Passover with his Galilean disciples like the synoptic Gospels suppose. But if we stay on the level of pure history, then how absolutely improbable these bizarre coincidences seem: man no more chooses the date of his death than the date of his birth. And how likely is it that so serious an event as a capital execution could have taken place in Jerusalem during the most solemn feast of the year? That, the mythologists say, is where respect for history leads to; critical minds err in following the Gospels on their level and according them the "natural miracle" of the almost impossible coincidence of the death of Jesus-the-Lamb with the death of the sacrificial lambs, his last meal with the Passover Meal.

But if we reverse the perspectives we shall make headway without falling back on the improbable or on faith.

Jesus died at some date or other. If he ate his last meal, that too was at some definite time. It is certain beyond the slightest shadow of doubt that the rite of the breaking of bread and the eating of this broken bread which the first Christians believed to be the actual Paschal Lamb did exist in those tiny communities which the Epistles describe. Therefore, the paschal myth is established in history. At what date, at what moment, are we to place this history and how are we to imagine it? That depends on the given points of the problem: Jesus died on the very day upon which the Passover lamb was sacrificed, there was no other possible day. He of necessity died in Jerusalem. He died violently and, in conformity to the sacrificial rite, not one bone was broken. So much for the time and the place. Finally, since Jesus obviously could not die and at the same time preside over his last Passover meal during which he mystically immolated himself, must he not have in some way anticipated the Last Supper? Might he not have been familiar with another calendar, the one used by the Dead Sea Community, which

fixed the Passover two days ahead of time? That is how
those events which seem to have the character of history
about them and, because of the improbable coincidences
contained in them, of a deeply significant history, or of a
history divinely arranged by an eternal power that is sovereign
over places, times and their relationships, — that is how, I say,
these events are *demythologized* and "dedivinized" by simply
reversing the movement of the intellect which proceeds from
the sense to the fact and not from the fact to the sense, which
also completely dissolves the harmony between *fact* and *sense*
which are accommodated to each other in an eternal plan.

That is the principle of the second explanation I call
mythical. Its practically untenable conclusion is the denial
of Jesus' historical existence. It is unsuitable to moderate
minds. But this excess does show what it tends to. It leads
us to think that had Jesus not existed, it would have changed
nothing.

The Essence of the Mythical Explanation

There are two ways of not existing. The first is simply
not to exist at all; the second is to be mediocre, banal, uncertain, doubtful, *insignificant,* as we say. (We may say that
but for a few exceptions we all are, in as much as we are men,
the latter.) We do not have to go to these extremes: barring
miracles, we may concede to Jesus some of the traits which
the Gospel attributes to him. We may even go so far as to
grant him death on the cross.

It is typical that this line of thinking recognizes in the
existence of Jesus, whatever it may have been, an *occasion*
of the belief in Jesus (if one is an unbeliever) or of God's
revelation concerning Jesus (if one is a Christian). This
ultimately, and therefore virtually, explains the genesis of
Christianity without Jesus who is but a spark, whose existence one can always insert between brackets and bypass in
order to give undivided attention to the essence of Chris-

tianity as it is presented in the faith. This is to imagine that "nothing essential would be changed if the name of Jesus were placed in quotation marks as a more or less conventional designation of the religious phenomenon similar to what occurred in the first Christian generation" (Bultmann).

I find that it helps my French mind to understand this approach if I recall what I know of creation. The general public is wrong to think that a novelist starts with something he remembered from the past and describes what he has seen. The novelist is astounded to hear it said that his novel was written about real characters who have been disguised. He is shocked to hear people name those who could have been models for the characters whom he could have idealized. This is not at all what the novelist does. Yes, a novelist needs a starting point, and it is true that he uses past recollections, historical persons, but only to set his creative powers in motion. When Balzac created Grandet he may have had a provincial miser in mind; that makes no difference. Grandet took his form, density and superexistence from Balzac's creative genius. In any case, Grandet cannot be explained by a real miser, but by the great legendary misers whom Balzac's genius invented.

The essence of the mythical explanation is that it proceeds from Idea to Fact and not, as the former approach, from Fact to Idea. Renan held that the ideal Jesus of the faith was the final embellishment of the real Jesus. Bultmann sees the real Jesus of history as the final expression of belief in Jesus Christ. That is something quite different.

The Difficulty

This approach contains a special difficulty which is best to overlook or leave unmentioned for it appears insoluble. The problem lies in the text of each of the first three *Gospels* and the *Acts* because these documents root Jesus into a particular time, a soil. They give him an origin, action and a human personality. These texts evoke a vast array of individuals around Jesus. They relate a web of true-to-life events. They insert the history of Jesus into the history of a highly pronounced milieu.

If we only had Saint Paul's Epistles, if the Johannine Gospel were merely a simple collection of discourses by the Logos, could we then find these views plausible? We have the concrete Gospel, the complex and contingent Gospel, the utterly human and topological Gospel, the Gospel in its historical form, and how are we to explain it from a belief in Christ alone?

If we take the example of the relationship of the Last Supper and the Passion to the immolation of the paschal lamb, what of the difficulties we encounter by supposing the four accounts of the Passion to be fabricated? Each Gospel is entirely distinct, yet so much akin to the others in its impassible and moderate tone, in its human plausibility and in its agreement with what we know of Roman and Jewish law.

How could fabrication reconstruct the Judeo-Roman world as it existed before the year A.D. 70, and reconstruct it so well when one stops to think of the enormous confusion among the ruling powers, factions and institutions? Judea, at first governed by Archelaus, son of Herod, was next administered by a Roman procurator subject to the imperial legate of Syria, while Galilee owed fealty to Herod Antipas, the vassal tetrarch of Rome. Judea was "an occupied nation." Because of the occupation of some countries during recent history, we are quite aware of the problems one meets in describing after the coup what the superimposed rule was like. Look how hard the task of reconstruction was in those Nazi occupied countries, even for those who lived under it. Now, the trial and passion of Jesus substantiate what we know of the ambiguous relationships which then existed between Jewish authority and Roman power: the Jewish microcosm, a unique structure which many chance events had wrought, this unstable universe swallowed up in the disaster of the year 70,

could hardly be described afterwards.   Now, in our four
Gospels the many branches of thought and factions bear close
resemblance: the Herodians, Pharisees, Sadducees, John's
remaining followers, the disciples of Jesus.

Fabrication and Attestation

I would like to approach this question from a different
angle.

Following Bergson's suggestion in *The Two Sources of
Morality and Religion,* I posit the theory that there exists in
human nature a faculty which adapts it to life, a faculty
which invents images and creates myths.   Now, by granting
that this power exists (and the fact of *mythologies* certainly
seems to prove its existence), one may study the character
of its products and the traits which distinguish them from
real things.   For, alongside this fabricative power, which
manifests itself at various times in life, there is also most
assuredly a faculty of observation and attestation: history and
social life presuppose it.   There must be some incontrovertible
sign that distinguishes legends from eye-witness accounts.

By asserting that we have within us, as two attitudes, two
faculties and two functions, I do not insinuate that they never
mingle.   We observe this mingling when we study the narrative
processes which man needs for transmitting what he has seen.
Every man who tells something is a narrator and there is, as
Pierre Janet said, a "code of conduct in narration."   The
narrator must follow an order.   He works within frameworks,
he uses older accounts as points of reference.   I have noticed
how the witnesses of an outstanding event are at a loss for
words to express it when they have neither the talent nor the
education: I have seen how powerless the mind is when it
must rely upon itself to describe what it has seen if it does not
borrow types, stereotypes and make slight exaggerations.
It is obvious that the more unique the event, the further that
it surpasses the bounds of expectation, the greater the need

4 *Jesus*

becomes for pre-existing elements in the narration of and
the understanding of the fact. We call this *true fabrication,*
and the study of the *forms* of evangelical tradition reveals
much about it.

It is even truer to say that the Gospel was in the beginning
a collection of anecdotes, facts and typical words used by
the missionaries whose memories were aided by rhythm and
form.

Moreover, since the meaning and import of a fact is more
important than its details to one who is teaching a doctrine
of life, the circumstances became obscured in favor of the
sense. Some features that were superadded or inspired by
like situations were mingled into the narrative. Barring some
kind of improbable assistance which one cannot deny on
principle (though it has got to be proven), there must be
some percentage of error in the Gospels concerning those
details which exist statistically in the human testimonies of
the same epoch and milieu.

May we take a further step and say that the essence of
the Gospel bears the stamp of fabrication? May we classify it
as a legend of cult? I wish to find out by making a comparison
between the process of fabrication and the process of history.

Examination through Places

We know how fertile the imagination is when left to its
own devices — as in the case of myths before a poet purifies
and transforms them. Myths take liberties with historical
fact and disregard any anachronisms; if their settings resemble
history, they invent the past in terms of the present. They
elaborate, enlarge, project and transpose according to the
regular process of fabrication found in every land and among
every people: we have moved beyond the realm of time.

Now it is an established fact that the places mentioned
in the Gospel coincide with what was written about them:

the people of Palestine recognize the sites, the distances, the differences in the regions, the descriptions of the holy city and its monuments, its surroundings and pecularities.

If we maintain that the setting for the Gospel stems from the mind's fabricative power, then one event in particular renders any possibility of historical accuracy even more unlikely. In A.D. 70, the Roman legions sacked Palestine, razed Jerusalem, destroyed its Temple and worship was broken off forever. Now, when the imagination considers the past, it cannot avoid projecting what it perceives in the present into the remote distance. Flaubert made intensive research to avoid any historical inaccuracy before he wrote *Salambo*. But Flaubert worked in his study. The mythical imagination of a zealous community that contrives the setting in which the legend of its hero is to unfold is something else. Because the people would be indifferent to it and because truth and local color might cause offense, just how accurate could that setting be?

I want also to reflect upon the paradox of Saint John's Gospel. Theoretically and according to what we have seen above, this Gospel would be least anxious to situate Jesus in his time and locale. The Gospel wanted to depict the Word in the flesh certainly, but it also intended to show his message present in time and co-eternal as well. We are able to date this writing from the end of the first century; that is, between the event and its redacting three generations had passed. Finally, the Gospel is addressed chiefly to intellectual disciples who had little patience with onomastics and details of forgotten places, especially now that Jerusalem had been laid waste. All these circumstances put the minute details of this Gospel on the times, the hours and journeys of Jesus into a strange light. How could the author of the Fourth Gospel be so fortunate as to invent descriptions unknown to synoptical tradition and which have been verified by excavations nineteen or twenty centuries later?

Renan recognized this characteristic of the Fourth Gospel which, stripped of its doctrine, had served him as a guidebook that permitted him to insert the humanity of Jesus into history and tell *the life* of Jesus. Excavations have confirmed his insight: the description of the Temple, the two pools at Bethsaida and Siloe, and the Lithostrotus. Of course, one may always say that the author of the Fourth Gospel used a Baedecker to situate his imaginary history into a particular locale which he wanted to substantiate like the authors of *chansons de geste*. The most probable and economical hypothesis of all is still to admit that the Gospel rests upon the accurate recollections of a privileged eye-witness.

We must point out that each one of these careful verifications of the Gospel by the earth, history, calendar and custom requires a great deal of time and absorbs the full attention of a specialist over a period of many years. Also, each type of verification is independent of the rest: for example, an expert on ancient papyri owes nothing to one who studies the times or locale, nor he to the specialist in Jewish customs, or the Jewish or Aramaic tongues, nor he in turn to the study of Greek vocabulary or the Hellenistic milieux. It is the whole fabric of such findings taken from many sources which have incarnated the Gospel once again in its "time" and place, in its moment, and situated it in life and given it a concrete historical dimension — verified everything not concerned with the assertion of faith which bears on the transnatural which is, in itself, unverifiable. [1] And, as I mentioned earlier, the time comes when accepting most of the data as historical except for the principle assertion causes the negative attitude to lose its value, for it becomes patently evident that denial is ultimately maintained by the will to deny, just as belief is maintained by the will to believe.

---

1. In connection with this point you may wish to read **The Gospel of Jesus Christ** by Father Lagrange (Newman Press), and **Jesus and His Times** by Henri Daniel-Rops (Dutton).

The Lack of Exaltation

A second characteristic of the mythical narrative is, I believe, the continuous adulation of the hero who is elevated above historical conditions by great prodigies. This is the typological, schematic and unilateral characteristic of the personage who is not so much a person as an example, a desire, a thought given human form in keeping with pre-existing outlines. Then there is the conventional and accessory character of the minor personages who are there simply to exalt the exceptional being, and all they have to do is to resemble and reproduce him.

Beyond doubt the first Christian communities which we know through religious or profane history had sentiments towards Jesus that were equivalent to adoration. Christ is a pre-existent and post-existent being who transcends the bounds of history. The earliest Christians believed that he had conquered death, that he was beyond human conditions — glorious, risen from the dead, supreme judge, the very source of immortality and the redeemer. Even if we grant that they had conceived the idea of furnishing this extraordinary being with a history, how likely is it that they would suffuse him in ordinary conditions of ignorance and mediocrity? At the very least, a Gospel made in this way would be filled with wonders, celestial manifestations and demiurgical operations. The imagination could multiply such prodigies without fear of hurting the faith which is always accommodating in matters of verisimilitude. If we admit that Jesus is God, then we may permit him to do anything.

I see nothing in the most ancient Gospels, particularly in Saint Mark's (the most primitive of the three) which responds to these desires. The personage of Jesus is not exalted beyond the human condition, so that when one reads the Gospels of Mark, Matthew and Luke with an open mind, one is under the impression that they are merely talking about an exceptional prophet and not a God become man.

It has become commonplace to note that the Gospel depicts for us a rural life with its Eastern traits and permanent structures which are like all the other rural areas on earth; for everywhere we find people setting out on journeys, returning back from them; people everywhere fish, gather the harvest, have burials, weddings; everywhere there are fathers and mothers, spouses, children, friends, enemies, and the return of the seasons and the beginning of things anew. Karl Barth puts it rather well:

"It is not a moral or Christian world, not an imaginary world that is here described to us, but quite simply and artlessly the ordinary world as it goes its way without a care for anything else, not interested in great events but concentrating wholly upon little facts, humble human relationships. Here is a typical ne'er-do-well, welcomed back by his father — after all, he is his father! — with quite incomprehensible kindness; here is a judge who feared neither God nor man, and a shrew who got the better of him; a king who embarks on an unwise war and beats a retreat while he still has time; a speculator who sinks the whole of his fortune in order to acquire a valuable jewel; a sly old rascal (a typical war profiteer) who contrives very cleverly to get possession of treasure he has discovered by accident; a sharper who deals with money as if the rights of property were non-existent; children quarreling in the street; a peasant sleeping comfortably while his fields do his work for him; a man who falls among thieves — such things do happen! — and has to wait some time for the compassion of a Samaritan, though the world is full of very pious people; a whimsical host, who in spite of refusals on all hands insists on filling his house with guests; a woman living alone, who loses a penny and is as much perturbed as if she had lost everything; a good man and a sinner side by side in church and both behaving quite consistently. How commonplace it all is, how free from illusions; from the point of view of eschatology, how completely pointless! But only because this is human life, something real, entirely surpassing the eschatological. No artistic style, no literary form; but a deep understanding of everyday happenings, in all their integrity, in all their rational necessity and perfection." [2]

I shall skip over these facts of general observation which make the hypothesis of mythical creation a difficult one to hold. I immediately come across others that seem to me stranger yet because they are observable only with difficulty and because they lie beneath the surface of phenomena and are hidden beneath their intricacies.

I open Saint Mark's Gospel and notice how Jesus is depicted in it. He cannot perform any miracles in the village he was born in because those who know him so well do not believe in him. His brothers and sisters accuse him of being insane. He is forced to come to grips with himself before he can perform a miracle. He objects to being called "Good Master" because, he says, only God is good. He declares that he does not know the Day of Judgment. He practices the Jewish religion punctiliously, no one sees him founding a new religion. He is obedient to Another to whom he surrenders his whole being. His passion is the passion of a man: before it begins, he is tortured by fear; at the end of his passion he feels himself abandoned by God. It has been said that these characteristics were deduced from the notion that the Messiah must be humbled, but was that man not a genius to have found so many unimaginable and yet so entirely natural episodical details to write about?

The apostles are often depicted as aghast, ordinary, incredulous or cowardous men. There is something like a settled prejudice to humiliate them. Divinity is couched in obscurity

---

2. This English translation is taken from M. Guitton's **Problem of Jesus** which quotes Karl Barth's **Parole de Dieu et parole humaine**, pp. 71-72.

and one can understand how Arius saw nothing in these earthy Gospels to attribute any belief in Jesus' divinity.

Resistance to Myth in the First Christian Community

A myth, finally, may be engendered in silence by a poet. Generally it is elaborated upon and augmented little by little by narrators living in touch with the people after the manner of the *Légendes Epiques*. But, in the case of the Christian origins, we do not have the necessary time required for this slow and gradual growth of a myth. Paul's activity — twenty years after the death of Jesus — reveals to us a "myth" already proclaimed everywhere.

We know that the milieu in which Jesus' history began was not one of crowds or zealous bands, but rather it was an organic community with a hierarchically structured organization that had twelve supreme leaders. A second group, the blood relations of Jesus, was alongside this first group and still controlled it. If Jesus were a mythical invention we should never have been able to understand how those delerious or possessed people could ever have gained sufficient mastery over themselves to form and set up a community of witness and want it so stringently arranged in a hierarchical order so that at each of its levels the possibilities of fabrication were held in check. As soon as history begins to record this Christian group, it is seen as a very small society under the guidance of the apostles, and the apostles themselves subordinated to an authority in conduct and in speech.

On the other hand, if we assume the initial event, then we can better understand how testimony organized the Church in order to preserve that event and draw inferences from it.

We know how resistant this strict group was to any kind of novelty — this group in which one was watched as much as he was loved. We cannot see how any fabrication could possibly have infiltrated this group and thrived; we can see rather strikingly what would have happened to an innovator. At heart, in spite of their many differences, these first Jews who became followers of Jesus were united by an element of opposition to every reduction or addition. Peter's supreme authority in these egalitarian milieux can only be explained if we recognize an unquestioned higher authority behind him.

The Gospel and the Earliest Expansion of the Church

There is still another consideration to be made, one that is perhaps more difficult to follow because it is founded upon the silences of the Gospel and it is no easy matter to interpret silence. But there do exist some improbable silences which are like testimonies without words.

The Gospel is a Palestinian writing which revolves within the framework and boundaries of the Jewish universe and treats of problems relevant to the Jews. Jesus was not presented as the founder of a new religion. Rather, he was the restorer of the Old Law in the spirit of the prophets: the first followers of Jesus were the more fully developed Jews. But circumstances were such that (chiefly the work of Saint Paul) the "good news" which was virtually intended for all men was proclaimed to the whole pagan world at the same time as the Church in Jerusalem was forced to cut itself off from the synagogue. This period of the Christian Church's separation from the synagogue, its development aside from it and its spreading abroad coincides with the period in which the documents of the evangelical tradition were being written.

Now we come to the hypothesis of mythical fabrication. How strange it is that this fabrication did not obey the laws of utility and propaganda which are its principle! How strange that in these fabricated writings Jesus is always wearing himself out over the extremely grave problems besetting the infant Church! We see Saint Paul grappling with these new problems, trying to clear up the new issues by drawing in-

ferences from the principles which Jesus set down for them.
How much simpler and more final for Paul to base his position
on a word of Jesus!   And how easy it would have been to
invent this word since it produced them all!   Plato had an
answer for everything with his pliant Socrates.   It would have
been quite easy to attribute to the synoptical Christ all sorts
of discourses on gatherings for worship, on authority in the
Church, on the conversion of the pagans and the problems
raised by this conversion, on the Trinity, the Holy Spirit. . . .
Yet, the redaction of the Gospels, especially that of the first
three which are the seeds, does not take up these needs of the
Church.   Jewish color and the Jewish horizon are always
prevalent.   Discussions on the Sabbath, of concern only to
the Jews, take up a large portion of these writings.   While
the world looked stable and had survived the destruction of
Jerusalem, the Gospels were not hesitant to proclaim the end
of the world which had not come.   What is more, how are we
to explain that the fabrication which came from the Church
did not make the Gospels conform to the exigencies of this
infant Church, how can we explain the fact that the Gospels
contained some highly embarrassing texts, some prophecies
(like the end of the world) which never came off, gaps of
silence over the essential rites, over the transmission of power,
— if there had not been an element of opposition to every
attempt at fabrication: words and deeds within living memory which no one felt he had the right to change?   If in some
cases they appealed to the Spirit of Jesus in order to develop
the thought of Jesus in the face of new situations, it is precisely
because there was a *seed that Jesus had sown* which was
considered as a seed capable of development, but already
fully present and contained.

Another thing: if there were no refractory element, how
could we explain the conflicting and divergent details on
several points in the narratives circulating among the Churches
without anyone trying to match them up?   Their indifference

towards these discrepancies indicates that they were certain about the essential points and that the rest was of no great importance.

The Portrait of Jesus

We can with difficulty explain the person of Jesus, to which we must always return, as the confluence of numerous and disparate themes taken from Jewish tradition or from the forms of thought and narration that regularly crop up in earlier religions. Here, I think the studies on *the form* (literary form) of the Gospels help us to specify the reasons for this difficulty. It is in effect the essence of this method to abstract the Gospels from a certain time, place and historical situation and to be interested only in the literary aspect of each of the fragments which compose them: here an anecdote, there a miracle account, a maxim, a parable, a didactic dialog. Then this method hunts down the sources of each of these bits either in an earlier tradition or in the life and exigencies of the first Christian community.

There are two possible hypotheses in this analysis of the living composition of the Gospels. We may say that all the themes of thought and piety and legend were heaped upon an unknown man called Jesus, or we may say that Jesus lived and produced an extraordinary impression on his contemporaries who borrowed these modes of expression to translate the reality of Jesus. In the first case Jesus is only the occasion and ultimately the effect of the work of faith. In the second case he is the cause and the result. Now we always find ourselves standing before the same capital problem of being able to distinguish *what is the cause and what is the effect*.

This, I believe, is how we must decide the problem:
The *Formgeschichte* has the advantage of being able to show and explain the mosaic which strikes the Gospel reader.

The Gospels are comprised of pieces gathered together with little regard as to how they fit together — like a rapidly dashed off biography whose written evidence is not blended. I am of the impression that its author spent little time planning the work: pieces are stitched together which often lack chronological order. But this is to be preferred because the hand of the author, the distorting prism, scarcely appears. The one who compiled them is effaced by his material. The same thing happens when a person who fired people's imagination dies and his letters written to various people at various times, his most important documents, anecdotes and remarks, are gathered together. This compilation is published for those who knew him in life. And, if his personality is strong enough, this patchwork compilation is more valuable than a scholarly biography even for those who never knew him, for through textual gaps, and thanks to the disorder which Pascal called an order in digression on every point "which one gets to in the end and teaches all the same," the real countenance of the dead person who was so unique arises in their minds. It will always be mathematically possible that all these traits were assembled by a forger or by the unconscious action of a religious community. But this possibility will convince no one. Beyond the calculus of the possible there is an intuition of the probable and of what is humanly probable. To use a prudent expression that is popular among the men of science, we may say that everything points to the fact that Jesus had existed before the Gospels were written and that these Gospels are like photographs taken of his face.

Conclusion

If we must come to a conclusion about the verisimilitude of the mythical explanation which is so alluring to a mind that is both critical and religious — a mind which desires to conserve the idea of the faith without forsaking the postulates of science — I would say that Renan's hypothesis seems much more reasonable to me because it is more in conformity to human experience. We start with a true history and, through time, we ascend to the legend by slight embellishments. Finally we pass to the greatest enbellishment, to the over-assertion in which love and faith repose. But how can we insert into history the opposite approach which, beginning with belief in the divinity, the resurrection, the redemptive passion, reconstructs the Gospel Jesus situated in the flow of history and who is almost contemporary to the followers to whom they offer this reconstruction, to people who lived in the same area as Jesus was said to have lived in? If they wanted them to accept the faith, why should they multiply the difficulties beyond the breaking point by telling them a very recent history which they knew never happened because they could prove it? This is unthinkable unless we are to assume that the Gospels were written in the second century and were never offered to the Jewish contemporaries of Jesus.

Strauss understood the necessity of a long time gap between the pseudo-fact and its account. He said in 1835: "Evangel-ical history should be unassailable (*but has there ever been an unassailable history?*) if it could be established that it was written by eye-witnesses or at least by men closely related to the events."

Jesus is too near in time to Christ to have been invented from Christ. The mythical imagination pushes back the origin of religious as far as it can in time. It makes this origin co-incide with the origin of the world in so remote a span of time that it is beyond the reach of proof. In this way the origin becomes plausible because it is unverifiable. Here it is not a question of myths loosely recounted by bards, but rather it is a question of one immediately preached publicly and in the very same time, places and circumstances.

And if this preaching was not refuted or confounded at once, it is because there were in the same places and beneath the eyes of those contemporaries some kind of strange, inexplicable but unquestionable event which thrust itself upon friend and foe alike by its overpowering weight.

Shuffle and reshuffle the problem as much as you like, to derive the history of Jesus from the faith in Jesus Christ which makes the origin of Christian cult and preaching incomprehensible, as if he were the result of it and not the first motive element and first source.

CHAPTER V

The Way Out
or
The Third Approach

> *"They are so constituted that they cannot stand by themselves because of their error, nor can they be united because of their differences. Thus they fall...."* — PASCAL

I BEGAN by examining the hypothesis which maintained that one could hold most of the assertions contained in the "Apostolic Memoires" as historical while rejecting the miraculous element and explaining it by causes that were purely subjective. But then I saw no real reason to retain what was left. I was also unable to understand how these subjective causes could have produced the religion in which Jesus was adored as God immediately after his death.

I then turned in the opposite direction. I tried to think that the essence of the Gospel, belief in the divinity of a man who overcame death, had first been present in the faith through a sublimation of the idea of messiah and that fabrication, working on the nebulous facts surrounding a certain Jesus of Nazareth whose execution was enshrouded in a mist of obscurity, had grafted the myth of the "dead and risen God" onto this experience.

But this hypothesis also seemed unfounded because history does not show me any transition from myth to history. It showed me instead, as the critical school would suggest, the idealization of an individual almost ideal already. And in both cases, but especially in the mythical school, there is not a sufficient lapse of time to explain how, in the Jewish world, a community devoted to the memory of a dead prophet could have crowned him with so un-Jewish a concept as a "dead God."

Onge again I am going to examine these two tendencies that correspond to the only two possible directions the mind can take: either Jesus was a great man whom the imagination fashioned into God, or Jesus was an ordinary man upon whom the mythical hypothesis of a dead and risen God fell after his death. In the first case Jesus is a man made God; in the second Jesus is a God made man.

Advantages and Disadvantages of
the Only Two Possible Approaches

I see immense difficulties in both cases.

The critical mind can never fully explain the sudden divinization of an historical figure.

The mythical mind can never account for the deeply historical character of a Gospel composed by the juxtaposition of myths projected upon an almost entirely unknown man.

The first school is up against the divinity of Jesus professed by the infant Church.

The second school has to face the humanity of the evangelical Jesus.

The critical school will satisfy anyone with an artistic sense of history and all its less obvious aspects. But it will not satisfy anyone with a grasp of the depth and of the religious sense of history.

The mythical school satisfies the religious or theological side of thought, but it offends the historian. It is unacceptable to anyone with a concrete sense of the origins.

The critical school may be said to elevate Jesus and humble his disciples. It paints Jesus with the beautiful features of the Gospel. But it degrades his disciples by depicting them as under a kind of spell equating a mere man to God. This is best seen by reading Renan; when one passes from Renan's *Life of Jesus* to his *Apostles*, one descends.

On the other hand, the mythical school elevates the disciples and debases Jesus. The first communities are the very finest being comprised of mystics and seers. And Jesus is their great dream. They re-made him. And no one is certain any more what he really was in himself. Goguel recognizes this. He speaks of the *Apostles* with more certainty than he speaks of *Jesus*.

The critical school took root in France. It developed in Paris where it found good soil. Renan's talent and knowledge were perfect for clothing it in the garments of the greatest plausibility. Now, it is necessary to re-read his *Life of Jesus* which appeared nearly a century ago and became the greatest literary success of that century. We cannot acclaim it so unreservedly because the transition from man to God is inexplicable.

The mythical school grew up in Germany. It was the choice land for this kind of thinking; the German genius lacks a feeling for nuance. But we must hastily add that it possesses the faculty of creating abstractions and making them come alive. Since we can find in Jesus all the types of the Old Testament, it is not difficult to take each of our values and see them in Jesus as their source. Jesus is the great dialectical moment. We could say that he is the apex of man's adoration by man. But once we have likened Jesus to an Idea which appeared in history, how are we to explain the circumstances

he lived under? We are going in the opposite direction, from
the Ideal to the real, which is incomprehensible.

✻

"What about chance events," say the supporters of myth
to those of history, "the chance that the idea of a suffering
Messiah was quickly imposed upon the Jews when their attention was drawn towards the image of a conquering Messiah;
    "The chance that this individual died at the moment of the
Passover to lend credence to his verisimilitude with the Lamb
and to found a new cult upon this misinterpretation;
    "The chance that this personage was considered equal
to God and that the Jews believed it in spite of their disposi-
tions to the contrary;
    "The chance that this belief favored the spread of a Jewish
religion which was in tune to the aspirations of the Greek
cults;
    "The chance, finally, that this man's preaching was rapidly
transformed into a mystery, that it quickly produced a dogmatic
which was opposed, to be sure, but was never considered
absurd in itself?"
    There are indeed many *lines of chance* that are independent
of each other and are coordinated one to the other. They
comprise an intelligible whole if the reality of the fact of
Jesus is posited. Of course each link can be explained on
purely natural and plausible grounds, but it is the totality of
all these lines and their convergence about a single point
which is so difficult to explain if one maintains that the Christian faith is without value and that there never was a divine
event. Such is, ultimately, the difficulty of every negative
historical explanation.

    But the Historians retort to the Mythists: "We accept
these coincidences, for coincidence is not in itself unheard of.
Now, your hypothesis is essentially absurd for it renders

unintelligible the growth of Jesus' divinity and the real origins of the faith, such as history gives us."

In both cases we are forced to acknowledge what would be ridiculous everywhere else. *On one hand the absurdity of the convergence of chance events without reason. On the other hand the emergence of an effect without cause.* The chief difficulty being that in both instances one destroys on principle prior to investigation the very essence of the given: *that to which* testimony *bears witness.*

To borrow a thought of Pascal on the mystery of man we may say that *these two views cannot stand by themselves because of their error, nor can they be united because of their differences. Thus they fall. . . .*

Attempts at Combination

It is true that we have and shall always have a way out by combining these two explanations in various degrees and attempting to correct the shortcomings of the one by the other. This is what I see being done in most cases.

The historically inclined mind will unite the *mythical* and the *critical* by putting more emphasis on history as Goguel, the master in these studies, did so well. The mystically inclined will prefer to go in the direction of myth and, like Bultmann, the humanist exegete, it will explain the theology of the New Testament by leaving Jesus in the mist of uncertainty. Of course an extraordinary man did live. This man attracted to himself myths like "life after death," "unity with God," "return to judge the living and the dead." Why this attraction? Because after his death there were surely some improbable phenomena (mystical, metapsychical or psychical) which led people to believe that he was still living and so they bore witness to their beliefs which, though begotten in good faith, were wholly lacking in truth.

It might also be said that the Jesus of Nazareth whom we know through history was a prophet put to death for reasons shrouded in mystery and about which a series of legends has sprung up. But in this connection God revealed to men the immensity of his love for them by the symbolism of a God immolated for the salvation of mankind, a mystery which is mystically presented in the liturgical rites. Faith is added to this temporal mystery whose historical anecdote was merely the causal spark.

Also, this vacillation between Man-made-God and Myth-made-man might be said to exist for Buddha as well, and generally for all great men. It is always possible to explain Napoleon through the critical method by saying he was a little Corsican who won wars and was adored. He could be explained through the mythical approach by saying that the myth of the Empire settled upon a fortunate soldier out of gratitude to him. One might even go a step farther and say that this double explanation of one's existence is applicable to any man were he but dead. Hence one can stand over a grave and say, "Here lies a worthy man who earned the funeral honors." One might also say that the myth of the good father, the good functionary, the faithful spouse, has come to rest over the poor creature like the tomb stone of the Unknown Soldier. But in the case of Christ and of Christ alone this rebounding from one explanation to the other goes on to the infinite, most certainly because the mystery of man is carried out to the infinite in him.

It should be rather easy to show that these ingenious combinations are not viable, for either these combinations take upon themselves the difficulties of the two types of explanation or they amount to one or the other of these two types.

I perceive at least one positive result. Whoever desires to suppress the mystery of Jesus must try one of these approaches, and I suppose that this necessity will exist a thousand years from now just as it does today and did yesterday. If one holds the postulate that *a priori* declares impossible anything

that surpasses nature and the laws of nature, then there is no
hope for a third type of solution.

The Profound Similarity of
the Two Negative Approaches

These two opposite and negative solutions, though they
conflict and are brought together with difficulty, have a way,
as contraries do, of secretly augmenting each other because,
as Aristotle said, they are of the same genus.

They both reject constatation in favor of a mental process.
The human intellect often takes a fact from experience and
reduces it to its ideal limits.   Often, too, the mind begins
with the ideal and expresses it in concrete metaphors; the
mind personifies the ideal.   The question then is to learn to
what extent our mental processes represent reality, especially
the reality of Jesus which is perhaps unique in its kind.

It is also striking that these two contrary explanations are
in full agreement on one essential point: they both reject
testimony.   It is true that they do not reject testimony in the
same manner.   One retains the grammatical subject in the
sentence uttered by the witness: *Jesus of Nazareth,* but
removes the predicate *is risen.*   The other explanation retains
the predicate but rejects the subject.   In both cases the verb
IS relates them, but it is void of any substance.   And yet it is
upon the verb IS that the whole force and act of the witness
was centered.   He did not attest that Jesus lived or died.
Nor that the idea of the resurrection had any profound
significance.   But only that there was an identity between
the dead man and the man risen from the dead.   I must come
back again to this essential point.   The question was raised
whether the intellect has the right in this case to fragment the
witness' act of judgment.   This act is fragmented by the
science of those who judge things according to the laws of their
understanding and idea of possibility.   Yet, these are the

positive minds formed in the disciplines of the sciences whose methods and their successes have conditioned them to be receptive to facts even if these facts seem inconceivable at first glance.

These explanations produce a sense of security if we pardon them for nullifying the judgment of existence which is the act of testimony! Its advantage lies in the fact that it leaves nature to nature and history to history: it economizes the unprecedented act of faith.

●●●●●●●●●●

If I were to resign myself to conceive of Jesus as "God and man" then the two solutions could join together without conflict. The "historical" side would represent human *nature*. The "mythical" side would represent the *divine mystery*. These two characteristics of Jesus' being would then be associated in unity just as the act of faith asserts. This act is basically very descriptive and positive, taking the fact as it is, respecting it, designating its contours, translating its structure, preserving its essence.

The Third Approach

But is this act within my power?

What is certain is that if I could make this instantaneous act that is at once and indivisibly an act of submission to a given and an act of faith in the transnatural significance of this given, I would set my mind at rest. Both the rebounding of my mind between the two opposite solutions which I consider in turn or mingle with difficulty and the anxiety this mental vacillation causes would cease. I would be adapting my mind to a reality where the opposites, instead of vying with or confounding one another as they do in my mind, would unite into a real subject which I could call a *mystery* from then on.

Father Lagrange once told M. Couchoud (and both men

told it to me since then in almost exactly the same way),
"Renan believed that Jesus was a man made God. You
believe that Jesus is a God made man. Don't let anyone
ever bring the two of you together, for then you would be a
genuine Christian."

That is the problem in a nutshell. These two movements
of the mind, the one proceeding from the man-Jesus to God
and the other from God to the man (the one following the
path of our knowledge, the other the deeper approach of the
divine humiliation) will always be necessary to the human
intellect's puzzlement over Jesus Christ. And since it is
difficult to maintain both positions at the same time, we must
eventually incline towards *one* or the *other*. Thus, the synoptic Gospels and the *Acts of the Apostles* tend toward the
movement from the man-Jesus to God, whereas the Gospel of
Saint John tends toward the movement from God to the man-
Jesus. I think that the "critical" school is a distortion of the
first of these movements, and that the "mythical" school is a
distortion of the second movement which is more religious
than the first because it begins with the idea of God and
descends but does not re-ascend. These two incompatible
movements, apart from recognizing the mystery of Jesus, tear
Jesus to shreds by reducing him to a mere product of the
mind: a product of the enthusiasm which created the hero in
the first case, a product of the mystic which created the myth
in the second. It is an ill-conceived blending of hero and
myth.

When in his *Church Dogmatics* Karl Barth began to study
the Eternal Son (from a viewpoint quite opposed to mine
since he rejects all human reflection in the immediate discovery of the Word of God), he found himself caught up once
again in the "eternal dilemma." As a theologian he observes
that these two tendencies have continually appeared throughout the history of Christianity, the one to inspire every theology that hints of Ebionism, the other to inspire every theology

tinged with Docetism. [1]   He wrote with his usual vigor that

> "The Church has fought off Ebionism and Docetism
> and therefore every modern theory which smacks of either.
> According to the Gospel, Christ's divinity has no meaning
> if we refuse to see in it the glorification of a great man or
> the personification of an idea of God or a divine idea.
> It forces us to reject the conclusions of this alternative.
> The New Testament in effect mainly considers the vertical
> where the two Ebionite and Docetan lines intersect.   It
> introduces a third dimension.   If we maintain only two
> dimensions, it is impossible to escape from the dialectic
> of history and of ultra-history; it is impossible to avoid
> thinking that enthusiasm or mystical doctrine alone explain
> how an historical individual was able to become a heavenly
> being or how a heavenly being was able to become an
> historical person."

Karl Barth was right to compare the real being of Jesus
to an object situated in the third dimension of space which
we would like to reduce to our two customary dimensions.
If the intellect applies its natural mechanics to Jesus it will
destroy his *relief* and will project him on a mental plane.

There are two images of Jesus Christ: the Nazarene prophet
depicted in the Gospels and the pre-existing Christ preached
by Saint Paul.   The obligation to maintain two images, two
norms, for the same being (symbolized by the division of
the Gospels and Epistles) is the whole problem of Christianity.
The mental rebounding between these two images, or the
acceptance of their mysterious union into a single being —
these are ultimately the only two possible solutions.

---

1. The Ebionites denied the divinity of Jesus in the third century
and the Docetans maintained in the first century that Jesus had merely
the appearance of a man. It is noteworthy that Docetism is the most
ancient of heresies.

Here I am standing at a threshold, as the life of the spirit sees it when, to be faithful to experience and to logic, thinking must step beyond experience — beyond, it seems, even itself.

If there really are three solutions and no more than three, then if the first two cancel each other out, must I not accept the third even without proof? This is what detectives and scholars do when they come up against what they think is an improbable solution when it is the only one left after they have eliminated all the other possible solutions save one. People often accept a doctrine not by its obviousness, not by its proofs, but out of the sheer impossibility of adhering to the other doctrine which would have to be necessary if the first were false. They are compelled to believe in God out of horror of atheism. The opposite is equally true.

It is up to me to decide what I want to sacrifice, for I shall not come to a conclusion without some sacrifice. If I am inclined to the third solution (which, by the way, was Bergson's at the end of his life and is that of believing exegetes) then I am transported into the mystery. But if I retain one of the first two solutions then I am acting in bad conscience towards the initial postulate as they both imply placing an injunction on nature in order to move beyond nature. They force one to admit *beforehand* that there has never been a single exception. But testimony is about this exception for it asserts that there was at least once at some point an interruption of the universal cosmic order. Must I deny this witnessed fact for the sake of a principle? Or, in the name of the testimonies, must I accept an event and a mystery which are unique in their kind? [2]

---

2. I wrote these same thoughts in 1946 in **Difficultés de croire** (pp. 109-194) and **Problème de Jésus** (I, pp. 87-137). By comparing these texts the reader will be able to see the corrections and complements that I have added to my thinking after years of additional reflection.

Part Three

The Problem of Believing in Testimony

CHAPTER VI

The First Discussion of Testimony: the Marvelous and the Improbable

I HAVE an apartment with a little room overlooking the Luxembourg Gardens whose rich foliage has already heard the whisperings of so many doubts. And there I invited some friends so that I might read to them this first *mémoire* on Jesus.

I think that it is pointless to journey alone through difficult matter if you do not occasionally check yourself by welcoming critical examinations of your work. My friends were not exactly believers, but I dare not say they were unbelievers. They were, rather, full of caution and belonged to that line of men whose will to believe immediately sparks a reason for doubting. Their hearts (this word depicts the intimacy of their spiritual being) dwelled continually on the problem, and they could all have quoted what Goethe had to say about Jesus: "All things considered, Jesus continues to remain for me a distinctly significant being, but a problematic one."

I suspect that they enjoyed these problems and would have been sorely distressed to find them resolved all in a flash by any kind of solution. Pascal's *Wager* was repugnant to them because they esteemed the intellect too highly for that sort of thing: nor could they have endured seeing faith or love appear at the conclusion of a mathematical calculation. I have a painting in my room that shows Pascal speaking with

Descartes. It reminds us that different approaches to all
things, as Plato said, are necessary and that embodied minds
are sensitive minds. My friends seemed to prefer living in an
umbrageous but human region rather than in one of certainty,
though with occasional bouts of uncertainty. They retained
certain aspects of the ancient faith: Job putting his hand up
to his mouth when the Eternal One spoke to him in the midst
of a storm and revealed incomprehensible things, or the
excessive prudence of the *Proverbs,* or the moderation and
languor, the repose of ignorance which runs throughout
Ecclesiastes. I observed them while I read my *mémoire,* for
the thoughts contained in this guide-book were not only my
own but often also those of other men which I had incorporated
as extra provisions at that moment of my dialectic when they
seemed plausible. I glanced at Olivier over the rim of my
glasses to see whether he had recognized himself and I
winked at him in a way which betokened friendliness touched
with a bit of irony and puzzlement.

In spite of his reservations about Renan, Olivier leaned
more towards what I call the *critical* school. He thought
Renan's approach was valid and that he could only be
censured for getting too personally involved in his work. He
lacked Renan's dread of anyone who admitted that there were
gaps in determinism. He had read the works of the modern
physicists in those days before Louis de Broglie was converted
over to determinism: he realized there was some indetermina-
tion, some play (in the sense one says that a lock has some
play), some degree of chance in the cosmos. And he said
that there could have been at the time of Jesus (concerning
Jesus or in the relationship between Jesus and his followers
after his death) some undefinable event or other analogous
to the material leaps in quantic mechanics (the Resurrection
could have been one such leap), or analogous to the abrupt
mutations among living species which are just on the verge of
transformation. He reserved therefore a part for mystery,
novelty or strangeness possible in history as it is in nature.

He once told me that jackpots come up only once, that the figure 247,821,601 must necessarily come up one day if one allows oneself "not," as they say, "infinite time, but a time which I take upon myself to calculate for you." For him there could be no strange event which lacked possibility or necessity even. I told him that the Resurrection of Jesus did not happen by blind chance with no consideration for place or time, but that it had taken place at a determined and precise moment, that it was improbably situated in space-time, in human history, after a series of events themselves inter-related and that one could not compare the advent of Jesus to a lucky number that finally turned up after millions of others. It is all the more a lucky number since the mechanism of chance which makes this number appear has no reality, it being like all the others. It is I who make it the winning number as I see fit by choice and rules. Assuming that Jesus was this improbable event men call lucky, it still must be explained why they consider him an infinite gain; why also, whereas the improbable number of the lotteries falls back into nothingness for millions of times, Jesus in his Church has begun to exist again without ceasing as though the lottery, mad and out of order in the case of this Jesus alone, had been turning up the same lucky number at every moment for some 2000 years.

Olivier began to smile. Though he found my reasoning subtle enough, it was unconvincing for, as he said, I assumed precisely what was in question: the ability to know the *incomparable* value of the phenomenon Jesus. "You will never convince me otherwise," he added, "that all things are explained naturally in nature and historically in history. If I don't believe that, then the whole framework of my knowledge and even of my conduct will collapse. And that is why so long as I have a breath of air in my body I shall keep the postulate of the sciences: the postulate of Celsus, Hume, Renan, Bult-mann. Only, I don't see why I should deny the existence of the man Jesus, why I should not put this man on a lofty plane and why I should not take him for a kind of superman which sometimes turns up out of satistical necessity. Let us call him a Francis of Assisi, a Joan of Arc, a Gandhi, of the highest magnitude."

But then," I replied, "how can you explain the very *sudden* transformation that made this man (nearly without any time-lapse) into an adored being, the object of worship? This is what we have to explain. The mystics whom you just mentioned are only explicable by the impact and imitation of Jesus. If you have read Saint Paul, you cannot have the least inkling of an idea that he was referring to a very beloved master (as a Las-Cases to a Napoleon, an Eckermann to a Goethe, as a disciple, as a son, as a lover), he almost never speaks of Jesus as a predecessor. Or if he does it is to say that he has no desire to know him according to the flesh. Saint Paul leaves us the impression that he was completely indifferent as to the color of Jesus' eyes. I believe that except for one discourse in the *Acts* he never once quotes Jesus. And that one time he quotes is a sublime but a commonplace remark: "It is better to give than to receive," which (it is original) is not to be found in the Gospels. Rest assured that Saint Paul could not describe the blood of Jesus he speaks so much about, and if Leonardo da Vinci had asked him to sketch Jesus' hand taking up the bread to break it, he would have been utterly unable to do so."

"But I am not denying what you say," replied Olivier, "Quite the contrary."

"You do not deny it," I said, "but you cannot truly reconcile it to your approach. If Jesus were but an ordinary man, how can you explain away the halo of glory, the *aura* which was immediately his light, how can you explain the instantaneous elevation of his person into the celestial sphere, of which there is no other example in any historical epoch? I have long reflected about this — so much so that if I had to choose I would be more inclined to the myth-making hypothesis. It has the advantage over yours because it preserves the explanation and lets us understand not so much the first three Gospels, but rather the thoughts in the *Acts of the Apostles.* I do not know whether you have been struck as I have by the *geology* of the New Testament.

"Here are ordinary, untroubled plains — the first three Gospels; then all at once the volcanos: in the book of the *Acts,* in the preaching of Saint Paul, in the *Apocalypse,* what you perceive is a Christ in glory, an eruption I dare say. His lightning flashes dazzle and make you doubt that he had been a man like us. No one can easily reconcile on the one hand the Christ, the Lamb, the Angel of God and on the other hand the Jesus of Nazareth upon whose cross Pilate, like a meticulous police officer, ordered his name and status to be inscribed to situate him in historical humanity."

OLIVIER

"You are describing here the transition from history to legend which we observe all the time in ourselves — our childhood memories for example. Read Marcel Proust again. As soon as the man died we idealized him. It is a secret apotheosis: every dead man is a god to those who love him."

MYSELF

"Yes, Olivier, I know. But look at the differences. What took place in the transition from Jesus Christ has its likeness in the operations of the memory. We are not content with vague comparisons. The idealized dead are not Ideas full of life mingled in our life and transfiguring it; they do not establish their love on earth, they do not become the only existent beings. And Jesus was scarcely dead before he attracted existence to himself. He alone exists in thousands of conciences being more present to them than they are to themselves because they live for him."

OLIVIER

"I say that he exists in the history of singular conjunctions, as in life there are times when misfortunes seem to pile up all

5 *Jesus*

at once.   And we call these encounters "happenings" in both
trifling and important matters.   The solar system, life on
earth, the moon lighting up our nights — these are improbable,
aberrant, fantastic occasions which are sustained.   They are
the things of chance which have become the substance of
history."

MYSELF

"We have yet to determine why *these* chances are sustained
and not others; a king of hearts drawn from a deck of cards
does not sustain itself.   You shuffle the deck.   The king of
hearts returns to its non-identity."

OLIVIER

"Grant me that there are strange encounters in history
such as that of the Corsican general who stepped in to keep
the Directoire from becoming a Restoration and then threw
France and Europe into an unexpected future — a soldier
without faith whom the pope came to crown.   But this chance
responded to the desire of France.   Who would think of
alluding to a providence guiding France or a spirit working
for her downfall?   It is sufficient to think that every now and
then some conglomerates of propitious chance and, as in
games, moments of chance come together.   The whole question is our knowing whether one must not reason the same
way for the moment of Jesus: the Jewish religion, vanquished,
dispersed, but exalted in its sufferings, prepared for anything,
awaiting anything.   The world unsettled here by too much
culture, there by bizarre secret cults; just when the Roman
Empire was taking shape it began to have doubts about itself,
and this drove it on to self worship, or rather to the desire for
adoration.   The need for a concrete, palpable Savior at once
a bit different and still simple, acceptable to all, especially to
the suffering masses.   Then Jesus stepped in with his proph-
etism which very simply condensed what the deeply Jewish
prophets had said.   Then something extraordinary and inex-

plicable happened which could be surely explained today had we been witnesses of it, just as we have explained the stigmata of Saint Francis: I am speaking of the reapparitions of Jesus after his death and of the encounter (which I call highly improbable but not impossible) of this improbable being, who was Jesus with the concourse, in itself improbable, of the state of mind of the Jews and Romans. To this you may also add the highly improbable Saint Paul whose conversion is *a priori* extremely unlikely, although such startling events are not rare. Have you read the account of Ratisbonne's conversion in the *Ara Coeli* which M. Goguel likens to what happened on the road to Damascus? But it was a circumstance in itself as unforeseeable as the survival of this organizing genius just when the party of Jesus most needed to be introduced into the West, joined to the pagan world, the Hellenistic culture and the imperial center. The first persecutions followed this introduction and right away produced martyrs who are the effect and the source of faith."

MYSELF

"I cannot be content to collect these encounters. The time must come when it is not the encounter which must be explained but rather the return of those concerted chances you call *encounters which* I see recurring in the same way or similarly and always along the same lines to the advantage of the same kind of people. If a young man dressed in black sits next to me, it is an encounter. If, stepping off the train, he enters another car with me, it is another encounter — amusing and curious. If he is alongside me at another station change, I will say that *I am being followed.* Right then the phenomenon changes in significance and plane by rising to another level of existence and value which is simpler to conceive of. 'The clock is out of order,' said a man nonchalantly, 'it rang six times for one o'clock.' It would have been simpler had he said, 'it is six o'clock; time to get up.' Let us take the word PAUL. Instead of imagining that P chanced upon A, that A encountered U, that U encountered L, I put them all together and say PAUL. That is our difference; you spell the encounters and find yourself pronouncing a group of four inaudible letters. *I read* and say that there is no encounter, but there is an encounter of encounters, that is to say a plan: it seems more economical to my way of thinking."

OLIVIER

"That goes to show you are already a Christian. You extrapolate. But I am content to describe: I tell you there are many stars in the sky at curious distances from one another and you put them together into constellations; you say: this is *Orion* or *Aries* or *Virgo*. That is your privilege."

MYSELF

"What I do you could also do with me."

HE

"I cannot do it because I am not a Christian."

I

"It seems to me that you have no reason to put me in your position as an observer."

HE

"And it seems to me that you have too much faith when you put me in your position as an extrapolator."

I

"I say that you do not see things exactly as they are, not that you have poor eyesight, but because deep inside you are afraid to see, that is, to believe."

HE

"On the other hand, you believe what does not exist because you are secretly afraid to see only what exists and hence to remain in a state of uncertainty."

I

"If you consider the whole order of human history on a broader plane from the origin of the Jewish people to the actual Church, you would have a better understanding of the sentence for you would see its whole sense, subject, verb, and predicate, instead of concentrating upon the individual events of Jesus."

HE

"If you agree to take a still wider planetary, cosmical, extragalactical stand and measure time in immense unities, you will notice that human chronology is but a mere point along an infinite line. You will begin to tell yourself that improbable conjunctions ought to occur rather often in the infinity of space and time."

I

"But if you grant for a moment that God wanted to reveal himself through artistically grouped chance events, there would be no need to look further. There is enough beauty in these prolonged encounters which we see throughout the minuscule history of our planet to indicate to us a faint whispering, a shadow, a presence of God, without our having to hunt for others somewhere else. In an instant of perfection there is something (I know not what) which satisfies and suffices.

HE

"You have stepped onto the plane of faith and love. But why do you want to prove them?

"I am going to take up your example of the false Joans and of the only true 'Maid of Orleans.' You almost answered the problem by wording it the way you did, for you, with official history, exalted Joan of Arc and devaluated the other prophetical women of that age so rich in miracles. Go back to Michelet's book *Joan of Arc* and instead of bringing up the disparity between All and Nothing, between the Infinite and

Zero, which is your constant approach, attribute to all those
Maids the differences of degree and quality inherent in
natural things — in ears of wheat for example. Could it be
that Joan almost missed being burned at the stake? Could it
be that the Pâtre du Gévaudan or the Dame des Armoises
almost succeeded? And if they had succeeded, if they had had
divine sanction and the consecration of success, do you think
that looking back at them we could not have discovered some
genius in them? What I call *success* is the crossing of a
threshold as a natural result of circumstances conspiring with
the subject's disposition. I am not denying that Joan of Arc
stood apart from all other maidens, nor do I deny that there
was, as with Bonaparte, an encounter between an outstanding
personality and exceptional circumstances. But these encounters are constant in history where periods of disorder snatch
up, so to speak, exceptional people."

I

"In my opinion, your explanation does not apply to the
full depth of the subject.

"We admit that it remains valid for Joan of Arc and Bonaparte, though I prefer to use the word 'genius' instead of
'exceptional.' But Joan and Bonaparte have no posterity;
they may have imparted a certain élan to people and to institutions, but they did not make this people cross over from one
order of grandeur to another, whereas that indefinable mysterious little difference which caused a higher form of animal
life to cross the threshold into humanity brought about a
change of genus, of quality and of value which the entire
species shared in — and that without even the slightest
regression or reversal: none whatever! I would grant you
that an exceptional animal might have been placed in exceptional circumstances, but we must insist that, in crossing a
threshold beyond the range of the ape species, this supercreature received a new faculty, the power of rationality,

which it was unable to give itself in spite of all its superior physical qualities.

"I believe that when we reflect deeply upon the human *origins* and *emergence* we all admit the direct, radical and abrupt transition from one *that is not* to one *that is*. We admit also that we have never been able to seriously think that an animal could have changed into a rational being little by little over a period of continuous, gradual and cumulative transformations. I would also add that this transition is indiscernible at the moment itself and must be concluded to after it is accomplished.

"I limit myself to observe that the case of Jesus apparently resembles that of Man, and that my analogy of Joan of Arc does limp, but the use of analogies is free.

"We see humanity rise above itself in its various branches of which the most singular example is the Jewish race. And in this race we find the almost continuous flow of prophecy from Amos to Esdras. Imagine that we have fallen asleep for five or six centuries. When we open our eyes again we see this same humanity has crossed a threshold and has been led by its greatest representatives into a new and previously unimagined sphere of existence; new moral values have sprung up, simple and final solutions have been given to problems that were until then insoluble. Let us go back over the past and imagine that they permit us to see the duration of the interval: we find the movement of Jesus. We tell ourselves at first that this transition took place through Jesus. Then we say that it is Jesus who crossed the threshold. You reply 'Yes, but accidentally.' Another, the Teacher of Righteousness for example, could have crossed that same threshold. . . ."

OLIVIER

"If, as you say, there do exists thresholds, if what we call the 'Christian atmosphere' had pre-existed Christianity just as Mount Everest pre-existed Mallory, or Annapurna had pre-existed Herzog, you would have to admit that someone besides Jesus could have crossed it also. If I am not mistaken, it was Proust who said that the Sonata existed before Vinteuil, but it was he who made it famous."

MYSELF

"True. But, in the case of Jesus the higher world he introduced is not separate from himself, and that to me is the exception of an exception.

"Annapurna is not Herzog. Look at how Herzog struggled to climb it! But I see no difference between Jesus and the world of new values he brought with himself. We may think of Jesus as a Herzog and imagine that, like an ultra-Socrates, he climbed up a slope so that he might reach this higher world. But the Gospels by no means give this impression. Jesus himself is this superior region. He does not cross the threshold: he is the very bridge, the sublime atmosphere. And that is why in my guide-book I have insisted on the impossibility of maintaining for any length of time a critical hypothesis which shows us Jesus as an exceptional being helping humanity to take that leap across the threshold. I believe it is truer to say that, from what we can glean through written evidence and people's belief, Jesus is presented as the *beyond* of the threshold, the mystery hidden behind it who humbles himself to our level. But it is futile to desire to compare him to any one person at all, were he exceptional. He is the ideal of a new humanity (conceived, I grant you, according to the concepts of the Jewish and Hellenistic mentality), but capable of being re-thought in every category possible. This is why I said in my *mémoire* that doubting minds like yours are inclined by their inferences to see Jesus as a myth. More than that even! The very type of myths. Contemporary disbelief resolves around the single thesis: Jesus is a myth. Today when we say *myth* we secretly think of Jesus. You shake off all the difficulties at once. Jesus becomes the projection of that model which every man has within himself. It only remains then to be explained how this projection of the Infinite, which could have come about in many different ways, since there are many disturbed people, was manifested only in these circumstances and for the sole person Jesus."

OLIVIER

"Jesus appeared as the myths appeared. The case you just mentioned of Joan of Arc is the best for showing how this comes about. Myths existed before Joan's time: the Virgin victorious over the Devil, France lost by a woman, saved by a Virgin, the myth of the Virgin Martyr, the myth of Justice and, above all perhaps, the myth of the Virgin Mary. But, in certain circumstances which I could easily describe, the myths solidified into a bulk and came to rest like a crown of doves upon the head of an historical being. This is how I explain the 'mystery' of Joan of Arc. I shall not go so far as to say with Anatole France that Joan did not know on which bank of the Loire, Orléans was situated, nor that Joan was a mascot in the clever hands of Regnault de Chartres. This excess is like M. Guignebert's when he called Jesus a 'piece-worker.' I admit that Joan of Arc was an indeterminate personality, as often very young girls are. Her history is a 'holy history'; she unites several ambiguous realities and the great myths of religion, royalty and the nation. In addition, it is notable that in the case of Joan of Arc, as in the case of Jesus, the myths have curiously taken each other's place."

MYSELF

"We must find out whether this explanation is consistent with Joan's action, with her statements during her first trial, and whether, instead of being superimposed on Joan, these myths did not on the contrary spring from her person as the only way for the human mind to explain her. Indeed, some of these pre-existing states of mind streamed about her, without which she would not have been understood or could not have influenced her milieu the way she did. I would concede that

Saint Margaret and Saint Catherine were the projections of her faith: they were saints well-known to her social environment and she saw their statues in the village churches. In my opinion, the facts seem to indicate that Joan received the inpouring of a higher power *through* these statues and images; that this power which gave her foreknowledge on certain matters and gave her strength and certitude also on occasion is a power transcendent to history. The other hypotheses fall short by neglecting the most affirmed, most decisive and most authentic point in this history. They neglect the conviction of the first highly educated witnesses who came from every walk of life and who are our only sources of information. Above all, they ignore the cry of the chief witness, the only witness with inside information, who, in order to back up the truth of her declarations, let herself be condemned and burned at the stake when a mere word from her would have permitted her to live. What about the problems that arise when one tries to reduce all these things to visions, legends and myths? Logically, it would be simpler to say, 'Joan really was what she said she was.'

"But I return to the idea that is an analogy between this problem and the problem of Jesus because in both instances it is necessary to choose, with all their risks and perils, between the *sub-human* and the *super-human*."

The Doubting Young Man

"I'll finish this matter off. You are looking for something absolutely beyond question which everyone can accept about Jesus. I would say that it is this: that there are books with printed letters and that some of these letters comprise two syllables: JE-SUS, and that, because of my background, these two syllables invoke within me an emotion of doubt or fear. And that is the first state of Jesus. The explanation you have just been giving me are like other appearances which you are superimposing upon the first. Why not keep to the first level and say that the problem of finding what lurks behind the word *Jesus* and these images is a senseless problem? It is never necessary to look for what lies behind the appearances of something. Many young people think along these lines today. It is precisely this investigation of an uncertain something behind the apparent that "Phenomenology" delivers us from. It is also the position of the man in the street. For him Jesus is nothing but a word, a statute or a vague recollection. He does not go beyond them."

MYSELF

"If that is the case, then why not apply the same attitude to what you have just now been telling me and affirm that it is nothing more than passing sounds, and that you yourself are but an appearance without any substance beneath you. Then, we could only say, 'Let's go take a walk in the cool night air. . . .' "

After this indomitable doubter had spoken, an embarrassing silence ensued.

HELENA

"While I was listening to you I asked myself whether we could not clear all this up. Do you really believe it is that necessary to put so much emphasis on the 'It happened'? My woman's mind has been looking for a more direct way to proceed right to the heart of the question without having to take your detours.

"Again, I say that you do not have to follow me, but I am going to tell you how I reached my conviction on this matter. And I believe I am no different than anyone else. I feel myself in communication with the simplest of people; the ignorant — with all people. While listening to you I got the impression that you were raising overly scholarly questions which few people could follow."

We were all in favor of hearing what new way Helena proposed to avoid all the unanswered questions.

First, some information about Helena. She was Italian by birth, but her father married a German; she grew up in England, though she continually travelled. With tongue in cheek she once called herself the "most intellectual woman in England." I corresponded assiduously with her until her sudden death in 1946. Her whole life and thinking were Catholic and, like Baron von Hügel, she now and then experienced *difficulties* of faith, but in a woman's way, as she said, without the embarrassment of intellectual doubt. A visceral faith, that familiarity with the beyond which is the Italian legacy *par excellence,* shielded her from possible doubts, while her inquisitive mind permitted her to skirt the very edge of the abyss. She found her delight in these ideas, but took no pleasure in their conflict or in their resounding clash. Or, at least, she looked for something else in these reverberations: the sounding out of the true. She did not raise objections. She was a wonderful listener. (She heard all that has been said in these discussions.) She was so keenly disposed to being open to others, that once you had her for an audience, you could not do without her silence which neither approved nor disapproved, but was receptive to all you said. Even in childhood she loved Scripture, as she said, more than she had ever loved Tradition. "In Scripture I find more of the *dulcis hospes animae.*" But she had no taste for the historical element in *Scripture* (I tried to pick a quarrel with her on this point); hence, she skimmed over the two books or Samuel which I find so enjoyable. "Scripture," she said, "is the *Law* and the *Prophets,* that is, what comes from above and what is to come." One should not *write* what is in the past: history is made to be bypassed.

We differed also in the fact that she did not appreciate biblical criticism, especially when this criticism distinguishes the levels of greater and lesser certitude, when it says, "This is true, this is an image; as for this, we don't know." She took all Scripture as a whole like the average Christian does, like Paul Claudel. The book of *Jonas* was for her as true as

Samuel, and Leo XIII's distinctions between revealed teaching
and words spoken according to appearances did not interest
her. She told me, "I am like the fisherman's wife. Certainly
I will help you mend your nets when you return from your
fishing trips. If criticism is a mending, I also criticize. But
you don't have to be a sailor to repair nets. Yes, I know that
every net breaks, that every creature is imperfect, that every
pot shatters as *Ecclesiastes* says; I let the menders ply their
trade and I accept what they say when they by chance agree.
That is why I love Lagrange for his work (you have tilled
well, oh biblical ox!) and I forgive Claudel his imprecations
(you have roared well, oh lion!). I evaluate creatures according to their species."

She often spoke to me in the vein. You have to be aware
of that if you are to understand what follows, to better understand what she said to us then, her face intent and serious,
slightly inclined to the right side like the statues in our old
churches which depict the Virgin-child reading the Scriptures
on Saint Anne's lap.

"I would like to speak for those who examine scriptural
writings by their own intimate thought and reflection with
no outside help. For it is certain that one can grapple with
the letter of the Gospel without having to spend one's life
in the study of languages and texts, and it is certain that one
can answer the problem of verisimilitude by methods as sure
as those of clerics and learned men. For this reason the
Christian religion is so original and democratic. It gives us
the texts of the Gospels and invites us to judge them not by
philology, exegesis, archaeological references, comparisons,
and so forth . . . the text by itself alone must afford each man
a response, for every man must be able to grasp in it that
particular something which is not to be found anywhere else.
It is something akin to what happens with works of art.
One may study them technically, but if the work has succeeded
in bringing across what it intended, if it is truly a masterpiece,

the ordinary man without benefit of instruction or comparison will realize that he has before him a thing of beauty
which is speaking to him on its own power.

"We may consider the Gospel in the same light: we must
judge its truth simply by reading it."

One of us then stood up and said:

"We don't question the Gospel's beauty, we only want to
know whether it is true.   That is our whole problem.   We
want to go beyond the question of the *Vicar of Savoy*, the
Génie du christianisme and even the *Life of Jesus*.   We are
trying to find out whether these things happened in the sense
we can say that the war of 1940 happened."

HELENA

"I think that what I am going to say will help you arrive
at my understanding.   Life has taught me to first set aside
the bothersome and only come back to it later.   A general
once told me this was how to overcome obstacles.   And a
mathematician whom I knew at Cambridge told me that all
algebra was like that.   This I do not know.   But I do know that
an obstacle holds one back and this delay is never good.
I am not saying I do not believe in 'It has happened.'   I only
ask you to make a slight detour.   Except by faith (which we
as a rule do not consult in this debate), or by scholarly
research (in which a mere woman will never feel at home),
how can one know whether these things actually happened?
— I desire a better approach.   And this approach suggests
itself when I am in the presence of a poetical work.

"I believe I have a sensitivity to a certain accent, a particular tone, an inexhaustible sentiment.   A beautiful text has an
eternal presence and its explanation is not left to the fickle
tastes of each of us.   If you let yourself be transported by it
for any length of time, if you do not recoil before its difficulties (even before certain necessary subtleties), if you

have discerned in its shadowy depths spangled with beams of light the diverse levels of a single sense — and you are on the verge of recognizing and defining the experience which is at once human and poetical, which is always its leveling source — if, after having tested it in yourself, you test it again with friends of a different race, temper and culture; if you appraise it by what the wisest critics in many countries of Europe say about it — then you arrive at an intimate, multiple and coherent truth confirmed by the experience of life. To be more precise, that you are from then on in possession of a truth which does not require the effort of *believing* in the same sense that the moderns give the word (which is not that of the Bible). No, here you do not have to give up a secure bank to jump across the river of uncertainty with your eyes shut. I do not see any stage of uncertainty in this approach."

ONE OF THOSE PRESENT

"Do you believe that people will ever be one in these matters? Look at how tastes change with time. The works of Béranger, the Abbé Dellile and Crébillon were honored by everyone, and who can say that Paul Claudel one day will not go the way of...."

HELENA

"One may err here as elsewhere. But do you believe that Béranger's admirers made the descent into him of which I speak? Look at Ronsard. His glory has had its eclipses. And now Ronsard is above reproach. I am certain that those of his contemporaries who had the necessary patience, calmness and depth to read him in a better light would not have been mistaken about Ronsard and would have been absolutely sure that they stood in the presence of a genius. I will return now to my idea. In a work of art there is a poetical and cosmical human truth that is both expressible and ineffable at the same time. And we can attain this truth in a way that does not depend upon our individual tastes.

"The sober (but not morose) accent of melancholy that is replete with good humor, with smiles and with gaps, the accent of Jacques the philosopher which is also that of Theseus, Richard the Second, the Duke Orsino, Prospero or Hamlet — the strains of a disillusioned grandeur that is still mindful of the world's humor — the renunciation of every kind of power to be worthy of finally obtaining the only Power which is spiritual by the supreme Art which is the theatre, wherein all forms of art come together, from song and pantomine, to epic and lyric, with accents of philosophy, music, and magic thrown in the background — all this is what touches me in Shakespeare. I am not occupied here with history, for (I sense it) on this plane everything is confused for me and will perhaps remain so forever. Besides, the example of Shakespeare is a wonderful one, for if it was this poor man, this simple man, of Stratford who wrote these dramatic works without having travelled, without vocabulary, without experience, without greatness of soul, then there is in him, as in Jesus of Nazareth, a mystery of a twofold nature and incarnation. Only history knows the mediocre nature of the man from Stratford; but the true being who was Shakespeare borders on the eternal. This is what I test and unite myself to along with everyone who appreciates the beautiful and the human."

HELENA PAUSED, AND THEN CONTINUED:

"Surely you are familiar with Irving, the admirable educator who taught Mallory, the young hero of Mount Everest whose body vanished on the highest point of the earth and was never found (the Greeks would soon have made him into a god). Very well! Irving said somewhere that Christ's revelation of the true divine essence quelled the fear which man, natural man, feels towards the solitudes of nature and that Jesus permitted access to the high mountain when he gave a new form to the universe by means of the Gospels.

"All this goes to show you why instead of word *historic* I prefer to use the word *authentic* for now."

ONE OF THOSE PRESENT

"Because you have not studied enough to know the historical, whereas you feel the authentic right away in your heart."

HELENA

"My heart? — I should rather say: *my mind at work*. But the heart — it is that. And besides, the heart, defined this way, can only exist in me through Christ. Christ on earth communicated to the pure mind of the Greeks and the stern mind of the Jews this fineness in work that yields blood and understanding which we call the heart.

"To assent to the understanding of a true miracle such as the multiplication of the loaves, I prefer to accustom my mind to them by reflection on *pure miracles,* as I call them, which at best are only highly unlikely encounters. Jesus needed to pay the tax of one didrachma. He said, 'Lower your net,' and in the mouth of a fish swimming by they found the didrachma. Nothing in nature was unsettled. Two currents of life and destiny intersected. I see the same type of miracle when Eliezar met the woman watering her camels at the well in Nachor. Rebecca was the only woman in the world who could please Isaac. Several times in my life I have known this kind of miracle. Without telling you my secrets I will say that it does not obfuscate but rather it sparkles. These silent encounters — ordinary and explicable — are like a word whispered to me alone; I guess at them without any effort of the imagination by that same portion of heart or mind which lets me understand Shakespeare and the Gospel.

"Now, let me return to the Gospels. You conceive that when I read them I believe I have so intense a poetical and human experience that all of Shakespeare pales into nothingness before it. There is a source of experience, of humanity and of poetry in the Gospel which far surpasses what one

could conceive in reading fictitious works. The experience
one can have in the loftiest moments in literature — the
moment of Homer, Eschylaus, Plato, Virgil, and Dante, the
Elizabethan theatre, the seventeenth-century French, the English poetry of the nineteenth century, Goethe, Balzac, Dostoevsky; or even the epoch of Péguy, Claudel, Proust, Gide,
Valéry — all of which have a considerable dignity, poetical
impact and repercussions — dissolve into significance before
the Gospels. For there and there alone, with respect to
presence, I find myself before a BEING who is to me at once
more intimate than the others, who surpasses me on all sides.
At the same time as I read, I am read. Truly, I am as though
standing before a 'God-with-us.' If the forgers of these texts
intended to arouse the illusion which animated them, so be it!
They are sublime artists! The Gospels emanate from a school
of geniuses far superior to the Homerides since, without being
skilled and without working together, they knew how to
transmit to me the magic of the eternal become intimate.

   "I have even greater admiration for the faculty which this
Being of mystery called Jesus has of giving vitality to those
rather mediocre people who chanced to encounter him. Far
and above the art which permits one to transmute colors,
sounds or words, there exists a still higher and truly divine art
whose object is to fashion other artists by giving an instant
of genius to those whom one encounters through an indefinable
something that is communicated to them. It is the privilege
of great educators. This is what happened in every encounter
between Himself and others. Incidental conversations set
down it seems in a haphazard way (or rather which are like
the puddles we find on our muddy country roads after a
storm — each one reflecting the entire sky become calm
again ... and each evangelical anecdote ought to be, Oh Lord
yes! ought to be enough ...). But, where was I? Ah yes,
I was telling you that I found if I relate the Gospels to my
life's experience and, at the same time but on another plane,
relate them to the key element in my life which is my poetic

experience, I find that in proportion as these two avenues of my knowledge widen I perceive in them a truth related to other truths, but one which is far higher in essence than these other truths.

"I sometimes wonder whether my idea of beauty — that accent, that melancholy and somber tone which is compassionate, sovereign, noble and a little distant, though intimate still, which I look for in a literary work as its interior inexpressible truth, does not spring from the same divine source which I recognized in the Christ of the Four Gospels.

"That is my way of *demytho* . . . (how is it?) *logizing?* . . . It puts me in intimate converse with the human element in Bultmann.

"This approach permits me in my unscholarly woman's way, untrained in exegesis, to distinguish between myth and history. I am quite sure that it is not mythical."

Because one of us asked Helena to go into further detail if she could and tell how she attempted to make this distinction by her approach, she continued:

"There is a verisimilitude of the true. It is a density, a plenitude, a kind of sweet brutality, a restless singularity, a bit of the strange in spite of everything that is respectable; I would say there is an imperfection of the true which helps me to distinguish between the *unreal* ideal of the philosophers and the 'true-falsity' of the myths. And it is this nebulous faltering characteristic of the really human reality with its surfaces, its blunders and its lacunae, which I see as a shadow of beauty. This lesser beauty is discernible, I believe, in what were once called the *synoptic* Gospels to distinguish them from the more ideal Gospel of Saint John.

"Hugo said that one can recognize a masterpiece because it gives to man 'all kinds of serious and sweet counsels.' Yes, in the Gospels I recognize these counsels of humanity which I know in great works of art. In addition the Gospels were written in a divinely intimate art, for its material is the most hidden elements of life and not exterior things. This master-piece is not only an admirable object placed in the light as one of Botticelli's paintings, it is, rather, like a sun; I mean it continues to be a source of light to man, a suggestion to painters, novelists and musicians of possible beauty. I think of Shelley's lines on intellectual beauty:

> *Thy light alone ...*
> *Gives grace and truth to life's unquiet dream."*

Helena liked to point out the similarity between truth and beauty. It is a fact that everytime we compare them we give more of a phosphorescence to truth, though we risk dissolving the solid body of the true into a kind of mist. Long ago when I read Abbé Bremond's comparison of prayer and poetry, I feared this possibility. *Pure* prayer, *pure* poetry are for me heights unopen to man.

Because of the lengthy silence that followed her remark, Helena began to speak once again:

"The beautiful and the true in the Gospels is the use made of silences. Poetry also lives by its silences. Music, which ascends from point to point with no transition other than an instance of silence, is woven with silences.... At almost every moment in the Gospel there are ruptures. Our supports are knocked out from under us as though we were arrows shot forward with no plotted course. Everything is strophe and music — until that final silence, until the interruption just before the end we were expecting, which is so obvious, notably in the Gospel of the Resurrection and in the last chapter of Saint Mark, as in the last chapter of the *Acts*. Writing (such as Saint John's Gospel) with a belabored ending carries the human mark and makes us aware of an author. The fifteen hundred verses of *Berenice* were written for the final silence."

CHAPTER VII

The Second Discussion of Testimony: Event and Person

WE parted company quite late that night and continued this discussion the following evening. Even after all that Helena had said, it seemed there still remained a great deal left unsaid about the problem of testimony. While going over the problem we came to see that the important thing was to know *the sense of the testimony*. It was not our object to determine whether Jesus had witnesses, companions and followers, for that had been well established. But what does the testimony mean in itself? What does the Christian testimony point to? Is it like any ordinary historical testimony?

To attack Christianity was at one time to put the testimony in a questionable light. "Deceivers or deceived," they said in Voltaire's day. Witnesses who must be believed because they gave themselves over to be slaughtered, they repeated twisting Pascal's observation — who, by the way, never said that dying for a cause was in itself proof of its truth over and above the doctrine for which one died. That, we are agreed, would seem rather gross for our times. All our wars and revolutions have taught us too well that one may die on both sides for wholly human causes. To be called "martyr" strikes us less than formerly. The crematory ovens, voluntary deaths, a better understanding of deleria permit an economy of the accusations of deception. The problem for a modern, especially for a psychiatrist, is to separate belief from delerium. Such a one is liable to think that he would get a deeper understanding of the state of mind of the first Christians by comparing it to the deleria he observes in his patients.

I wanted to start this discussion off with a few observations on mental illness as related to genius and faith. As usual, I accepted the hypothesis contrary to my own; I was not opposed to the supposition that some of the apostles were abnormal from a clinical point of view. But I looked ahead to see what would follow.

"Let's admit for the sake of argument," I said to them, "that the first propagators of Christianity were mentally deranged. After all, this is not impossible. Saint Paul complained of a sickness difficult to pin down which stung his flesh: he described himself as one stunted, a man afflicted by fear and dread. We know that the first Christian communities in Greece experienced the phenomena of "speaking in tongues" which are now known as disturbances rising from damaged areas in the brain. According to Saint Luke, Pentecost seen by the spectators resembled drunkenness. We come up against a general problem: what exactly is the relationship between genius and certain abnormal states of the nervous system?

"We know that there is some connection between certain maladjustments and the highest manifestations of the mind: Caesar, Dostoevsky were afflicted with epilepsy. Schubert, Schumann, Chopin were sometimes struck with bouts of madness. I would like to understand what connection there is between mental illness and ultra-humanity. Until now no one has afforded me an explanation I consider helpful. It may be that certain illness predispose the human mind to new syntheses because of their ability to disturb, to unsettle and to dissociate. It may be that our nature finds these superior gifts insupportable, that it becomes bogged down like an albatross by its giant wings. But, even supposing that some of the apostles had suffered from such weaknesses, it still remains to be solved how such sick men showed more wisdom, effectiveness, prudence and courage than normal people in good health. All throughout the long history of Christianity we find the same phenomenon of *the weak made stronger than the strong*.

"Grant that one could determine what is normal and define what is healthy (a difficult task even for a doctor), and that the first propagators must be classified as abnormal, nevertheless, if one is faithfully to describe the appearances, one must say that these abnormal men were able to challenge and convince level-headed people. Who would not want to be ill as they? There comes a time when the word *sick* no longer means what we want it to. What is normal? Would not this so-called normal man reputedly of sound mind, but slow, thickheaded, skeptical, would he not be the *true* sick man because he does not correspond to the full model of humanity?"

Olivier said he would not for an instant dream to call the apostles deluded; he realized that this would resolve the question. "My difficulty," he added, "is more delicate than that. I believe it touches upon a graver point. The apostles were unquestionably believers: they announced a mystery of faith; they thought to *proclaim* it to those whom God had already chosen to believe it, who were predestined to this faith, to eternal life. I do not say therefore that the apostles did not *see*, did not *hear* in the faith what they say they saw and heard. In their faith is kindled the faith of those who listened to them, and this faith was transmitted down to the present. But why do you want to force me to admit more than this? Why should we have to enforce in the domain of faith a spirit of historical or scientific verification? This is quite uncalled for. By forcing me into this position you are succumbing to the positive mentality which has taken ahold of you without your being aware of it. Do you believe that one day there will appear in religious matters, as an outmoded attitude, an ill-conceived fruit of the scientific spirit and the spirit of belief, a product of the nineteenth century in its decline, incapable of grasping the depth of religion which lies in adherence to bare faith established beyond the realm of experience? Why do you insist on leaving the solid ground of faith to do battle in the field of experience and historicity where you will always be vanquished?"

MYSELF

"I open the Gospels and observe that the faith in them is always a result. The Gospels which are the residuum of the Word proclaimed in the beginning are not a collection of articles of faith, but an account of what took place. I open the *Acts of the Apostles* and find the same very condensed accounts in the mouths of the apostles. I open to Paul and I see that he refers to symbols more condensed yet which suppose facts.... You, you study these very same texts while concentrating on the final expression which is the moment of summation: faith in Jesus. I concentrate upon the initial expression and the whole progression. And I find myself in the presence of a reflection based on facts, centered on an experience which has a history for its primary matter."

HE

"You used the word *experience*. I question your use of the term because in the ordinary meaning of this word in your vocabulary I do not see that there is any experience here."

MYSELF

"Then I ask you to let we know what more you require for it to be truly an experience."

HE

"A cross-examination. I require an impartial, accurate and impassive testimony; a testimony similar to what a university

educated man, an upright enlightened individual, a scholar,
a prudent man, a Greek philosopher, an Egyptian sage, a
mandarin, a yogi, could have given. A testimony from a
disinterested mind, lacking assent, simply and deliberately
observing, an impartial judge who prepares a civil action by
weighing both sides of the case. It would be an experimenter's
testimony. Now, the testimony of the apostles is nothing of
the kind because they are shown to be convinced and because
they speak the language of faith. An historian could never
use the Gospels as documents because they are the solutions
of faith and because we lack the other side necessary which,
in this case, would be a report by an unbelieving witness,
such as a Roman administrator whose only concern would be
to observe and understand so that he could submit the matter
to the proconsul or the emperor. No true examination is
possible under these conditions. It remains for us to wager
pro or con at our own risks and perils, as Pascal felt. What I
am telling you here is not simply Pascal's thinking; I am
convinced that I have been telling you the personal opinion
of the majority of the moderate minds of our times."

MYSELF

"In an inquest a good and upright man, submitted to an
accusation he thought unjust, wanted to bring witnesses for
his defense. The judge interrupted him, 'We're terribly sorry,
but we cannot accept your witnesses whom we know are your
friends and who could never give us a really impartial testimony.' The accused demanded why the testimony of those
people who had been involved in the events and who alone
knew what really happened should be excluded by the court.
They very gently answered him: 'These people are on your
side, you admit that yourself; the reason according to the
notion that our sort has of justice and honor. What is more,
they consider you innocent of that which you are accused.'
The accused was caught in a paradoxical situation; he had to

find witnesses for his defense among his adversaries: it was a quandary. He was summarily condemned.

"It is the same thing here. The unbelievers deny that the Gospels are historical documents because, they say, they were written by the faithful, that is, by men who did not believe before the events took place but who changed their minds because the events they describe forced them to alter their first state of mind. Admit that the unbelievers are being difficult. What do they want from us before we can be historically honest? They require documents written by witnesses who saw these same things and assigned no particular value to them. They are setting a condition beforehand which is contradictory to the case in question. For, if they insist that the only scientifically and genuinely valid testimony is that of one who has not seen what the witness (now a believer) has seen, it is tantamount to saying that the case was judged before it got started, lost before it was brought to trial.

"Certainly now is a good time for you to tell me that one could nonetheless compare the testimony of one who says he *saw* and the testimony of one who, also being there at the same time, claims he saw nothing. I am not saying that if one could compare the testimonies pro and con it would not be extremely interesting. Nor do I say that it would not be desirable to have a report written about the apparitions by an ultra-Thomas who was present when they occurred and did not believe them. Alas, this possibility is cancelled out by the nature of the religious fact which is not a laboratory experience. Suppose we had the account of a skeptical apostle who had not seen the one risen from the dead, though the others saw or thought they saw him. You would still have to choose one of two accounts and reject the other. And we have the same problem all over again. *Who are we to trust?*

"I am not saying that you are wrong to reject the witnesses who have the faith. After all, each man is entitled to set his own conditions. But I am fighting for the sake of clarity:

I would like you to see your conditions for what they are:
conclusions without premises, plea-in-bar postulates, debar-
ments raised before the examination — which from then on
is not strictly an historical examination as you insist it is."

OLIVIER

"I can't help but think that the requirement I share in
common with many of my contemporaries — a requirement
for a critical examination — remains perfectly objective. Why,
in the demain of the spiritual and eternal life, can you not ask
for the same warranty as in those serious questions which
concern us most, or in those cases where we risk condemning
the innocent? Is it too much to hypothetically desire that
there be alongside the Four Gospels held by the Church a
Gospel according to Thomas, according to Pilate, or according
to Judas, or according to any indifferent person whoever he
might be, and then to compare these four with the other four?
Why do you object? Why do you condemn me for having
only nothingness or infinity before me; the nothingness of the
absence of witnesses, or the infinity of the four witnesses of
faith."

Olivier continued with the same demand. I realized we
were getting nowhere. His criticism touched the very heart
of the debate. Confronted with an abnormal event which is a
sign for some and nothing for others, could one settle the
question scientifically? The question boiled down to whether
one could see a miracle. Mme Saint-René-Taillandier told
me the other evening that she once had dinner at her "Oncle
Taine's" house with Renan. Renan had said during the course
of the meal that he would gladly believe in an apparition of
one risen from the dead if it took place before a commission
set up by the Académie des Sciences. Mme Saint-René-
Taillandier insisted that, in spite of her inexperience at the
time, she felt Renan demanded an impossible condition. She
wanted to object, "Nothing would ever come of it." In effect,

the commission, while admitting that it had seen "the apparitions," would at once have withheld judgment and proclaimed that it wanted to study the matter more thoroughly in order to establish through expert advice and investigation whether natural forces until then unknown or a chance combination impossible till then, the intervention of a quantic number . . . might not have explained what at first sight had no explanation.

I am following the physicists very carefully these days. Since the Solvay Congress of 1927 they believed they could speak of indeterminism in matter. Indeterminism was verified, or plausible, on a certain level of experience. But indeterminism might rule on another deeper level of this same experience. Rigorous minds like Einstein's have never admitted there was no appeal against indeterminism and that determinism was not sovereign. Einstein, classical and Cartesian in spite of everything, withheld his judgment on the reasoning of the indeterminists. He called what seemed impossible to him in a deeper reality that remained entirely in the power of determinism an indeterminist "miracle." We have seen Louis de Broglie, who began to mistrust his indeterminist disciples and doubt even himself, propose a theory which explains the wave phenomena without indeterminism. Thus, confronted with a fact of indeterminism, the human mind will always be able to reduce it to an appearance, to explain it by a resignation or a confusion of the intellect seduced by a probabilist illusion, and appeal to a future explanation able to explain the appearance without compromising the postulate, which alone is deemed intelligible, of natural necessity.

If you are absolutely certain that such and such a person is dead and someone tells you he has just seen him, you will not even consider the possibility. If you are a die-hard atheist, no report of miracles or mystical testimony will convince you, no 'experience' of any kind. Your first intimate certitude will destroy all experiences and cast them off into the zone of illusion or into the realm of the 'unexplained-as-of-yet.' Consequently there is a preliminary condition to every religious experience: it is to admit that it is not impossible.

OLIVIER

"I do not say that this cause or this presence is *a priori* impossible. But, aside from these interior incommunicable facts which cause Paul to believe and not Peter (I tend toward Peter's side), I ask you how, our reason being what it is, there can be any kind of revelation; I mean historically."

I then asked Olivier if he had thought about what a testimony really was. I did not mean testimony as the judges in the world take it, but, because it is necessary to reflect on the most common words grown insipid through overuse, by taking the words of the language in their fullest sense, their heaviest and most pulpous sense. If we open a dictionary of the New Testament we see that the word *martur,* meaning "witness" from which we get *martyr,* is taken in the full sense of which I speak. I shall even go so far as to say that for Saint Paul and Saint John, testimony is an affirmation involving one's entire being (making one a *false witness of God, if he lies*). And what affirmation? — An affirmation bearing ultimately on the presence of an eternal element inserted into the temporal historical world.

I began to develop for Olivier the idea that the moderns have lost the meaning of what it is to be a witness of even the commonest events of daily life. When an accident happens at an intersection, people scurry away for fear of giving testimony. Olivier raised the objection that the *engagement* which is at the very heart of testimony is much extolled these days. "Yes," I replied, "but our epoch which speaks so highly of *involvement* is not so involved as it claims to be. It courts only the semblance of involvement by being committed to the cause which cannot fail." Olivier mentioned that he had never taken up the problem of testimony and that for him it was a particular matter of assent or belief.

"Indeed," I said, "it is a belief, but one proposed as a certain kind of experience: believing in a testimony is really to believe in the experience of another."

Olivier acknowledged this point and said, "You agree that perhaps the need of this kind of testimony is rather barbarous. One day you will see behavior tests, the probings of psychoanalysis, electroencephalograms or other recording devices replacing testimonies. A picture taken with a telephoto lens, a tape recording will become the only valid witnesses since they preserve the incontestable traces of what was seen or said."

"But," I objected, "a witness is not a passive tape, a strip of inert plastic. The essence of testimony is in the relationship between this tape or this band and the person who placed them before an event or before a spoken word, the one who later proposes to show these things to other minds like his. The camera was aimed at a particular scene by a human mind which chose one of them while eliminating all the others it could just as well have selected. The essence of testimony is present in the taking of these worldless pictures. The camera equipment was but a means to widen the compass of the senses. But the testimony consists always in this voluntary relationship established between the self and what the self has seen and heard about other selves whom it judges. No mechanical device can bear witness.

"You cannot see the impotence of these devices because the testimonies to which you refer are testimonies without involvement which, actually, could have been made by machines. Suppose you have filmed a crime: it will only be a testimony when you have said: "I have captured a crime on film." In reality one never *sees* a criminal, one does not even *see* a man, but only patches of grey and white light mixed all together, animated by a movement among other patches. It is your mind which judges that this spot of light is a man and it is your conscience which says that he is a criminal. If you say, "I have seen a man in the act of killing someone," the testimony

bears on the crime, that is on the crime against justice, which
is not visible, though sight is necessary to denounce it.
Machines will never tell you that an act is blameworthy.
Ultimately, testimony is a judgment bearing on value which is
intimate and invisible.

The act of bearing witness helps us to understand our
most ordinary judgments. I ask you to think about the phrase:
Snow is white. I ask you on which word your act of judgment
revolves. Obviously it is not on "snow," nor a "whiteness" for
we know these are whitenesses which are not the whitenesses
of snow. If you judge that snow is white, yours is a strange
process: you are neither in the realm of snow nor in that of
whiteness, but you are asserting that this particular snow
participates in the quality of whiteness which may include
other species — such as the whiteness of milk, a flower petal
or a face. Your thought then centers on the word IS which
designates this act of judgment that no electronic computer
will ever make.

"Now let us apply these observations to an analysis of
faith. I say that the faith does not focus upon Jesus, nor upon
any miracle. It focuses on '*Jesus IS risen.*' The object of
this judgment of faith is not Jesus as an historical man. Neither
is it the mystery of which the Resurrection consists, nor any
miracle of the multiplication of loaves. Profane historians
give accounts of ordinary men similar to Jesus. Images or
legends give us mysteries or myths, metamorphoses, the
multiplication of matter, exceptions to natural laws, people
leaving their tombs, apparitions. The originality of the Christian message is, therefore, neither in the historical element nor
in the mysterious (or mythical element). It is in the line, the
indiscernible, indissociable joining together of both. In other
words, it is not Jesus the historical Nazarene historified who
is of concern to me, nor is it the theme of the multiplication of
loaves. It is *Jesus multiplying.* The object of testimony is
Jesus HAS multiplied. In the same way, Jesus dead, condemned or crucified does not concern me, for his trial was like

all other trials, his death like all other deaths. Nor am I particularly concerned with the apparitions which, if by themselves, detaches and separate, would resemble the apparitions of the gods mythological legends tell us about. What interests me in that this Jesus historically dead IS the Jesus mysteriously living after his death. As the testimony in the first case centers upon the bond between Jesus and the multiplication of the loaves (Jesus IS multiplying), so the force of the testimony points to the identity of the crucified Jesus with the risen Jesus (Jesus dead IS Jesus risen). An agony and a death in themselves would not be religious, nor could apparitions by themselves be the object of the belief of Christianity. These must be united in an intimate union in the concrete, in reality and in historicity before there can be a foundation to the Christian religion, that is before, on the one hand, the Incarnation can be a real mystery, and before, on the other hand, it can be known by the human mind in the act of testimony.

"To the incomprehensible act of divine power which brings together the eternal and the temporal into the unity of Jesus Christ there corresponds the stunning act of apostolic testimony which asserts that it has verified through experience (also unique in its kind) that the historical has been penetrated by the eternal mystery — or to put it more simply, that here the human experience is miraculous. Essentially the idea of miracle is the idea of this intimate presence of an element superior to history in the very heart of history: this presence is necessary, impossible to deny, and it is that to which the whole weight of the facts bears witness.

"If you think about it, you will see that this is where the originality of Christianity lies. This is what makes it resemble both *histories* and *legends*. But this is also what radically distinguishes between histories and legends.

"Because of this presence the Christian fact will never be fully grasped by purely historical minds, neither will it be understood by purely mythological minds. Both believing the study the Christian fact, they exhaust and dispel with the presuppositions of their approaches the one thing that makes the essence of Christianity irreducible: the Incarnation on the part of God and testimony on the part of man.

"The strange thing about the final chapters of the Gospel (we all feel it on Easter when the Passions are read before the feast and the Christophanies are read after it) is that the narrator, whoever he was, keeps the same impassible tone of a town recorder recounting events as plausible as the death of a man and also as unthinkable as the apparitions of a dead man.

"In the episode of the disciples on the road to Emmaus this liaison (without a double exposure of the ordinary and the strange in the very same account) is more obvious still, for the reader cannot immediately distinguish between what is probable and what is not. We could believe that Luke, if he is the author of this account, was the pupil of Mérimée or Edgar Allan Poe, both of whom delighted in working a mysterious impossible event into a true-to-life account rich in everyday details without your being aware of the transition. Read Mérimée's *Venus d'Ille*. It is an absolute masterpiece of sleight-of-hand."

Olivier asked me what I was getting at.

Myself

"Quite simply to help you put your finger on the nature of the Gospel.

"You see that we are coming back to the two schools I described earlier. Only the account of Jesus' Passion is of value to the *historian* since it has natural and historical verisimilitude. For the *mythologist* this account tends to become a legend of faith composed, as legends sometimes are, by the juxtaposition of several themes drawn from prophecies or from the necessities of propaganda. But neither of these can face up to WHAT is precisely the sole question at hand. It is as though to resolve the problem of man we are faced with

6 *Jesus*

either the (radical) positivists who see man simply as a
biological and social being, or the (absolute) idealists who
admit no other conceivable existence than that of pure consciousness and its images. Neither can see (I do not say it is
beyond them to explain) what is precisely the heart of the
problem: this inconceivable existence of man who is at once
fully material and fully spiritual, this total concourse of spirit
and body in the unity of the human person. Why I reprove
these two schools of the *critics* and the *mythists* must be clear
enough to you by now. I would say that the criticism of
miracles in either school leads to dissolving beforehand the
essence of the testimony of the miracle, the knowledge of the
bond between the natural *event* and the supernatural *event*.
It destroys this bond prior to every historical experience by
virtue of a preliminary judgment beyond which there is no
appeal. Hence, the unbeliever attached to these schools may
sleep peacefully, eternally certain that the FACT will never
cross his path.

"Whenever he encounters a testimony he will easily and
necessarily strip it of substance by the skillful action of his
method. I do not mean he will deny it. Everything the
witness says will only serve him as a documentary on the
circumstances, as a test concerning the state of mind of a
believer and his delusion. He will see it as a poor compound
of observation and illusion, void of what makes its substance.
Under these conditions history will never encounter the faith.

"In other words the critical mind theoretically states that
the witnesses only bear witness to their own impressions:
which means that they are mistaken. Yet, the critical spirit
is prepared to favorably receive every testimony for the
prosecution. Fontenelle once said, 'The testimony of those
who believe something verified is powerless to substantiate it,
but the testimony of those who do not believe it has the power
to destroy it: those who believe cannot be given reasons for
not believing, but it can hardly be that those who believe
nothing cannot be given reason for believing.'

"Because of these reasons I wish to approach the question from the opposite end. You have your reservations about the witnesses because you are sure he is wrong. But it is this preliminary presupposition which now seems questionable to me. And I wonder if we might not begin by putting ourselves in the witness' frame of mind. . . ."

OLIVIER

"Certainly. But the frame of mind of which witness? Do you believe that a religious witness, an evangelical witness, a witness in religious matters is comparable to what you and I call a witness? Saint John tells us of the disciple who saw the blood and water flow from Jesus' side on the cross. And he adds with unusual solemnity: 'These things he saw, and we know that his testimony is true.' But does this mean that he *saw* in the sense I can say I see you at this very moment? Blood and water are rightfully called the sacraments of the Church: the Eucharist is represented by blood, baptism by water. Now, can that *be seen?* And then we can say *this man* is bearing witness only if we give 'witness' a meaning altogether different from the ordinary sense."

MYSELF

"I realize that this is a difficulty, or rather one aspect of the unique difficulty of this debate on 'reason' and 'faith.' To reduce the obstacle to size, I propose to tackle the question of what a witness is and approach it by setting aside for the time being those religious themes that divide us, and proceed by an analysis of what each of us feels in himself when he *bears,* as they say, witness. This question is always neglected. The text you quoted from Saint John is troublesome. He who so solemnly attests that he saw the water and blood seems to give them a certain mystical significance. However, this text is not typical of the first Gospels which lack this symbolical character."

He

"You are rejecting the text most to my advantage because it shows me what an undisputed witness says he *saw*."

Myself

"I do not reject it. I simply set it aside because if you want a truly fair investigation, you cannot begin with a rare, perhaps a unique, instance. You must start out with a common one. Let's examine the everyday circumstances we become witnesses to *in spite of ourselves*. I believe them to be highly representative, for are we not always more or less involuntary witnesses and somehow compelled by the event because we saw it without wanting to? We have witnessed a chance occurrence, perhaps the sovereign and repeated chance that is the behavior of a sage or hero: and we must speak out. Or we see an innocent man condemned. . . . Actually we see neither wisdom, heroism nor innocence, but only the signs of them, just as blood and water are signs in Saint John's Gospel. What has happened?

"Our being has come into contact with another being occasioned by an act that puts into play our whole way of conceiving the moral life. A secret, intimate contact — and it immediately quickens within us as a seed of thought, the idea of difficult obligations. And of course there are all kinds of degrees between the stealthy perception of a pedestrian who suddenly *finds himself seeing* the collision of two cars at an intersection, and the impregnation of one entire soul by another during a long shared life. In the case of a witnessed accident, the observer is by definition in a state of surprise. He has no preliminary perception. He finds it hard to fully realize what he has seen.

A relationship of friendship or hatred is required before you can give testimony in every case of strict observance over a long period of time. The necessary perspective of an audience growing ever larger and without limit is required. The act of testimony, which already has an antecedent history in you, is assured through you of a union of what was most personal and most diffused. This is the rare moment when the transition from the most solitary to the most public takes place. When all is said and done, testimony is not judgment alone as I have just now told you, it is speech at its profoundest.

"I bear witness to an event that I alone have captured on my retina and within by being. If everyone saw it as I did, then of course I would not have to make the almost sacrilegious substitution of bearing witness. Sacrilegious, I say, for it implies in the depths of myself an inarticulate summons to the power of truth that is transcendent to my consciousness and which tells it, *Destroy me if I am lying!* I am not destroyed. This ordeal is ineffectual and I go on as though the truth abided within my testimony.

"Remember also that the fact we witness is a fragment of secret history which will never occur again; no experience of any kind can bring it back. The event is not inscribed in the seasons of the stars which are repeated over and over, year in and year out. Let me reiterate this. When what you have seen is something exceptional, when the speech you have heard is solemn, veiled or mysterious, you become like initiates. It is like a mystery religion founded all at once where you initiate another, asking him (senseless thing) to see with your eyes and not with his. This is what it means *to believe*. Your companion's inability to see and know without help, the necessity of a mediator, is an attitude of religious essence in the life of the most worldly individual.

"Once again I would like to point out the paradox of testimony. The matter of the testimony is that secret confided to you, though only temporarily, in order that you might make restitution of it. You feel, and rightly so, that you are but a channel. You are soaked through and through by a sap you have not secreted and which is going to spread throughout your body by the assertions which involve you. You must bring out into the light of day what was said to you in utter darkness. This secret that has entered into you without your asking for it is like life itself, for you did not choose to be born. It is deposited in you as a seed for retransmission. It must be *brought out*, as they say, in spite of all the risks it may entail for you, the greatest of which, if necessary, is to die.

"But we moderns scarcely understand this characteristic of testimony. For various reasons we have lost the sense of responsibility that one must have if he becomes the temporary custodian of a truth destined for others. But you will tell me that the moderns have a deep sense of advertising. And that to such an extent that everything has become so public that no one can write a letter, a personal diary even, without the fear that one day it may be plastered all over the magazines. Hidden tape recorders record state secrets and private confidences. What the moderns have often called *openness* was not the effort made to transmit a truth in their keeping, but rather the act of disclosing the ordinary or shameful episodes in one's life, like Rousseau or Gide, in order to confess them and equalize everything. Cynicism replaces hypocrisy, but for the same end: to put ourselves at ease in evil. That is no testimony at all."

Olivier

"What you say concerns testimonies people make, but do we see testimonies like these in the Gospel? Do we hear the sound of a voice telling us: 'I was there and this is what I saw? Your analysis would be more suited to the account of Saint Paul's journeys in the *Acts* written up by his companion. There we believe we can hear the kind of testimony you describe: secrets revealed, personal experiences recounted to others. But in the Gospel accounts I do not see any like assertions of the narrator. I see only a sequence of often marvelous anecdotes or narratives. All of it resembles literary works that are supported by imagination and not by testimony, as you say."

MYSELF

"I am not saying one can defend each fragment of the Gospel from the point of view of testimony. There are instances when it is quite difficult to figure out the connections between the witnesses and the author of the narratives: the Gospel's concerning Jesus' birth, for example. But, if I consider the Gospels of Jesus' public life *in toto,* I see them offered the reader as established facts. I call your attention to the opening lines of Luke's account written with the harmony and precision that is *the* charm of the Greek tongue:

> 'Inasmuch as many have undertaken to draw up a narrative concerning the things that have been fulfilled among us, even as they who from the beginning were eyewitnesses and ministers of the word have handed them down to us, I also have determined, after following up all things carefully from the very first, to write for thee, most excellent Theophilus, an orderly account, that thou mayest understand the certainty of the words in which thou hast been instructed.'

"This text raises a moral and human problem. If one who speaks like this is a forger (for he is too much aware of his task to be accused of illuminism), he is a consummate forger. One cannot assert more explicitly that a document is historical in the most modern sense of the word 'historical.' There is no more emphatic way to say that this account is based on witnesses, on 'having-seen-by-themselves' (*autoptai*), as Luke calls them. Besides, would it help much to consider an account of the Gospel as 'testified to'? We usually say that Saint Mark's Gospel is a résumé of Saint Peter's preaching. Now, if for every place you see *Peter* you put the pronoun *I,* you will get the impression of hearing Peter testify.

"Saint John's Gospel is written wholly in the idea of testimony. John presents himself as the witness *par excellence.* He says, '*I saw.*' And he redoubles his assertion: '*It is I who have seen,* it is I who give testimony.' He appeals to *Him who knows whether his testimony is true.* When Renan contended that the Johannine Gospel, as we have known it since the Ecole biblique de Jérusalem, contained much information, people objected telling him that it also contained many miracles, citing the *Fioretti.* Renan replied, A biographer like Francis of Assisi's may tell of a great many miracles without ceasing to be for all that the most ingenuous man on earth. But, if this biographer had said: 'I was his closest friend, he preferred me above all the others, everything I wrote down is true because I saw it' — unquestionably, one would have to call him something else.' This is being logical. It is superficial to take the Gospels for collections of miracle tales. I know that the preachers formerly insisted above all on miracles. But we see that Jesus spurned the exercise of this power to perform wonders just as he spurned temptation. We see him criticizing the Jews for desiring wonders and signs in the heavens. He would give no sign but the sign of Jonas — the Resurrection."

Helena began shyly to tell us what she thought about this matter. She worked out, she said, from the *divine ways of acting,* from elegance and discretion carried out to the ultimate degree and which belong to God, a conception strikingly different from that of the average man.

It seemed to her that if God wanted to offer Himself to men, He would do it neither by causing amazement nor by admiration (at least if it were too sudden), but rather He would slowly reveal Himself through veiled signs, through whisperings, she said, instead of loud voices. From this point of view, Helena preferred Saint Luke's approach to Saint Mark's, though they both speak of the same events. Marvel (it would have to come some time) should not explode into the lives of men but evolve gradually as a necessarily slow conclusion, as springs flowing along our countrysides are undiscernible but for the lush verdure of the meadows. And

I believe that these overly sensitive, exacting and grim minds ("Perhaps," said Helena, "too exacting, for what they demand is too difficult to realize.") would prefer the miracle of Emmaus. Here we see a light growing brighter little by little during an ordinary conversation, a meal taken together at twilight and the moment of God in a furtive gesture, in a departure.

"I realize," Helena added, "that various kinds of minds approach this subject. Certain spirits simply cannot yield to this sort of self-abandon demanded by the testifying act either in becoming aware of a singular fact or in transmitting it to others. Goethe, for example, was too clever for that. He knew some exceptional people and saw many unique events: yet the battle of Valmy did not strike him, did not transpierce him. He remained a stranger to it, although he was a spectator, indifferent to that moment of history which he nevertheless considered of great magnitude. When Goethe recounted his life, no one could say he gave testimony either pro or con, even in his favor: he witnessed his life with a regal indifference, without passing judgment on it. On the other hand, take Pascal. He is just the opposite of Goethe. Pascal even finds ways of considering physical or mathematical objects as singular beings and almost as personages. I have always been surprised to hear people speak of sections of a cone, arithmetical triangle, or the sines of a quarter circle, as though they were facts. Pascal was at heart so intensely a witness that he carried out this quality of being almost to physical experience — this quality given once only, once and for all. We can picture him setting the stage so that the famous experiment of his brother-in-law, Périer, on the Puy-de-Dôme would resemble a battle that Périer would recount. [1] With this same historical heart Pascal became attached to the solitary religious of Port-Royal who were as the *last witnesses* of the faith. The further Pascal advanced in life the more he wanted to be,

---

1. Périer confirmed Torricelli's experiment on air pressure — Tr.

if it were at all feasible, a more of a witness than one of the
faithful. Pascal's faith kept guard over the memory of well-
dated events. He wanted to found his apology on *facts* which
his method permits one to *see* with the eyes of the spirit in
the same way one sees people in the street."

I told Helena that I shared this highly spontaneous sentiment so long as it would not become a system imposing
preliminary conditions on divine freedom. We were of one
mind in recognizing that the Gospel is not a literary work
like those that recount the lives of wonder-workers.

"This still won't change the fact," Olivier said "that miracle
tales were for centuries the chief argument for the faith.
Miracles supported what the apostles had to say. This is
true even with Paul as we see in the *Acts*."

I replied that the very rapid spread of the faith could
not be explained without admitting that the imaginations of
the Jews and especially the Greeks were fired up by some
striking element. I said also that because neither of us could
discuss each miracle account individually, it would be better
to put them between parentheses and consider only the fundamental miracle — the Resurrection. Saint Paul said that if
there were no Resurrection then all the rest was meaningless.
I offered to show Olivier a *mémoire* I had written on the
Resurrection, and he was delighted to see it.

I asked him not to pass judgment on miracles just yet.
I agreed with what he said about the importance of miracles
in the Gospel, but I went on to say that Saint John puts less
emphasis on them and only considers one miracle of each
type from which he immediately draws a religious teaching.

"Already in the first century we can perceive a development
of the spirit. It seems that in Galilee right from the outset,
the healing of the possessed struck the people most of all.

If this were not so then one could not explain why the affair of the pigs of Geraza possessed by the devil *Legion* could hold so prominent a place in Saint Mark's very concise Gospel. But the testimony does not solely and by preference bear on these miracles which, I reiterate, were written up only after the Resurrection and in the wake which transformed everything."

I added that, "Jesus did not begin by showing his power. The extraordinary events blended into the rest of the Gospel and were mentioned only in addition to the rest. First of all there was HIMSELF. It was life with him, the familiarity with him, with his person and the secret of his identity.

"The Gospels proclaim these new relationships to a single being who stands visibly over man as his creator. It is *friendship* in the fullest sense, a word given us by the ancients, but now has become so trite in our times. We see that the Gospel is built like a pyramid of friendships, large at the base, but rarefied and increasingly narrow the further one ascends.

"You find the seventy-two disciples, then the twelve apostles, then the three favored, Peter, James and John. Then in the midst of this trio, the Two, Peter the leader and John the beloved disciple, each being preferred in his order without the preference of primacy ruling out the primacy of love. At that point, at that juncture and instant when the pyramid of human friendship is consummated in the Three, the Two, another region begins — the unparalleled, indescribable and inconceivable region of love and testimony wherein the Son bears witness to the Father and the Father to the Son — the Son of whom John says that he reposes on the Father's breast as the disciples at the Last Supper reposed on the Son's.

"Thus, when you look for the essence and the interior truly secret movement of the Gospel, you perceive always the testimony which one person makes on behalf of another because he alone knows what is intimate and unrevealed in him, and it is this something which he transmits to other spirits. The source of all these communications lies in the first testimony Jesus makes to his Father, the reason for his existence.

"That, in my opinion, is the force of the Last Gospel which, coming after the others, brings out what was implicitly assumed in them: the act of bearing witness not merely to the more or less inexplicable events, but to a BEING from whom the inexplicable emanates as from a wellspring. Testimonies bearing on one fact or another cannot be separated from the global testimony, and this testimony centers upon one mysterious personage, upon a Being who is both at the same time Flesh-in-History and Spirit beyond flesh and history.

"In much the same way the enduring foundations we see in history occur. They begin with neither idea nor chance nor even an encounter between chance and idea. But chance and idea are assumed in an historical being. For example, the habit of thinking about causes and ends called strangely enough in the West a "philosophy" derives from Socrates. In Christianity we have seen these foundations develop from one individual who gathers witnesses around himself in the beginning. The reproduction of the Gospel is not simply "the appeal of a hero" as Bergson called it, but familiarity being transformed into appeal without one being able to say when or how. We perceive neither pure facts nor ideas as you tend perhaps a little too much to suppose. But *fact-ideas* or *idea-facts*. I mean ideas incarnated in beings.

"That is why I think Plato's way of evaluating things, rejecting them in the 'state of flux,' retaining only their 'ideas,' is an intellectual error. As though the Idea strode above the thing resembling it in a sort of distant heaven, as Proust said of the Idea of a sonata. In this case the idea would not be incarnated in nature, since it could be detached from nature. I am looking for a more intimate relationship which does not separate the visible from the invisible like the dualism of catharsis. I desire a relationship which discovers and contemplates the spiritual within the concrete and carnal, the spiritual glowing as a presence and capable of perception by an intuitive mind.

"I am only too aware of how difficult it is to avoid this separation. If you replace the dissociate method of Plato by what is called the *positive* method which retains only the little facts, like Flaubert, Taine and many historians and novelists, you are even less further ahead. The "little facts" do not exist in an inert and indifferent state. They also are charged with meaning. The *Journal* of the Goncourt brothers, who regarded themselves as machines to record conversations, is much more malicious than Saint-Simon's *Mémoires* which bear the deep imprint of his personal bias and petulance. I think this explains that a genuine artist, because he is looking for the fact impregnated with meaning, the spirit present in the forms of things, stands before a reality much like the one the Christian calls WORD-MADE-FLESH. The cosmos is before his mind and his art, in its immensity as in its details, without confusion or separation, imprescriptibly all matter and all spirit. It is not enough to say with Virgil that the spirit stirs up the crowd; it is a more interior abode, and we are incapable of knowing where it begins and where it ends. Therefore, you will not be shocked that I find a similarity between the act of seeing, in which we capture the form and the color of a thing at the same time as its essence, and the act of testifying, through which the apostles placed themselves at the point of junction between the eternal word and the 'flesh.' Neither realism nor symbolism will ever satisfy me. For I know too well that we never perceive either a brutal existence or a symbol, but a reality full of significance. We see an incarnate idea.

"And if we suppose that the Incarnation of the Word is real, we understand that testimony is the necessary organ for knowing it. For this testimony does not only reach the flesh, but, as Saint John's Gospel says: the Word made flesh. A witness is one who sees the real *and* the symbol, the temporal *and* the eternal, at the same time. In one glance he sees a being as it appears and as it actually is.

"Hence, in a testimony there is much more than a simple verification: there is a grasping of that which is signified. Plato was not present at Socrate's death, but he is more a witness than Cebes or Phaedo because he understood that death.

"This is also why Saint John's Gospel, though further removed in time from the events than the others, is nevertheless more of a testimony than they because it depicts more deeply the meaning of the same facts. He adds nothing to the facts. He adds to their significance. Therefore, as I see it, he bears witness more fully."

OLIVIER

"This is tantamount to saying that one must believe in order to bear witness, and in order to believe one must have borne witness. This is simply one more instance of the enchanted circle of the faith."

MYSELF

"Yet, if there do exist some events whose supreme sense can only be grasped by rising to a higher plane of existence, you must admit that if you are to understand them clearly you cannot refuse to believe in them if they are offered to you. That is the whole problem of religion. Faith is not essential for coming to see, as though it alone gave sight and as though you can only see with the eyes of this faith. What is required is that the answer of the faith be not condemned beforehand, that a pre-existing philosophy, a prior conviction, an idea in the back of my mind, does not render the faith impossible to the eyes of reason. It is essential that the testimony be not implicitly refuted before giving it a fair hearing. Testimony is a human act that has faith as a consequence but not as a premise. Testimony is the apex of the life of the mind when

this mind stands face-to-face before being, not being understood abstractly, but the singular temporal being, the personal,
truly existing being, who is engaged in flesh and in history.

"The Gospel carries out to the ultimate intensity this act
in which man captures the spirit present in flesh and in
history. Unfortunately, it can be said that human thoughts
are not favorable to the understanding of this great act. They
were not among the ancients. Neither are they among the
moderns. . . ."

Part Four

The Two Unknowns,

Resurrection
Divinity

CHAPTER VIII

The Event

IN my previous study I wanted to define the eternal element in the difficulty which Jesus presents to our minds; inevitably, I gave this examination too ivory-tower an approach. I had to come down to some applications.

I shall pass over the minor points which are infinite and often insoluble. To consider some miracle story, to compare it to other accounts of the same type in other religious traditions, to examine a text and see "the levels of comparison" — these are the problems which interest the scholar and researcher in me and that part of my mind which likes to conjecture. "Maybe. . . ." I delight in hovering from possibility to the other. I will not give in to it.

I want to keep the rule I set down for myself. I want to ascend as far as possible to the summit of it all (*solvitur in excelsis*) and not turn back.

Besides, the apostles' method was a global one. They did not dally over minor details. We see that when they lost Judas they wanted to bring their number back to the full twelve. So, they cast lots for the twelfth one from among those who *had seen* Jesus from the time of his baptism until the ascension. The testimony covers his entire public life. Saint Paul still more emphatically sets up a hierarchy among the facts and from them he selects one so basic that if it were

questionable the whole structure would crumble: "If Christ
has not risen, your hope is in vain." This is thinking in depth,
in perspective, in terms of the strategy of the true, for nothing
ever has exactly the same importance. To defend a position
according to its details and its contour is to render it vulnerable.

A friend once told me that when he had a Gospel in his
hands, he immediately flipped over the pages to the Resurrection. I can understand why he would. The last phase, the
last instant shed light on what came before them. When the
redactor of a Gospel wrote the first word he had the Resurrection in mind. The Passion narrative which lacks all hope was
written by a man who believed in the Resurrection. The
Gospels, just as any life when it is recounted, were considered
backwards from the death to the beginning, and by men who
know from the first how everything would come out in the end.
This law of every narrative is especially applicable here.
The Resurrection is not the final point of the Gospel, but the
envelope into which the Gospel is placed and where it finds
repose.

How am I going to tackle this essential problem which
differs enormously from every other historical problem in its
dimensions, perspectives and import? How shall I obtain a
result that many people will find useful? How can I do this
by applying my own unaided reflection to the givens of that
problem as is my wont and my method? It seems quite a
problem indeed. At least I am going to look for a starting
position that will be acceptable to everyone.

Description of the Appearances

I am going to take for granted that I already know through
history the beginnings of this new religion which claims Jesus
as its origin. Let us describe the appearances:

About the year 33 of what will later be called the first

century I see emerging outside the pale of the Jewish community a sect that worships Yahweh, but one more different than a prophetical school or even the Essene community of the Dead Sea. The disciples of Jesus believed him to be the Messiah whom the Jews were awaiting. The indifferent administrators described Christianity as disputes among the Jews over a certain Jesus. Something happened. Proudhon will say: "A primitive, organic fact enshrouded with mystery, encased in obscurity." I do not know whether we can, whether we must, go that far.

What is this primitive fact? It is obvious that all I can say is that I am resigned to remain in ignorance of it.

I can do no less than learn what the Christians say about their beliefs. And I am faced with the affirmation of the article of faith: *Jesus died for our sins, he rose again on the third day.*

That is the first sign and first vestige which the tides of history washed ashore upon the sands of consciousness, the first emergence. We have some well-dated documents which appear in the middle of the first century — about twenty years after the events they describe.

But here the obscurity begins, just as in every domain where one, not content with observing what appears in realm of signs, seeks to go back from the *emergence* to the *origin*. We have no non-Christian source of knowledge with which to study those mysterious events at the origin. We cannot verify them by any firm monuments or independent reports, such as a foreign history alluding to these events, or a statement from Herod or Pilate. Our sole source is the account that the faithful made of them, a narrative which for a long time was passed on by word of mouth and which finally came to rest in a single memory. Then someone wrote it down and assembled these fragments which I have before me as I write.

After all, it is not strange that a religious movement, appearing like a secret society, should alone know its own past and that we can have no information about it except from its members and followers. Who can tell us of the life, the journeys, the thought of Lenin before 1917 except his own companions? Whatever is germinal, closed in on itself, private and secret is by definition unknown to history. The *Gospels* are the embryogenesis of Christianity written by the evangelized. Nothing can justify the gratuitous assumption that the history they wrote about their origins is false or falsified. Nothing? Almost. One single thing gives us room for doubt — the marvels they report in these origins. The difficulty does not stem from the life and wretched death of Jesus, but from his resurrection from the dead. Obviously, Jesus' religion, as Proudhon said, needed a *primitive fact,* but what nature, what proportion, what kind of existence must one give to this initial impulse?

If I am to get a clear idea of this original X, I shall have to use a negative and indirect approach. I decide to omit the knowledge of the first article of faith, or at least I shall omit what seems obscure in this article which causes me great difficulty: the Resurrection. I allow myself a Jesus reduced to the barest minimum: a Jewish prophet executed. In short, a destiny quite similar to that of the "Teacher of Righteousness" whom the Dead Sea Scrolls have revealed to us.

The precise difference between the "Teacher of Righteousness" and Jesus is obvious when seen from the point of view of their posterity. The "Teacher" inspired a sect, a school, a closed community which little by little shrank in size, then died off, and its documents were stashed away in a cave as previously it cut itself off from the world by becoming a kind of village-monastery along the Dead Sea and the desert. No universal religion emerged from the Teacher of Righteousness and preserved his name.

The special feature of the party, the movement, of Jesus seen from the first sketchy perspective I consider it, is the astounding and lasting effect produced which is so disproportionate to the smallness and insignificance of its origins.

The Emergence

Whether it is a question of fact or myth, or a combination of the two, I notice a sudden chequered and powerful emergence.

We almost have to resort to the imagery of explosion, of a cone of fire, I should say of an atomic mushroom cloud, to describe the extremely rare phenomenon's brevity and force of propagation.

And, as happens in atomic fission, the explosion occurs throughout the course of history in mitigated forms; foundations, reforms and renewals come to mind. All of this would lead us to suspect, if it were a question of a physical phenomenon (a powder-magazine exploding at a distance), that in the beginning there was an extremely concentrated energy. Consequently, I shall go on with my examination and, without using the disturbing word "resurrection," I shall study only the gulf that separates Jesus from the Church. I seek to plot out the edges of this crater as exactly as I am able.

The Crater's Edge

Even though the Passion narratives are unreliable as to date, circumstances, the conspiracy of the authorities, the kind of death, still no one who wishes to use the method which will permit him to write the history can reject the death of Jesus.

As several critics have pointed out, the only event that one may assert without fear of contradiction in the "life of Jesus" is that Jesus died, condemned as king of the Jews and the Messiah, that he died on the cross after a very brief career.

I would include as well that Jesus died a death which was infamous in the Roman and particularly the Jewish mentality: the death of a runaway slave who was nailed to a cross and exposed beneath the city walls. A slave Jesus was not. He worked at the free trade of carpentering, at his free prophet-

ical activity: he was a slave on the night of his death, exposed
to the glances of people who wagged their heads as they passed
him by on the cross.

No one could make a start from so total a defeat: no
worship could spring from the sight of a wretched corpse.
The appearances must be radically changed. Now, the story
teaches me the state of mind of the "poor people of Jerusalem"
after the death of Jesus: they were convinced that he was
more than a living being: present and operating in the midst
of them. We have no proof that this feeling of ultra-presence
evolved over a long period of time, that it cropped up only
after a lengthy state of confusion. We see on the contrary,
immediately upon the death of Jesus, an extraordinary
intensity of faith and activity. This leads one to suspect
that there was something else besides a sudden and bloody
death at the origins of Christianity.

I want to carefully examine this first point. And to keep
this examination restricted to this much I shall not burden
myself with the details. I wish to omit everything except the
form of a void, as one would study a lock to figure out the
shape of the key. I say that in order to explain this resurrection of joy, hope and enterprise after so heartbreaking a death
we need *something* strong enough to efface the impression
of downfall, infamy, abandonment on the part of God. We
need (whether it be true or only illusory) a kind of experience
that is at least as powerful as this death. Jewish tradition
held that crucifixion was God's solemn declaration condemning whoever was executed in this fashion. The Jews, so
attentive to signs, interpreted Jesus' death on the cross as the
sign that he was a false prophet. The spectacle of the cross
blocked to some extent people's memories, and excited anguish
and doubt about everything that happened prior to it. We
know the power of suspicion to cast aspersions on our estimation of someone. Suppose a husband finds out after his
wife's death that she had been unfaithful to him. Suppose a
subordinate officer deeply admires his superior officer and is

forced to conclude after certain reports that he is a traitor.
I believe that what I now advance is implicitly admissible
in one way or another by everyone concerned with the problem.
Proudhon, for example, strangely enough supposed that Jesus
did not die on the cross and that his disciples took him down
from it and that he was still present in the underground movement, inspiring and spurring his followers on. This hypothesis is unthinkable but, from my point of view, it does respect
the boundary lines of the void.

"The rapid spread of the Nazarene propaganda after
the apparent death of Jesus is the strongest argument for
his presence among them. Everything took place quietly;
the work went on as though underground; it steadily
advanced, expanding throughout Galilee, Samaria, Syria,
then into Asia Minor, the Isles and Greece. Less than
forty years after the death of Jesus it reached Rome. As
soon as all these communities were founded and affiliated,
it became indestructible.

"Now, it is just as difficult to conceive the death of
Jesus as it is to conceive its development in his absence.
He alone could save his work killed along with his body
on Golgotha; he alone could give it the increase after the
dispersion of the flock.

"At this point M. Renan took a particularly wrong turn
by not discerning in these matters what stems from individual initiative and what stems from collective influence.
For me, Jesus' action is not less necessary after his reputed
death than before it. Could Peter or John have steered
a straight course through the outbreak of gnostic sects,
before a Simon Magus, a Paul, an Apollo, the Nicolaites,
the Cerinthians, the Ebionites? Jesus' fundamental thought
survived them all. It was not understood until the resurrection; later, after the destruction of Jerusalem, it was
altered and exaggerated; therefore, from the year 29 to
the year 70, he lived among them.

"Jesus would have kept silence about his resurrection, attributing his return to life to the work of God, convinced, he the first, that he only escaped death through the will of heaven. Condemned never to show himself in public again and no longer able to follow his disciples, they become his successors in the work of the ministry. Placed also in a deceptive situation after giving them encouragement and additional instruction, he had to slip away out of their sight and only communicate with them from further and further away, and finally to suddenly disappear without them realizing that he had become: *Dominus quidem Jesus assumptus est in coelum.*"

I like this text, this thought — in my mind unthinkable — yet it does describe the *effect*: a clandestine operating presence of a dead man believed to be living.

His death had to be annulled. How? By an element I call X which could transform defeat into a sign of triumph. This X must be convincing enough to everyone who had seen the corpse — it must also be very closely connected to the events, for one sees the historical Christianity rising immediately upon the death of Jesus. Certainly, this X had to be accepted by many people, for it is beyond our understanding how anyone, if he alone had experienced this X, could communicate it to others. Let us say that there simply had to be some kind of manifestation of Jesus as no longer dead. We can say no more than that, but we can at least say that much.

The description of the *void* I have tried to make does not contradict what the Gospel relates, since its message is that Jesus, after his death, showed himself to be living.

However far we ascend, this faith is affirmed with the shining clarity of a diamond.

Today, the basic documents have been thoroughly classified. The Gospels thought to come at a later date are not taken into consideration, at least not in their actual state. But specialists on the primitive liturgies and acient symbols of the faith have discerned and isolated — especially in Saint Paul's letters — the most ancient formulas of Christian cult. They encounter on all sides, like a foundation stone, the assertion of the Resurrection in either clear or mysterious terms, according to whether it is mentioned in juridical definition or in the mystical spirit. The most notable of these formularies is to be found in one of Saint Paul's Epistles which exegetes believe was written in the year 55. Saint Paul says it was *received before him* in the churches and was uncontested. Next would come Peter's discourses written in a very ancient style and which are included in the *Acts*. Finally, the Gospels, the latest of which would be Saint John's or the little résumé that concludes Saint Mark's Gospel. I pass over this point which no one questions. History shows that to be a Christian and to believe in the Resurrection of Jesus is one and the same thing. One may question Jesus' divinity among the Christians, one may doubt the historical nature of the Resurrection; but there has never been a Christian who did not believe that Jesus arose from the dead.

But in what sense is one to understand this new life of Jesus that he manifested after his death?

To admit a continuation of his former life, as Proudhon supposed, is so unlikely from the viewpoint of verisimilitude that no one can maintain it for long. To say, as did Renan, that the love of his followers made Jesus raise up from the dead in their hearts, is to fill this void with words: so great an effect could with difficulty depend on so poor a cause. To say that they made up tales of apparitions with the prophecies woven in to proclaim the Messiah's resurrection would be more probable. But this takes for granted that earlier messianic tradition contained detailed resurrection prophecies: which is precisely what we have not got. Besides, a recomposition of this kind would be a scholarly literary work which is improbable in these first communities. It would seem much more plausible to say that this myth was borrowed from the pagan world, from the cults of dead and risen gods. But then the mode of this borrowing is difficult to conceive because of what we know about the Jews who were so utterly unyielding to pagan influence. Anyway, here once again *time is lacking,* for all our information points to the fact that belief in the Resurrection followed immediately upon Jesus' death. To say, finally, that in spite of all the difficulties one encounters in trying to grasp the chain of cause and effect, in spite of the human mind's repugnance for hypotheses without proof and improbable concourses, it is absolutely necessary to explain the Resurrection by fabrication even though one would not understand the mechanism, simply because there is no other explanation outside this one. This kind of approach resolves the problem by a philosophical negation: that of *a priori* impossibility. Such a negation has nothing to do with history which only judges whether a fact is established and not whether it is possible or impossible. Perhaps it is reasonable to say here: I do not know.

Mystical Explanation

I believe nevertheless that for a man of my times and of my spirit there still remains one rational approach that explains the *void,* the original gap, without a direct appeal to the impossible: the approach examining mystical phenomena. It is my hypothesis that a real experience took place in the mind of his followers after his death. This experience was so powerful that it assured them forever that he was living.

The mystical explanation seems to be in accord with what the Gospels have to say. They show us Jesus *appearing* soon after his death to one person, then to a group, sometimes a small group, often a rather large one. Then, all of a sudden these apparitions ceased. The disciples clearly understood that the last apparition was the final one. Their mystical period, if we may call it that, came to an end. We know that it is often the same way in the mystical life. Visions have their day and then cease abruptly. They are like a phase of visitations which form an integral part in life, in raising the mind to God. When the visions have ceased forever the mystic nourishes himself with their memory and meditates upon their meaning.

But what of the questions that arises here in the case of the apparitions of the Risen one? What is the nature of these apparitions? Must we believe that Jesus really came to life again; was it not merely his image that impressed those who were merely witnesses of their state of consciousness? Was there actually a unique exception at that particular point in space and time, an experience from beyond the grave that was unique in its kind? If so, what kind?

The rule that extreme caution has led me to formulate for myself is against having recourse to a hypothesis that introduces mystery except when I am backed up against the wall. I must use these aids sparingly. At this particular stage of my present study I can say that in as much as it is impossible to explain the sudden birth of Christianity because of hallucinations, so too it seems feasible to explain this birth by an original mystical experience. For these apparitions, which certain persons experience and can only communicate to others by testimony, are not really perceptions.

Any object I perceive thrust itself upon me just as much as it does upon other people. I see the Cathedral of Notre Dame in front of me; others see it as well. And an atheist, a denier, an infidel, will see the two towers, the galleries, the rose-widows just as clearly as I, better perhaps, aided as they are by hatred or indifference. And let us suppose that I imagine I am dreaming these things. Just a few simple tests of description are all I need to assure myself that I am not dreaming — for instance, I may ask my neighbor what he sees so that I may measure up my vision alongside his; or, I may step up to the

cathedral and touch a part of its structure; the cathedral is
but a formless and sombre cliff, a grey rock, rugged. If I had
an insect's eye, each jagged bit of surface would be like a
lunar world.

The experience of a constant change in perspective as I
approach the object, the rising up of a new and unrelated
universe as the eye skims the rock — these things assure me that
I was not dreaming, for dreams never have such changes of
perspective and such control.

The Risen Christ could not lend himself to such experiences.
And even if Thomas had wanted to, it would have been
impossible.

Jesus chose to *appear* to those who were able to accept him.
He showed himself first to some women — fabrication would
not have been able to include this account in the Gospel, for
in those ancient times the testimony of a woman carried no
weight at all. But, from the point of view of the pedagogy of
faith and love, one can understand how Jesus would first
reveal himself to a creature who is characterized by faith
and love. In the Johannine account, which summarizes all
these movements, John sees the empty tomb first, not Peter,
even though he was the leader, because John acquired
faith through love. The disciples of Emmaus were in doubt,
but they were not impervious to an experience if the experience
were but presented them. In this sense their state of mind
recalls that of the moderns. It was that of the receptive critics.
In fact, tradition has never mentioned an apparition to Pilate
or Herod; Jesus only appeared to his apostles, to his disciples
and to a small group of faithful women. It would seem that
if his followers had decided to submit Jesus to a commission
of inquiry or to a "bureau of investigation" Jesus would not
have appeared. The permission given to Thomas (which
Thomas does not seem to have used) is an extreme condescendence and Saint John's Gospel attaches no blessedness
to it.

The Work of Reflection

Nearly every document presents one rather strange feature (which is difficult to explain through the hypothesis of fabrication, for we would have to imagine the fabricator as too subtle a man): the disciples did not at first recognize their Lord.

Some believe; others doubt. It is astonishing when you think about it that Peter did not recognize his Lord, though he had lived in close familiarity with him. Mary Magdalen took Jesus for a gardener. Others thought he was a ghost. The disciples on their way to Emmaus did not recognize the stranger walking with them even after they had talked together for quite a while. If we pay close attention to these accounts, we come to realize one thing which remains constant throughout, though differing slightly according to the individuals and the circumstances involved. The man they encounter is not directly identified as Jesus, but only after a time of puzzlement. It is not said that this confusion resulted from ill-will or even from mere surprise. Jesus rebuked his disciples for incredulity and hesitation, for their slowness of faith. These accounts also imply that it was difficult to recognize him. Jesus had to resort to convince them (as on the road to Emmaus); he had to augment the fullness and intimity of his presence among them by eating with his disciples, by permitting Thomas to touch him. At other times, we are of the impression that Jesus disguised himself as a gardener, a travelling companion, a stranger walking along the shore.

An analogy of mystical phenomena will shed more light on this problem. The mystics are also confused when they behold an "apparition" — they demand signs, assurances. If they are as guileless as Bernadette, they ask the apparition to name itself and they hold out a pen and piece of paper to it!

Here we see no clear evident perception, no photographic likeness, nor that communication, that immediate and matter-of-fact recognition that occurs when two lifelong friends meet, much less a person whom one has just seen a few days before.

If it is essential, as I believe it is, to see in these notations the recollection of a most singular experience, we must say that the event was not as forceful and obvious as a physical fact would be. The consciousness of witnesses only attains a certain balance and assurance over a long period of time and continuous practice. I perceive another characteristic, one that is hardly to be expected in religious documents that arose in an environment of enthusiasts — and Jewish enthusiasts at that — given to believe in sudden theophanies. The four Gospels show us that the witnesses found their certitude only after they had thought it out first. Perhaps it might be better to say that this thought process was in some cases the process of verification similar to the one we spontaneously make when confronted with the unusual. We try to verify the data of one sense by those of another sense.

The best analyzed case, from the point of view of what concern the modern mind, is that of the disciples journeying to Emmaus. I will come back to this point later on. Let it suffice for the time being to observe that Luke indicates the difficulties of recognition. Before *recognizing* Jesus, the two travellers saw him with their eyes as they saw any ordinary person. But they only came to recognize him when their eyes *stopped looking at him*. One could say that a perception in depth not only sets one's complete memory in motion, but also one's whole power of judging.

I know what the objections will be here: that it is precisely to give the stories some verisimilitude that the fabricator or fabrication conjured up these difficulties, hesitations and delays in recognition which I see as a sign of the credibility of the experience which is actually nothing less than a highly artful device on the part of the narrator. But such skill demands a scholarly fabrication — and this presumes a great deal of reflection, art and discretion.

It is most unlikely that one would find a workshop or school in the first communities of the fervent and chiefly uneducated and uncultured followers which could fashion the Resurrection narratives with such artistry. If there were fabrication here, it would have been one of apocalyptic visions. But my observations of these evangelical texts on the christophanies is rather the exact opposite, since I find in them the smallest details, improbable and useless in themselves, especially to the reader of those times.

An Appeal to the Scriptures

Another trait of these accounts must be stressed which our modern mentality finds strange and misunderstands: the fact that Jesus appealed to the Scriptures in order to dispel the last doubts of the witnesses and assure his followers of the full reality of his presence.

The Emmaus incident shows us that Jesus prepared his disciples for the experience he was about to give them of his risen body by explaining to them what "the Law, the Prophets and the Psalms" had said about it. It would be interesting to know what passages Jesus quoted. But is it not a question of looking at the whole history of Israel from a global perspective, conceiving this history as a series of disasters and periods of thriving, of declines and upheavals, rather than a question of isolated verses? Or perhaps a still more intimate light shed on the relationship between death and life in man? Because the Jews were accustomed to see the shadow of the future in the past, the story of Adam had become the annunciation of a second Man vanquisher of "sin and death." These questions are mere pointless conjecture. Perhaps the disciples understood in an instant the meaning of their people's history. Sometimes an instant is all that is necessary to understand the meaning of history and a whole lifetime. Perhaps, as the Gospel suggests, their attention was focussed on a popular image, such as that of the prophet Jonas who spent three days in the belly of a whale, which Jesus, according to several Gospels, applied to himself. Perhaps Jesus used the "sign", the "figure" of Jonas as a starting point and interpreted "the Psalms, the Prophets, and the Law" from it. But I am not interested in the number, the value or the sense of such and such a passage that Jesus quoted or clarified. Rather, I am interested in Jesus' obligation to make himself known where he was and perhaps even to let himself be recognized by recourse to the past. Without this past, his total presence which was shortly to appear at the liturgical moment of the "breaking of bread" would not have been understood: it would not have possessed the sweet plenitude of certitude.

This appeal to tradition proven by warranty finds an analogy among the greatest Catholic mystics. As powerful as Teresa of Avila's experience and the impression of its obviousness was to her, she was only assured of the authenticity of her visions after comparing them to earlier religious experience as it exists in the official memory of the Church. If the orthodox mystic persistently turns to the Church's authority for a confirmation of his visions it is because he thinks that obviousness by itself is not a definite sign of authenticity (obvious impressions do sometimes err). The orthodox mystic wants to compare his visions with what other souls before him have experienced, all of which have been condensed, tested and interpreted by a living authority. In the same way, we examine our past experiences to see whether we can find anything comparable to a new and strange perception we have encountered. It is understandable how the witnesses, when confronted with the unprecedented experience of these apparitions, wanted to insure themselves against deception by demanding confirmation in the official tradition of the Church and people, that is, in interpreted Scripture.

We must point out one exigency peculiar to the Jewish mentality that is utterly lacking in our contemporary mentality. In the eyes of a modern the final and decisive sign of the reality of an event is what the existentialist school calls "factuality": the event looms up before you, brutal, unexpected, an admitted fact. Comprehensible or not, there it is. There is no need to seek confirmation of its existence.

There is a closer similarity between the state of mind of the Jews living in the time of Christ and that of the Marxists. In Hegel's dialectic the definitive sign for the truth of an event is its conformity to the logic of history, its ability to be replaced in a development whose law the mind sets up.

Surely it is because the modern mind despairs of being able to render the event intelligible by placing it in a logical progression that one passes to the opposite conclusion and declares it incoherent and absurd.

The Jewish mind was governed by the sacred texts to which it freely ascribed a prophetic sense. For the Jews, the author of the historical or prophetical books of Scripture communicated with the eternal Act by whom God created the past, present and future at the same time. From that time the supreme warranty for the existence of an unheard of improbable fact was its being foretold somewhere in the collection of books that the supreme religious authority guaranteed as coming from God and inspired with the Spirit of God coeternal throughout all time. In addition to this, if the event were to be consecrated as historical, as *having really happened,* a sworn testimony of contemporary eye-witnesses who had seen, touched or heard it was not enough. It was still required that this same fact be confirmed by the *witnesses of the future perceived in the past,* by the witnesses of eternity who were the ancient prophets. When we understand this state of mind that is at once deeply religious and metaphysical, we are no longer amazed at their reference to the ancient texts — an act that seems artificial and vain to us, but which to the Jewish mind was the warranty of existence.

Vocation and Mission

Another similarity between apparitions and mystical states is the presence in them of a summons, a destination.

Every apparition contains the element of bestowal. Jesus reveals himself to give commands and at the same time to confer powers.

Sometimes these commands are limited and concern a particular mission. This is true with private apparitions as, for example, when Jesus revealed himself to the women, to Mary Magdalen in whom, for Saint John, all the women at the tomb are summed up. The apparition on the Emmaus road seems to take exception to this rule because it is a preface to the collective apparition where the two going to Emmaus rejoin the Eleven gathered together. And, when Jesus appeared to the apostolic college, it was to transmit to it official mission to bear witness, to communicate the Holy Spirit to it, to invite it to a preaching mission that is without assignable limits and cuts across all of history. There is no perception of God in the Old or New Testament outlook without a call to a mission from God — a mission that is, after all, an eternal mission for it has salvation as its final goal. The Easter perceptions do not escape this law: they also are summons for the one most universal work of testimony there can be: the foundation of a spiritual society capable of extending itself throughout every age "to every creature."

The explanation I have just given draws its strength from pure mystical experience, and has the great advantage of being grounded on facts and of being still acceptable and coherent. It appeals to a kind of genius of the species, or more precisely to the faculty that certain privileged individuals have of entering into relationships with a transnatural existence. But it does not, at least necessarily and at the same moment, put into play an energy transcendent to nature.

The world we have stepped into would delight Helena,

for it is not unlike the world of art in which we see man being elevated and surpassed by the divine in his work. If we are believers, we expect God to be sparing with miracles and act through the simplest means according to the analogies of nature. Now, is it not simpler to act directly upon the minds of certain individuals by conjuring up visions and apparitions in their minds in much the same way a musician presses the keys of a keyboard, rather than to upset the natural order of matter and life by *really* giving life to a corpse and by withdrawing it from the inter-connected unity of the elements that compose the universe?

The Difficulty of this Hypothesis

I would like to be satisfied with this hypothesis, for it is in keeping with the facts, it embraces them, and goes no further. It only remains to be seen why this explanation would have been unacceptable to the witnesses, the actors and experimenters. For as I see it, this is the greatest difficulty.

The first witnesses affirmed they *saw* Jesus. And what they meant by the verb TO SEE appears to have been something other than what we mean by the phrase: *to have a vision*. They were acquainted with "visions" and never spoke of "visions"; they employed a word from the concrete and current language: TO SEE.

They asserted that Jesus' body was no longer in the tomb. They insisted that this was a certified fact. But from this point of view it is clear that the body's absence from the tomb is meaningless because the mystical experience of Jesus risen from the dead has nothing at all to do with an historical experience. It is a considerable difficulty. I lack the courage to disregard it. It is annoying to offer an explanation unacceptable to the people who were in contact with the reality they describe to you under oath, particularly when you possess no other testimonies outside their own.

It is embarrassing to offer Christianity an explanation

which empties it of the principle element, as Saint Paul would
say. Therein lies the whole problem. In most studies I have
read, this problem is hushed over. It is treated by preterition.
In all other instances like this one the attitude of the mind
which consists in eliminating without discussion and without
bothering to touch upon the issue, is what makes the center
of the debate seem unwarranted and false. Why turn the
experimenters right away into mythomaniacs, and hold the
witnesses suspect?

It is clear that the choice I am constrained to make here
engages the whole of Christianity: Its philosophy, logic and
history. Might it not also involve the whole problem of
existence?

I can make several probes into particular issues in order
to test my arguments. Thus, I may ask myself whether, in the
Jewish mind at the time of Christ, there was a distinction
between a purely *subjective* mystical experience and a real
objective experience that initiates a historical testimony. In
what category did the Jewish technicians of prophetical
phenomena place "apparitions"?

Beyond doubt the apostles and their first followers did
not conceive the apparitions of the risen Jesus as pure mystical
visions. Perhaps in the earliest times there were purely subjective visions of the risen Jesus which later on were assimilated
to the official apparitions. But there is a difference between
apparition and *vision*: vision supposes in interruption of
one's normal life, a state of wide-awake dream. The Jews
knew that as well as we do. Thus, when the *Acts of the
Apostles* tells of Peter's miraculous escape from prison, it
says: "And he followed him out, without knowing that what
was being done by the angel was real, for he thought he
was having a vision." The apparitions of Jesus did not take
place during sleep, at night, or in dreams. Nor were they
angelic apparitions as the Old Testament and the Infancy
Narratives knew. We can give an account of them. Most of

them, without being public, took place before several witnesses gathered together.

The Jews believed that God could communicate to men in dreams. But they made a distinction between this entirely intimate way and the official and visible way of events inserted into history which Scripture evinces. Sometimes the Eternal works through dreams or ecstasy by visions (more commonly in Israel by voices); sometimes he works by signs visible to all. The first phenomena are outside the pale of history and of all individuals. The second phenomena are history itself.

These distinctions exist in the new economy. Although the Evangelists saw Jesus as *the* Son for whom "the heavens were always open," there is only one passage in which he testifies that he had an ecstatic vision ("I saw Satan fall from heaven like a lightning bolt"). There are only four instances in which Jesus is thought to have been in direct contact with heaven: his baptism, the temptation, the transfiguration, the exaltation. Now, the apparitions of the risen Jesus are not of this ecstatic type. Instead, they are event-signs inserted into history, but reserved to a privileged group.

Differences Between Apparitions and Mystical Phenomena

Now I wish to probe deeper into the problem. It is not enough that the founders distinguished their experience of the risen Jesus from oneirical visions or ecstasies. I want to see whether their accounts on these experiences permit me to distinguish them from mystical phenomena.

These visions came to several people at the same time. I would add that they came to the leaders of the community and to several disciples. These visions impressed them deeply. I am not speaking here of visions that come to a secluded, unknown, feminine, childlike mystic which the Church, without making a pronouncement of their authenticity, recognizes as valuable from the point of view of morality and faith.

This we see in those particular revelations that the Church approves of because of their theological content or their pious import, without saying whether they are true or illusory. They are generally collective visions, or more exactly, collegial. If they are particular to one individual, he must then find the leader, or the head of the community for verification of what he experienced. From the mystic's point of view these almost contemporary multiple visions, differing in each case by circumstances and details, but substantially in agreement as to their significance, are phenomena altogether unique in their kind in the annals of mysticism.

Moreover, several senses are affected by the visions, as in perception — each confirming the other; especially does the sense of touch confirm the sense of sight. Jesus is not an immobile, diaphanous image who speaks as in dreams from which the dreamers were shaken awake. Jesus' disappearance *does not awaken* them. He takes meals with them; he speaks with them. What he does and says is analogous to what he did and said before. They find him as before, questioning, instructing, gentle, firm, severe, hard, master of the future, lawmaker, friend of all, but still holding some friends dearer than others. They see his old way of teaching, more concise now, but still with its lacunae and repetitions and his former gestures such as lifting his eyes up to heaven while breaking the bread. Is there perhaps for the first time in Jesus, usually so serious, a kind of interrogative irony and a smile?

All these traits indicate an historic existence. By that I mean mobile, astute, adapted to events and questions. No individuals seen in visions act like that, for only their essence is present beneath an image full of symbolism, and not their existence. Visions acting upon the interior life of a subject, giving it even a new impulse, are interruptions in one's historical life. During an ecstatic phenomenon one is entranced, one is outside this world into which he is going to return and find so insipid. Besides, the being which he has seen would seem outside the realm of time and space.

In the Gospel narratives there is no ecstasy. There is, however, an *enstasy* (if I may coin such a word for this one instance), precisely insofar as it is a reality of a higher order which is inserted into the familiar experience of a little group of men and, though transcendent, is related to their history and adapts itself to it.

By way of summary we can say that the Gospels dispose us more toward the Jesus appearing as a stranger walking along the road, than toward a Jesus coming upon earth in the way the Bible describes angelic apparitions. The Gospel shows us a traveller making himself known to his companions through prior historical experience, one who enters mysteriously into the framework of their actual existence.[1]

I have studied these passages myself without attaching myself to any school whatever and by guiding myself along on the mystical phenomena which, at first sight, resemble what is recounted.

I have come to a purely "phenomenal" description which I could sum up by the following characteristics: a strong impression of reality; a being, as it were, surreal though singular, and able to be the object of doubt; verification sought in the past by reference to the official religious Tradition, which is a capitalized experience; an impulse in the direction of future times, the desire to relay a message to a group of privileged people and, through their mediation, to all men. And finally, above all, the new life of Jesus being identified with his former historical life as though after his death he was again inserted off and on into the history of that little group of men he had chosen to be the leaders of the community, who were, therefore, able to give the same kind of testimony to these apparitions they had given to his historical existence before his death.

We may say further that if somebody wanted to put together a single story from all the accounts of the four

---

1. See **Problème de Jésus**, II, 174-180. See also **The Problem of Jesus** (P. J. Kenedy & Sons, New York, 1955), chapter V — Tr.

Evangelists, he would meet with almost insurmountable difficulties, especially with regard to chronological order and
the location of the apparitions. Exegetes have been working
long and hard over these difficulties. Thus, we see that Luke
only knew (or only singled out) the Jerusalem apparitions,
whereas Matthew writes of the Galilee apparitions. I almost
prefer that there be different traditions concerning the details.
They are unimportant anyway.

What does matter, though, is the sudden appearance of a
belief without there being a moment in which it did not
exist, or in which it existed only in sketchy form. *The idea of
the Resurrection had no gradual period of growth.* From
the moment we come upon Christianity in history, it is
professing this belief and claims to draw its power of
propagation from it.

Christianity does not flaunt this belief. On the contrary,
it gives it the least place in all the texts. Its articles of faith
express it in the most lapidary of formulas. The accounts of
an event so important to the faith lead one to suspect they
were reduced to such an extent that one may question whether
Saint Mark's Gospel contained one apparition account! Without exception, this story was reduced to one or two instances.
The contrast between the considerable importance of dogma,
the concern over it, and the terseness of the traces that the
Christians left of it in their texts bears much food for thought.
Man uses length, exaggeration and color in inverse ratio to
his certitude. In fact, when you know something, why be-
labor the issue?

Interpretation of these Facts

The most difficult part of my work is still to come. I must
interpret these facts in the light of my personal norm, that
is, by my intellect without relying on outside assistance.

Fortunately, the reflections I made earlier on the *Eternal
Dilemma* considered in its entirety afford me an avenue of

approach. Those reflections convinced me that the human intellect has but two directions to take in order to explore enigmas without appealing to a cause transcendent to history.

Attempt at a Critical Explanation

Let us turn to the commonest and simplest idea first: the body was never put in the tomb because it was thrown into a ditch. If it was in the tomb, his followers removed it. The evidence of the empty tomb gave rise to the notion of an assumption or a resurrection which could explain the fact that the tomb was indeed empty. The apostles, beginning with this assumption, believed they saw Jesus appear to them because of some extremely slender bit of evidence. We note the same phenomenon when, after the death of a close friend, we sometimes think we really do hear him if we give too much credit to garbled sounds or shadows. So intelligent a man as Renan sought an explanation in this direction. Superstitions originate through a confused admixture of states of mind, illusions, almost subconscious deceptions all entrenched into an unshakeable dogma in the same way a child believes a deception. Renan did not resort to the causality of mental illness either because he wanted to keep to the human level as much as possible, or because he knew very little about psychiatry. But such an explanation can be proffered: "Eidetic images, hallucinations, were transmitted from one person to another. You are headed in the right direction by studying mental illess and religious deliria."

Or, one may have recourse to metaphysical phenomena.

One may also, as I myself have done, simply say, "This is something mystical. There is no cause to look further."

These explanations have the advantage of conserving the historical appearance in the Christian beginnings, and of being grounded on the Gospels. This way, things are changed as little as possible and you deny only what is absolutely inadmissible: the reality of the fact, the object of belief, the testimony. I believe I have said enough on why I think this approach, from the point of view of mental health, is quite insufficient.

Difficulties

It is certain that if, around the year 100, Christianity had ceased being a religion known to history, if its ability to convert people were not regenerated throughout the ages among the common people as well as the élite, if it were buried with the "poor people of Jerusalem" or the visionaries of Asia Minor, if it had been a fanatical sect, and if, moreover, they had given us these apparition narratives out of context, then this explanation, which is the most plausible, would be the most reasonable.

But, the fact of diffusion, posterity and growth compels us to ask whether we can, without doing violence to reason, step away from this great tree grown from such a spoiled seed. Can we reasonably explain away by illusion mingled with falsehood, by clinical experience and telepathic phenomenon what this history shows us right from the beginning? Certainly we can, provided we do not go into detail *as to how*.

As soon as we examine *the how* with great care, we step once again into the realm of darkness and we are obliged to say, "We do not always know what happened in the beginnings."

We can only do as the philosophers and say prudently, as I have in this study, "It is an hallucination, a mystical phenomenon, but one that is absolutely unique in its kind."

We are quite familiar with this manner of defining. It considers the genus directly below that of the being one wishes to define, and it includes finding one attribute of this being which sets it absolutely aside in this lower genus. To define man, for example, we first look for the genus of beings to which man is inferior: *animal.* Then we add the attribute which contradicts this genus: *rational.* Now we say that man is an animal unique in his kind whose proper characteristic is precisely (since it defines him and is his essence) this *rationality* which animality excludes. To define the act of perception, we begin with hallucination and say that perception is a *true hallucination.* But, as it is the attribute of hallucination to have no relationship to truth, the adjective here again contradicts the noun.

It is permissible and sometimes helpful to use definitions of this type. We could say, in this vein, that faith is a *genuine delirium.* Or, to get back to the subject at hand, that "apparitions" *are mystical phenomena which have an objective existence to which one can bear witness historically.* But the question arises whether, by adding this last characteristic, we are not entering into such a new area that the term "mystical phenomena" becomes deceptive, as it would be misleading to continue to consider man as an animal after we have defined him as an animal endowed with *rationality.*

I hesitate at this point, for I do not see how one can explain, without a creative intervention, such a genus of historical and real mystical experiences.

Attempt at a Mythical Explanation

Now I must try to apply the second kind of explanation which I call *mythical.*

It begins with, as I have said, a pure belief in the Risen Jesus, and then gives this belief, through the various processes of literature, of speech, of liturgy and only apparent testimony, a density comparable to that of the events known to us through history — as though what is believed had actually taken place in the same way human events take place.

Next, we must explain how such a belief in the historical

reality of what is merely a subjective reality can arise in a
given society. And lastly, how this belief is able to assume
that quality which likens it to a history.

It might be thought that locating the origin of the resurrection image is a simple task, for after all it stems from the
mind's recoiling at death which is part of the conscious
existence of incarnate beings. Particularly with regard to Jesus,
how can it be admitted that the Perfect One, the Holy One
of God had been tainted "with corruption"? God's Holy One
cannot die. HE STILL EXISTS in spite of all the denials of
experience. Since he is alive, he must be able to show that
he is. He must *appear*. He has no reason not to, and if it is
expedient, then he will appear.

The inability of the mind to comprehend, to accept, the
death of the "Prophet of prophets" could induce visions, could
prepare an atmosphere receptive to any legend of survival
after death, at least among the concerned and faithful souls.
Furthermore, the notion of the gods surviving after death
was deeply rooted in the people of the Mediterranean area
— this idea was surely connected to the rites of April, after
the winter, when seeds begin to germinate and change the
bleak face of the earth. The mysteries of Eleusis were celebrated at planting time, and wheat was harvested in silence
as a symbol of resurrection.

Whatever may have been the origin of the myth (its
sway over the minds of men stems from the fact that it
unites the sublime and the common, thereby insuring a com-
plicity in all social milieux and in all parts of our soul), it
hovers, one might say, in the air, uncertain of its points of
application, just as the idea of power in a devastated nation
exists prior to the dictator. Surely there was a person whose
name may well have been Jesus with whom we can relate
certain incidents of the Gospels. But whether Jesus was cunning
enough to use the myth to his personal advantage, whether
because after his death his companions consciously or unconsciously applied this myth to him, the symbiosis of the

person and the idea did occure. And this idea increasingly grew to the detriment of the person. The stories of Jesus were fabricated in a way that the imagination could feed upon the canonical Scriptures which were thought to foretell the future and already contain this divine history.

Certain non-essential aspects of Jesus' life were to be fixed later on in the same manner, such as the date of his birth, unknown, forgotten or neglected in the beginning (when the faithful began thinking about his birthday), but was fixed at the winter solstice, not that there was an historical tradition to this effect even in the Gospels, but simply because the pagan feast of the first increasing day had to be Christianized; it was valid to think of Jesus born in the image of the Unvanquished Sun.

Difficulties

The mythical explanation is not in itself unthinkable. I believe it is more worthy of investigation than Renan's proposal which I mentioned above. However, if an hypothesis is to be acceptable, it has to be more than simply possible. It is essential that one understand in detail how the hypothesis tallies with the certified facts of history. And, in the case at hand, this hypothesis must help us bear witness, without rousing in us the sentiment of the unthinkable, to the transition from myth to concrete and historic belief in the various Christian communities — a transition that is entirely assumed with no evidence to support it and is reconstructed by mental deduction alone.

To say that Napoleon is a mythical character modeled after the great conquerors, with his campaigns into the desert and the snows, his birth and death on an island, etc. ... is a view which may be plausible three thousand years from now if an atomic war destroys most of our sources of information. But, whatever the future historians of the "twentieth-century myths" think, it must have some historical basis and must tally with the few remaining testimonies on politics, war, or with some memoires saved from the atomic hollocaust — for instance, the memoires of Mme de Rémusat and a few letters from Napoleon to Marie Louise.

This type of explanation has one inherent difficulty. It does not correspond to what we know from irreputable historical sources and it is unable to enter into the sequence of the great events: Jewish People, Jewish messianism, Jesus of Nazareth put to death under Pontius Pilate, the origins of a community that believed in Jesus, the success of their propaganda. How, except through subtle inferences, could one make it sound plausible that the myth of the Resurrection had become abruptly implanted with no preparation or prior connection and that it had been absorbed into their recollections of Jesus during the very brief time lapse from Jesus' death (whatever it may have been) to the preaching about Jesus, if in the hours, days or years following Jesus' death *something* had not occurred which was indefinable but persuasive and undeniable in the eyes of both the believers and their opponents?

Some will doubtless object that Paul's conversion, after a "vision" of the Risen Lord, indicates that the origin of this cult rests on mystical "appearance". But Paul was on his way to Damascus to put in chains those who already believed in this same Resurrection.[2] They will insist that the Christians believed in the Resurrection because of visions or revelations parallel to the one Paul was about to be favored with. But we encounter again those difficulties I have already pointed out: we would have to posit a whole constellation of convergent visions to people who differed from one another, and some who, like Paul, were radically hostile. We would also have to admit that all the first articles of the faith that affirm the apparitions, especially those detailed accounts of

---

2. For a discussion on this point, see **Problème de Jésus**, II, p. 183. Check also **Problem of Jesus,** chapter VI, p. 190 ff. — Tr.

these apparitions and of the empty tomb, diffused by primitive oral tradition and fixed later by "The Gospels," are entirely the products of legend. That is hard to take.

To uphold the mythical thesis, one must also declare it probable that the idea of a "dead-and-risen-God" was transmitted from the pagan religions *during this infinitesimal space of time* to the milieux of the Jewish converts in Jerusalem before these early Christians had emigrated to the great cities of Asia Minor or Greece.

We would also have to assume that a small group of Jews who were just as devoted to Jewish tradition as to the still very near person of Jesus, all at once borrowed the notion of a cosmical God dying and rising again with the seasons — an idea absolutely foreign to the Jewish mentality which was familiar with the sensuous vegetation cults. We would have to assume that these first followers grafted that idea onto the religion of Jesus which would suddenly have undergone a metamorphosis.

This quick transformation must be posited through logical necessity and pure deduction without the history of the first Christians (so abundant in minor details about their disagreements on usages, rites or methods) giving any inkling of so improbable a borrowing.

Or, one must posit that when these first propagandists of Jesus had arrived in an archpagan city like Ephesus, dominated by the temple of Artemis, they immediately began to preach the religion they should have been fighting, preaching it by blending it either consciously or unconsciously into their own. It would be tantamount to saying that the first Jesuits *buddhized* Jesus as soon as they landed in Japan and the Indies. It is tantamount to saying that communists in New York City began preaching a Leninism based on banking, gold and capital which they had incorporated into the doctrine of Karl Marx. I do not say that the improbable never happens: or that it has to *happen*. But, here we would like to have proof that the improbable did occur.

This corpus of difficulties raised by the mitigated mythical doctrine (positing an historical Jesus around whom the myth "died-for-our-sins-and-risen-from-the-dead" could have grown) has driven some logical minds to suppress the historical existence of Jesus. Its one advantage is that it permits them more time in which to explain the genesis of the myth, since they no longer have to contend with Jesus' death under the Procurator Pilate and are thereby given a fifty year period — a blank space of time we know practically nothing about: a span of time in which they can situate the development of the Jesus myth of birth, death and resurrection. It will become a question of one revelation transmitted like particular revelations. If this excessive thesis interests me, it is because I see a bitter fruit in it, but one masterfully deduced from the other theses. It breaks through the darkness by replacing the *unthinkable* with the *impossible*.

The Figures and the Awaiting

It is always possible from the point of view of the mythical hypothesis that the texts of the apparition narratives might have been written from the prophecies contained in Jewish Scripture and not from personal recollections. Or, at least it is possible that the prophetical figures might have superdetermined and fulfilled their vague and ambiguous recollections. Strauss thought so. This notion deserves fuller examination, particularly because the most ancient Resurrection formula did not stem from the prophetical argument: *Resurrexit tertia die secundum Scripturas.* He rose again, the third day, according to the Scriptures.

The foretelling of the Resurrection, the figures and mental expectancy of the Resurrection could have sketched out the event in advance: the account would merely be a filling-in of these figures and hopes.

This approach lacks any support by the facts. The first

Christians, the redactors of the first article of faith were formed in the Jewish mentality which, as I have said, means that a religious event was only fully guaranteed if it were foretold. Besides, they were shrewd enough now that the event had taken place to find verses which could be interpreted as predictions. They had an immense reservoir of nebulous images and often obscure texts which the Holy Book put at their disposal.

But in reality it is extremely difficult to find a detailed and precise Old Testament text which would facilitate or even induce a resurrection account. One is hard put to find a text that could be taken as the source for those we read in the Gospels. Few critics question the authenticity of the Passion account, and it contains many more antecedent figures (the casting of lots for the seamless garment, the bruises, the unbroken bones...) then the accounts of the empty tomb or apparitions.

It is not easy to say where "the three days" find their initial source in the prophecies. Indeed there is a text in the Psalms that is classic as well as prophetic: "You will not abandon my soul to the netherworld, nor permit your holy one to see corruption." This text did become clear to the faithful when they looked back to it. Perhaps it also induced the redactor of the first article of faith to put *tertia die* after *resurrexit* — when you consider that the Jews and especially the Palestinian Jews believed the soul only left the body on the fourth day after death when the body began to decay: *the third day* would therefore mean that Jesus did fulfill the prophecy of incorruption dear to the *Acts of the Apostles* and to Saint Peter. However, "Your holy one will not see corruption" is in itself too short and too vague to have been the germ of the accounts we possess.

Another verse is quoted, one from Isaiah, which says that the Servant of Yahweh, the figure of Christ in his humiliations, "was buried with the evil and that being dead, he is with the rich." But this verse is rather contrary to the

Gospel which tells us the body of Jesus was not buried with
the evil and was not found dead with the rich, though he
was placed in the sepulcher of the rich man Nicodemus.

Now, we must learn whether the devout Jews believed
that the Messiah would rise up again after his death. "I
know," Martha said to Jesus about the dead Lazarus, "that
he will rise again at the resurrection on the last day." This
clearly expresses the idea of a communitarian reincarnation
professed by certain Jewish schools, of a resurrection of the
dead, as Ezechiel described it, with flesh, sinew and skin, in
the Valley of Judgment. But this resurrection, otherwise denied
by the Sadducees, was not distinct from the image of the
end of time and the new people of God. Their idea of the
resurrection was not this sublimation of a single being for
a spiritual existence, but rather the final moment of history,
whereas the solitary resurrection of Jesus would re-begin
history.

Once again I would have to say:

"There may have been a mysterious event which seemed
to indicate that Jesus had been preserved from death, and
the accounts may well have been colored by the Jewish conception of resurrection. This is possible. But we scarcely see
any evidence of it. The vague expectancy and those rare and
sibylline texts were not in themselves forceful enough to
produce the account given to us in the form of testimony."

At least these reflections show that purely natural explanations also have their difficulties. They also have their
own particular brand of mystery, and they also demand
some movement of human faith either in the deductive faculty
of our intellects in order to reestablish invisible relationships,
or in the action of still unknown natural forces, or in an improbable conjunction of chances.

Therefore, it cannot be said that the modern historical
technique has solved the problem of Jesus' resurrection and
solved it in such a manner that the faith must forevermore

hide behind faith and forego every claim to be a rational faith founded on experience and testimony.

The Human Character of My Investigation

Since I first began these studies, this particular problem has interested me as a real and human problem, as a means of learning something new about my own mystery.

I had preconceived ideas of my own: I did not in advance relegate the history of the Resurrection to the realm of fantasy, as a student of Gérard de Nerval would have done, or to the realm of mythology or pure ideas, as did Alain in his book *Les Dieux,* whose frequent comparisons of Jesus to Apollo, the Virgin to Artemis, and Easter to sun and Spring festivals, are so foreign to my approach. If I had a preconceived notion, it was to place the Resurrection in the realm of human experience and not in the realm of concepts.

I was not interested in abnormal human experiences such as mental telepathy or the use of mediums, although I certainly did not overlook the possibility. Nor was I concerned with experiences of the mystics. I kept in mind certain experiences I am able to have with my own body, of the space in which it moves, of the way this body serves me.

The experiences recounted in the Gospels give food for thought on one more point — the question of defining what *to perceive* means when what is perceived is not an object, a thing, but a being endowed with interiority, another consciousness. Bergson once asked what would happen if man, instead of being first concerned with matter, mechanics and technique, were to study spiritual manifestations: an ocean liner or jet aircraft perceived from a distance by this wholly spiritual humanity would seem like an apparition, like some incomprehensible ghost. But, without speaking this utopic language, one might wonder what would happen if, in place of studying the perception of a piece of wax, a tulip, or the color red as being the simplest types, if in place of introducing another perception and thereby complicate this elementary case, one had begun by considering the perception of one incorporate being by another incorporate being, especially when these two beings are drawn by the body or the spirit (but where is the body and where is the spirit?) one towards the other. When the body we perceive is that of the other sex inhabited by a spirit, we are well aware that there is an immediate impression of its *presence* in us and, more, a coincidence with the bond which, in this other person, the flesh has formed with the spirit. Is this not analogous to our perception of a work of art?

A work of art resembles an *apparition* in so far as it astonishes by an excess that at times seems an excess of being, and at other times an appearance. It also gives you the impression that you can unite yourself to it through your senses. If ever this communion took place fully and far more than in desire alone, it would elevate you to a mystery already present in the work: it would force you to your knees, like Saint Thomas. But even now, confused, to be sure, the work of art initiates you into a higher level of existence beyond the ordinary conditions of this world. Similarly, the experience of a "glorified body" during those "forty days" after Easter.

It might be asked how a body that is neither enclosed within our space nor limited by our time can make itself visible across this space and time. There is much to think of and to work out on this point. Without yielding to the absurd concordism that tries to adjust the sciences to fit the Bible, one can say that the actual speculations of scholars on space, time, mass, on the relativity of space and time, on the relationship between matter and light, this whole re-thinking of old concepts has resulted in dematerializing them, as many philosophers of the past had suspected it would. We are standing just at the threshold of this new scientific spirit. We can only guess what would happen if the physical "absolutes" — speed of light, acceleration of gravity, quantic numeral —

should suddenly change their proportion, measure and relationship. Perhaps one day we shall understand that the shocking case of the apparitions is more in harmony with experience than it seems. And, if I had to explain what today is sometimes called the "phenomenology of perception," it would be easier to begin by considering the perceptions of the Risen Christ, to devaluate them to our own perceptions by charging them with density and materiality.

Of course, no one can fully justify God's actions. He seems to be keeping humanity in a twilight world of sunlight and shadow. Pascal said that if He revealed Himself continually, there would be no merit, but if He never revealed Himself, there would be no faith. If there actually are extraordinary events, they must be exceedingly rare. Might it be that the most extraordinary event has to be unique? Now, since death is the most pressing point in every human life, the one point most impossible to know and most necessary to penetrate, we are beginning to think that if ever the sovereign power were to shed light on something, it would have to be on death. And what possible light, if not the example of an existence which, while preserving its identity to ours, would transcend the biological order and move beyond death?

CHAPTER IX

Difficulties
of Believing in the Resurrection

*Exerpt from one of Olivier's letters
in which he expresses his doubt concerning the
historical character of the narratives*

"**Y**OUR cautious approach to the Resurrection seems a
new one to me in virtue of its prudence. You are like tongues
of fire that recoil so they can leap all the higher. One does
not know whether to admire your daring or your prudence.
At least, you are courageous enough to fix an unswerving
attention on the essential problem of Christianity. I have
found little help in what has been written on this problem in
the past.

"As you might suspect, I do not find your *mémoire* entirely
to my satisfaction. These are extremely lofty questions and,
as you say somewhere, questions so dazzling that it is better
not to look them squarely in the face. Life is short. And since
I have so little opportunity to satisfy myself in this life, it is
painful, for the both of us, to think about the disproportionate
time at our disposal in which to solve these problems. It is
typical of our age that the impossible is necessary and the
necessary is impossible. We must become reconciled to it
and advance a little each day, as the Gospel says, while we
have the light. You try to show that the Resurrection narratives lack the ear-markings of fabrication; that if they had

been made up, they would have been far more dazzling and unquestionable. You are trying to give these accounts the aspect of a progressive existence on which a kind of human reflection is exerted with mysterious grace. I tell you I am not absolutely convinced: for I know, much less than you, what the Jewish minds of the first century considered as possible or impossible in these matters. Next, if I put myself in your shoes, if I borrow your method which is generally to consider the texts in a chronological sequence so as to get a better understanding of the development, I think I recognize in these series precisely what you reject in them: the work of the inventive imagination. And I am going to attack you with your own weapons.

"I suppose we are both agreed that the earliest written and dated vestige of the Resurrection is to be found in Saint Paul's first letter to the Corinthians, chapter fifteen. Here he mentions an even older symbol of faith and he tells us of his own christophany on the Damascus road which he likens to all the other christophanies, though it is the last of them. If I stick to what is said in that confession of faith and first commentary, I see affirmations of faith there. Certainly he is speaking of apparitions, but they are summed up in the formula: 'Christ died for our sins; he rose on the third day according to the Scriptures.' Mark's condensed and interrupted account comes next in the order of time, followed by Luke's and those mentioned in John's Gospel. Now, if I arrange these documents in this order of sequence, I begin to perceive what I might call in rather barbarous terminology a growing *historification*. In Matthew, Christ is seen — he speaks. In Luke, Jesus is seen to be eating, and events come into sharper focus, at full length, in the Emmaus account. In John, chapter twenty, Jesus was almost touched by Mary Magdalen; in the second epilogue — perhaps the last text of the New Testament — Jesus eats some fish and shows his glorified body to the doubting apostle who was getting ready to put his hand into Jesus' side. One might wonder whether, in the course of the first century, the religious spirit did not add corporeal density and anecdotal details in order to destroy the purely visual character ('He was seen') of the apparitions which they experienced in the original period.

"Also, from this point of view, if we consider the stories of the discovery of the empty tomb on the third day by the woman and the apostles as it was told — a discovery that plays such an important role in the genesis of the faith — might we not attribute this story to the backward and greedy period when they wanted to touch and assure themselves by undeniable facts that Jesus' body had been really, materially and historically, taken out of the cosmos and had disappeared from the outset?

"This would incline me towards what you call the 'mythical hypothesis' in your *mémoire*. Of course, there may have been some vision at the root of the faith, but very shortly the Idea of Resurrection, of bodily Resurrection and, as you say, of testified events, or at least of testifiable events, sprang up among the faithful — presumably because of objections hurled at them by unbelievers seeking proof. The genesis of this belief could be similar to the genesis of all great conceptions: a vague presentiment at first, but a captivating one, which grows and develops through constant repetition until it assumes a concrete, living and authentic appearance. It is a work of art dear to Helena. Unbelief falls silent before it. They tell the unbeliever, 'Say anything you want, but you can never change the fact that it happened since it is entirely accurate even to the details.'"

An answer to Olivier's letter:
Awareness of the event

"Olivier, I am writing this to answer your questions which are always so keen, subtle and discerning, penetrating as the Scripture says, even to the division of soul and spirit, of

joints also and of marrow. You raise a formidable problem
concerning human knowledge: how can the observing mind
capture an event at the very instant it occurs and in sequential
order? You suppose that, according to the tendency which
draws me towards the analysis of genesis, I am led to believe that the human mind's grasping of the event passes
through stages growing richer as time moves on. I am astounded, you know, that no one has ever drawn attention to
this point, that no one has ever distinguished between
fabulatory developments and genuine and veridical developments. I would like to tell you something that happened to
me once — even if it scandalizes you.

"I remember a blue painted room filled with peace and
light deep in the countryside, where, while I was pinning little
flags on a map going 'from the Somme to the Vosges,' in
September 1914 I learned of Péguy's death. I was about to
enter secondary school (I prefer to call it a school of
humanities after the superb name given this level of education by the Jesuits). My teachers never mentioned Péguy.
I knew that Péguy had existed when I read Maurice Barrès'
article on his death in the *Echo de Paris* — regrettably too
late to sing his praises. I was first impressed by the words, or,
to be more exact, the themes: *Poet killed on the field of honor.*
It was a formula, an idea, as also would have been 'poet
executed,' 'consumptive poets,' 'poet in exile.' There are not
many possible poetic destinies. For the impressionable and
uneducated child that I was, to perceive Péguy's death in
September of 1914 meant (every Frenchman felt it) to draw
out of the storehouse of equally possible destinies one destiny
which could be applied to this unknown man with so fresh
and lively a name as *Péguy!*

"Twenty-five years later I was taken a prisoner of war, I
had a young poet, Patrice de la Tour du Pin, as a companion
at Oflag IV D. In 1939, Mouriac's article, like that of Barrès,
proclaimed his name and the fact of his existence to the
French people; he was the *Poet-wounded-in-the-head.* Some

Belgians rashly added, in the cause of beauty and legend: *Poet-killed-in-battle*. Patrice de la Tour du Pin kept in his wallet the article about a funeral service held in Brussels for the repose of his soul, and he showed this little notice to me every now and then after dinner.

"The initial theme surrounding Péguy was quickly enriched with a prophetical theme because he had prophesied his own death in *Eve*. No one during World War I could speak of Péguy without quoting the lines: *Blessed are those who died in a just war. Blessed is the wheat that is ripe and the wheat that is gathered in sheaves.* Péguy seemed fated to die in battle. He died because it had been prophesied, because he himself had predicted that he would be cut down, ready for harvest, gathered in sheaves: he died in the second month *secundum Scripturas*. Twenty years later people began to gather up the ever-increasing detailed accounts of his death which were finally summed up in the four canonical gospels of Tharaud, Daniel Halévy, Romain Rolland, René Johannet.

"Imagine, if you will, that twenty centuries have elapsed, and that Charles Péguy's every existence, for any reason you want, is the object of passionate debate. The critics of that epoch might propose a schema along these lines: in the beginning there was an ideal, a symbolical theme, perhaps even the mingling of several themes such as Poet-who-died-young, Phophetical-poet, Poet-soldier, Poet-martyr. Starting with the verse: *Blessed are those who died,* and noticing that mention was made of ripened wheat and wheat gathered into sheaves, they might conclude that the legend arose from these first images and that Péguy died at harvest time. Then, the critics would say that, as people later wanted more information about Péguy, the need to 'demythologize' this first vague theme appeared and was responsible for several contradictory accounts.

"Yet, we know that this hypothesis, though credible, is false. What actually happened? The few witnesses did remember the distinct details of Péguy's death, the beet field in which he died, and his attitude in death — he was, if I am not mistaken, lying on his back, his left arm folded over his head, his beard grey with dust. . . . But these witnesses were taken up with more urgent things at the time and after all when you consider that they hardly knew who he was, plus the fact that no one ever questioned them about Péguy, they had no cause to even think about what happened. The first awareness was not of the narrative type, but a fact already embracing several mystical themes. Only the brutal fact was known. Precisely because the information was scanty, this fact was seen in its essentially truest and simplest significance: Poet of the Fatherland. As in all our perceptions, the significance came first, the details lastly.

"This is what happened here. The first awareness of the Resurrection showed up in quasi-abstract theological themes. The first witnesses were not experts; they saw the significance. An idea, a theology was already contained in the first assertion. Death could be verified, but not 'dying for sins,' which is no more a sensory fact than 'dying on the field of honor.' There are only fields of grain. The eye of the mind sees the honor.

"It is probable that the rapid stylization of the event in the beginning allayed any curiosity about the particulars of the Resurrection, as happened with the details of Péguy's death. And, perhaps, when the second generation saw the first dying out, they began to gather up the details, but they were late, for the favorable moment slipped by them. This is why we know really so very few particulars about events, such as wars, which have influenced us most.

"Perhaps we are too concerned over 'little facts,' we moderns who confuse the historic with the documentary, and practically with what is televised or what can be televised. Instead of transmitting to us these concise acts and words reduced to the condition of maxims, suppose the Evangelists had left us some reports and described Jesus by saying, 'He wore a white outer garment, his face was swarthy. His hair

was black and gleaming ... ,' would we be more enlightened?
The spiritual man in us does not want a description. Rather,
he wants, as one reads on tombstones, a definition: the
essentials of a man being condensed into a few words.

"I was mulling over these thoughts when by sheer accident
I stumbled across this text in Joubert's *Carnets*, written in
1793. We must remember that Joubert witnessed the execution
of Louis XVI. This is what he says: 'All of a sudden there
appeared before them a ghost.... It held its head in its
hands, and its head began to speak. It said to them: "Yesterday
a universal peace reigned over the regions from whence I
came. Today, killed in the prime of life and struck down by
a whole people in the offices of my rule, I arrived before my
hour, stunned and innocent by this untimely departure.'

"As he spoke, an infinity of others arrived at the same
time, all mortally wounded as he and rising up from the
earth unceasingly and rapidly as if rain were falling in reverse.

"This is the style of the *Apocalypse*. Then I began to think
that the first write-up of an historical event one has been an
eye-witness to is entirely figurative (there were no others in
Joubert's *Journal*). Perhaps the Johannine *Apocalypse* was
the first kind of narration and recording in an age when
narratives should have appeared and did not for some unknown reason.

"The fact was not preached at the beginning of Christianity,
but only the mystery and the message. Only after the first
persecutions did they take the leisure to write this history.

The Enigma of the Empty Tomb

"I look upon the instance of the empty tomb as a new
illustration of the mind's rebounding between the *critical*
and the *mythical* — two contrary signs. Historical exegetes,
animated by what I call the *critical* spirit (Paulus, Strauss,
Renan, and so forth ...), retain the event of the empty
tomb. What of the miraculous content: some women hasten

to the sepulchre and find it empty! What could be more vouched for in the four Gospels? What could be more plausible than walking to a tomb? The fact of its being empty certainly does not transcend the natural laws. The genesis of the faith must be explained by some catalyst or other. Why not select what all the traditions posit: the discovery of an empty tomb? This episode is like the others in the Gospel text, forming one body with the apparition narratives and cannot easily be separated from them. It seems so unadded that, in Mark's Gospel, it is on the contrary the account of the empty tomb which is alone presented and the account of the apparitions which was superadded to it, or which, more likely, was lost. All of the above, which is an argument from historical or textual criticism, also from the argument of plausibility, speaks in favor of the critical hypothesis.

"You realize that this undisturbing explanation which respects everything (except the radioactive element of miracle) runs into difficulties if ever one reflects upon the sequence of events that it assumes.

"If the apostles made off with the body to prove the Resurrection by this negative proof, we come back to the eighteenth-century notion that they were imposters. But the hypothesis of able and swift sleight-of-hand experts acting together is unlikely when you consider their zeal in preaching, their courage even in the face of death, and their highly communicable conviction. If the body had been removed for any other reason, how could the apostles have preached the Resurrection when it would have been so easy to confound them by taking them to the body itself, to the burial place of Jesus, or by calling upon the witnesses of his disinterment?

"Remarks of this nature tend to unhinge the problem from any historical basis and attempt the opposite explanation which is that of the mythists (who in our days say they *demythologize*). They do away with a real resurrection and put in its stead a fabrication that is subsequent to the supposed events. Then, everything comes into sharper relief, for they have done away with the historical problem of verisimilitude.

"By this second hypothesis the empty tomb becomes, as you say, the final endeavor of the legend, the piece of defective evidence revealed at long last.

"This thesis has difficulties of its own when we want to make it coincide with those elements of historical order we can scarcely question. It is understandable how they might have wanted to prove the *reality* of the Resurrection in the face of those who scoffed at them, in the face of the criticism of their opponents or wavering faith, and it is possible that they contrived the story of the empty tomb. But how do you explain that this account is found in all strata of tradition? How do you explain that it is so prominent? One must then assume that the tradition of the Resurrection was very late in coming. But this assumption is fraught with difficulties (it is unlikely that the story of the empty tomb suddenly appeared at the end of the first century in an already static tradition). Was not the idea of the body's removal already present right from the beginning when the earliest preaching stressed the celebrated text, 'You will not let your Holy One see corruption'?

"Perhaps fabrication was used from the beginning to give consistency to some vague apparitions. But if fabrication were so powerful in the beginning, how is one to explain that it was never applied to the very essence of the Resurrection which is not mentioned in the official Gospel: *the body of Jesus in the act of going out of the tomb?* Rather than to invent a proof that could only have been indirect, insufficient and vague to the earliest faithful (Jews and Hellenes infatuated with tangible realities), a proof which was simply the discovery by several women of an empty plot, how much simpler it would have been for the apostles (and how much more convincing and profitable for the popular audience) to describe any kind of scene of the *coming-out-of-the-tomb.* They could have described a great earthquake in the light of apotheosis or apocalypse, a scene which had to be described later on and which has since inspired so many painters! But it is not at all evangelical. It would appear that a discreet guiding force had thwarted its existence from the beginning. It cannot be assumed that this force was concerned that the evangelists or authorities of the first churches should foresee the austere taste of the twentieth-century person and his aversion to prodigies.

"I will admit that the mythical hypothesis has one unique initial advantage in that it avoids the historical difficulties of criticism. It affords themes, types, rhythms and images that are more tensile, more pliant and more supple for our erudite and comparative spirit, for the fabrication of our scholarly hypotheses. Its shortcoming lies in this very facility. One may reconstitute and explain everything with myths as with concepts and simple ideas discerned from every contact with experience, *everything*, save *this merest essential trifle* that is the original event, the motivating force, the germ and point of ignition for the fuse.

"To be sure, I have no more knowledge about what happened in the beginning than you. However, to use the simple formulas of the learned, I freely declare that 'until otherwise proven' *everything happened just as though* the first Christians had certitude of a *real* resurrection, of a resurrection implying to their minds, and in keeping with their conceptions, the absence of Jesus' body from the sepulchre, the absence of his corruption and death. In the Jewish mentality of Jesus' contemporaries, a man's survival after death was not the Greek conception of the soul's delivery from the body-tomb, and its solitary freedom from then on. Instead, it was the subsistence or recomposition of the real complete being, body-soul. The Greeks believed that the soul was alone immortal and still lived on after death. The Jews, being more concrete, did not conceive of a real existence without the 'resurrection of the flesh.' The Sadducees denied this resurrection, the Pharisees upheld it. But all the schools agreed on the postulate: *no survival without flesh.*

"Even by assuming (which I think is almost impossible from the point of view of textual criticism) that no account of the empty tomb existed in the first state of the faith, but only apparition accounts, the Jewish mentality of the first converts to Jesus would have been obliged to conclude that the tomb was in fact empty (whether there was proof of it or not) at the moment Jesus appeared to them. And, by reducing these things to their ultimate logical hypothesis, that is by supposing that the episode of the empty tomb was a story fabricated to satisfy their logic (as indeed the Assumption narrative seems to have been, for this event was unwitnessed), the account of the empty tomb should be considered as an explanation of this profound necessity already contained in the Jewish belief in the Resurrection.

"But that is a useless hypothesis contrary to critical examination of the text. The verses in the four Gospels which recount the episode of the empty tomb lack all signs of later addition to an account which did not include them at first. These verses are so much a part of the text itself that they become the focal point, nearly too much so, for our desire to understand. The episode of the empty tomb is so much a part of the apparitions that I do not see how anyone could detach it from them. Therefore, they must be accepted as all of one piece, or rejected *en bloc*.

"I find the account of the first evangelic tradition very plausible in the human context which I always endeavor to reconstruct. The women on Easter morning had a *negative* experience like Michelson's experiment on the speed of light. But the *positive* experience of the apparitions immediately occurs. The two experiences, one empty, the other full, balance each other out. Without the apparitions the empty tomb would be utterly meaningless. But without the empty tomb the apparitions might seem like dreams, having no extra-mental reality. The non-existence of the body of Jesus proves the *reality* of the christophany, proves the fact that it was not a vision. Without evidence that the body was removed, one might think that the apparition was non-substantial or that there were actually two bodies of Jesus, one which corrupted and the other which was seen.

"Yes, all that is plausible, you are going to say, and perhaps I would accept it had I not first assumed, like Jaspers, the radical postulate: the resurrection of a body is scientifically and philosophically impossible and unthinkable, however strong the arguments or proofs may be in its favor.

"I ask nothing more from you, Olivier."

Olivier's second letter in which he relates his inability to see the relationship between the Resurrection and the spiritual life

"I want to bring to your attention what is perhaps an even greater difficulty because it touches upon the substance of the Christian faith more than upon the problem of its foundations. It is difficult to express, not because it is strange or subtle, but on the contrary because it is, as I see it, pre-supposed by most people today without their daring to mention it and without believers realizing that it even exists. I doubt that I could bring it up to you in conversation — a letter permits of more impudence. So, here it is:

"Christians base their faith on the Resurrection which they celebrate every Sunday; you look for reasons drawn from history to substantiate this faith, but what troubles me is not the fact of resurrection, assuming that it exists. I go as far as you do by agreeing with you that it is plausible, even that it is real. But this event in itself does not interest the religious side of me. It ought to interest me as a curiosity, an oddity, an event that is, as you so often say, 'unique in its kind,' but I do not see how this miracle could have any influence whatever over my mind as it approaches to God. I see death as nothing world-shaking. Death seems less a stupidity, as the gloomy existentialists say, than a biological event that we must not pay too much attention to and which is certainly necessary if we are to enjoy this life and endure time. I do not look at the body as something so very precious. To have a body again does not, therefore, seem so desirable! Nor, for that matter, am I exactly longing for a future society in another world patterned after our own. I could even tell you that I do not see why we need a body to be with God.

"It seems unworthy of divine wisdom to give a history of apparitions to a very small group of Orientals who lacked our sense of control, and then to make this the foundation stone for the greatest and most spiritual religion that has the best chance of surviving through the ages, a religion which is, as you say, most closely bound up with the progress of the spirit on this planet? You reduce the religion by binding it so tightly to the resurrection of the body who no one either desires or understands, or perhaps understands all too well: it is the dream of beginning life all over again. But can this end of life in its carnal mode be the central dogma of the religion of the spirit?

"You realize that here we are confronted with a more formidable difficulty because it does not deny resurrection, but only that it is unworthy of God. It is a far more vulnerable point. You are powerless to stop the idea of God from growing in purity and precision. What might have been suitable to a God of yesterday ceases to be as the idea men have of God ascends and matures."

Answer to Olivier's letter:
Sublimation of the body and superexistence

"Dear Olivier, I have received your letter. As brief as it is, you were correct in thinking it would give me much to reflect upon, since by degrees you are coming to the problem of eternal life and its relationship to resurrection — a problem which has always been of great concern to me.

"And other problems, too, that we hardly recognize, although they seem so familiar to us, problems such as, for example, the ability to know just what is this body, this hand and everything I feel or touch and sense, everything I call my flesh, expression, language, body, ultimately — which Paul Valery described as that 'unique object which screens us from the dead.' How am I to answer you except by falling back on my own resources, all doors being closed to the thoughts of others, and tell you how I face up to these questions that can be investigated?

"I need hardly say that you have avoided the very common error of confusing 'Christ's Resurrection' with the other resurrections mentioned in the Gospels — Lazarus' for example — which are of people returning to their former lives after a period of sleep, and a re-animation of the corpse which, now that it is alive once again, drinks, sleeps and goes about its former mortal affairs only to have to die once again, and this time for good. I do not say that the resurrection of Lazarus occurred (this is another area of investigation reserved to the Johannine exegetes), I restrict myself to say that the Gospel distinguishes the multiple returns to life from the one and only Resurrection: Christ's. Jesus by no means takes up his former life; he entered body and soul into a new mode of existence, from which he condescends to make himself seen and touched. He appears across space, time and matter, but does not experience any of the limitations that space, time and matter have for us. If we are to believe the Gospels, we see Jesus passing through obstacles, we see him being present in several places at once and making sport of what is opaque in this cosmos.

"I sometimes go back to Henri Poincaré's allegory on the fourth dimension of space in order to give a clearer picture of what I mean. Imagine some infinitely flat beings or, if you prefer, some animated points moving about on an orange without knowing and without being able to feel or even conceive the dimension of depth. Imagine also that one, only one, of these thinking points had by a *death-and-resurrection* passed into the third dimension and that it henceforth sees

the orange as a sphere and not as an extraordinary and incomprehensible curved surface. It decides to return to the
realm of the animated points, its less-wise brethren on the
orange. All it has to do is alight upon the orange like a hel-
icopter. The thinking points would be unable to understand
how it appears and, rising, suddenly vanishes from their sight.
They would be compelled to form the notion of *apparition*.

"Enough of these clumsy images. I only used them to re-
mind you that, according to Paul's very ancient interpretation,
the 'Risen One' is not a 're-living one,' but a spiritualized
being. 'Agreed,' you say, 'but with a body.' Yes, with a body.
What body? Paul says, '*What is sown in corruption rises in
incorruption; what is sown in dishonor rises in glory; what
is sown in weakness rises in power; what is sown a natural
body rises a spiritual body.*' A natural body like Adam's *rises
again a life-giving spirit,* a body no longer having the *Psyche*
as its principle, but the *Pneuma,* which in the Scriptures is
perhaps the word most charged with meaning and mystery,
translating into our language what is proper to God, since
God is *Pneuma,* according to Saint John. And I will say
that Saint Paul could not in any way favor those images of
printers which depict the corpses awakened by the trumpet
blast and struggling to lift up their tombstones. Paul taught
that from the seed placed in the ground, a new body, wholly
penetrated by the Spirit, will appear by an act of the living
God who is truly re-creator. And a body which will be to the
mortal remains of the first body what the seed in the act of
decaying is to the ear of wheat rising straight up into the
light. This is what Claudel meant by having inscribed on
his tomb at Barangues: HERE LIES THE MORTAL RE-
MAINS AND THE SEED OF PAUL CLAUDEL.

"I can hear you saying, '*Quid mihi et tibi?* What is it to us,
spiritual beings that we are, to have a body again?' I reply
that this superinvestiture could be called *sublimation* — an excellent term for it — had it not been profaned by psychoanalysis. Besides, all this is more clearly understood by

making analogy to the many examples of evolution that nature affords us.

"Look at a mineral and a flower at the same time. The flower contains no elements that are not to be found in the rock, but these elements in the flower are raised to a superior genus of existence. Leibnitz said that everything which is inferior is found to be in the superior, but in a more noble manner than when it was simply in itself. Thus, oxygen and nitrogen in the living being, or the living being in the human. I am the constant center of this ennoblement, I who live a corporeal life but who assume this corporeal life in the sphere of thought and love.

"Now, who can tell me that this very general movement by which what is good is assumed without being destroyed does not occur elsewhere? And why could not this imperfect sublimation which nature shows us at every turn reach its plenitude after death? You say death is the result of biological generation and that, therefore, the corruption of the body is of no interest to you. That is perhaps true for whoever looks upon life and death as one watches a spectacle. The paradox is that I who am essentially spiritual, am inv014scerated into this growing and dying body, subject to all the successions and outrages of time. The paradox of my incorporation into the world of living-mortals is present at every moment of time, but most of all it is by death that I become aware of the paradox. Now, if we believe in a Creator why, once he has made something, should he annihilate it? Why in particular, should he destroy this body-spirit creature we call Man, or only save one aspect of his nature? Why should not the body be called in and by the *Pneuma* to this existence and 'kingdom in which God will be all in all'? At least why should it be kept out of this kingdom once it has undergone the mysterious unimaginable transmutations that are the condition for another life? I do not pretend to give you any proof of what cannot be proven. I only want to remove from your mind the notion of impossibility which is indeed a most paralyzing one for the mind: but what is the impossible and how do you define it?

"Can you tell me what a body is? We know what the mind is because we are it; the body escapes us in all its parts. We define it like doctors: by its functions. It is, we say, a self-maintaining, self-reproductive apparatus. All one has to do is look at a face, a hand, a character written by this hand to affirm that there is some other element in a body besides its functions, that the body is not only an organ by which I register myself in the universe, in the biosphere and in history, but that it also is an image of my profound self. An essential and primordial language, the mirror of my spirit in as much as it is given to me and in as much as I give it to myself by molding it and transfiguring it by my acts and thoughts for better or for worse; a second self in the form of flesh that existed before the awakening of my consciousness and in which I see my virtual nature and condensed history. In addition, it is the only access for those whom I love to know and to love this mystery which I call *myself,* and which at this moment is tracing arabesques on a sheet of white paper for you to grope through. In view of these things, can one determine what death is?

"Is death the destruction of the body as experience seems to bear out? Is it not rather the moment when, according to the law of living things, the body ceases to be an organ for the spirit's insertion into the universe when (after a period of time whose duration, whether long or short, perhaps instantaneous, is of no consequence) it ceases to be the symbol and support of the life of the spirit as well as a means of communication, which language makes impossible by its very opacity, but to which we aspire, since in this world what we call society is a juxtaposition of solitudes? Of course, biological death contradicts all that, but it is a question of learning whether this deceptive experience must not in turn be contradicted and overwhelmed. I freely admit that I have ended up by finding some truth to the idea that the spirit is easier to understand than the body, eternity than time, and existence than non-existence. What are supposedly the most obvious things now seem the most obscure to me, for they are composed of two elements: the one come from the Creator and made to his image (which we are able to penetrate), and the other come from the bondage of the creature-state which always remains opaque to us, even though we are immersed in it. You will pardon my thinking that the idea of the spirit is opaque, whereas the idea of a reconstitution of the whole man, body-spirit, in a superior unimaginable existence is a clear concept, except naturally as to its times and modes. But time and mode are indifferent.

"But rising to a higher plane I began to realize that death and even 'the immortality of the soul' are not the ultimate objects of our thought, that we must proceed still further and ask whether *what exists will not exist in a more perfect manner*. Seen in this light, resurrection would be the incomprehensible and supernatural completion of the genesis of beings.

"I would ask you also to reflect upon the highly aesthetic side to nature which presents privileged moments and exceptional cases.

"I should not put these words *moments* and *cases* in the plural, for on each level of existence or of art there is, if we observe closely, but one masterpiece. When nature attains it, it reposes in it and goes no further: after man's creation, the *élan vital* comes to a halt. It proceeds to develop only what is in man.

"In human lives which I look upon as the privileged area of being and experience, I find moments of enlightenment and courage or pain that are recapitulation of all the others. Here, I wonder (assuming of course that God IS and that Jesus is an historical being) whether the most representative moment, the most significant and truly complete moment of Jesus' life might not be that of his relationship to death.

Listen carefully to what I mean: I do not mean the summation of the circumstances of his agony, his spasms, his derelictions, his execution and final cry. Certainly it is well to know these things, but they are not essential. It seems to me divinely probable that on the occasion of the death of this Servant of God, the mysterious power which governs all things and which makes life triumph over death and existence over nothingness made it really and uniquely apparent that this power is not 'the God of the dead, but of the living.'

"It was, in short, a question whether the maxim *Vita mutatur, non tollitur*[1] might not be specially applied and find a singular illustration at this particular moment and place and for that being alone. Since man's *spirit* is joined to his biological *life,* this would be the time to show once and for all that man is not swept away by biological dissolution and that the spirit within us *could* sublimate the body and not be destroyed by it. Such a sign could be given, would have to be given, in the death of the greatest of men. You asked me to explain how resurrection could be related to the life of the spirit. I believe I have answered you.

"Let me go one step further (maybe I should say 'plunge still deeper'). You speak of the 'life of the spirit', saying that death is of no consequence to the spirit and, as L. Brunschvicg told Gabriel Marcel, you seem to think that there is some pride and a little materialism in wanting to go on living immortally and, like Jean Paul Sartre, die to boot. However, the human mind cannot stop thinking at the moment of death just because it seems ridiculous to go on thinking. One must really go out of his way to trick himself into this indifference of years. The most natural thing for the spirit is continual progress, greater self-possession, knowledge without limit, intimate interior love. You tell me that the human mind can only attain its infinite goals by progress though

1. Life is changed, not taken away.

time and by transmitting to future generations what it has
acquired so that humanity might ultimately attain what
each individual desires. You say also that in the short space
of a human life there are imperfect instants of love, discovery,
happiness, esthetic joy, when, for a moment, the human
mind imagines that it possesses a glorified body through which
it reaches out and grasps the infinite. But you cannot deny
that these moments of eternity are fleeting and exist in
one's memory and hopes as impossible myths.

"The spirit in man actually desires something else which
it calls *eternal life*. Now the profoundly mysterious experience of Easter signifies that this life is possible in the fullest
sense and that it may even have already begun in the limitations of temporal existence. The faithful believe that the
season of the Resurrection is not only the sign of victory over
death, but also the pledge of a new life. And the earlier
Gospel miracles pale to nothingness before this one that
bears directly upon the human condition itself, showing that
our present state is not the final one and *that we are not yet
what we shall be*. We use the word 'experience' to signify
the ascertainment of sensory data. But, if ever 'the other
world,' as we say, could be experienced, it would be much
more helpful. It might be said that experience of the life to
come is really the only kind of experience we long for.

"The Resurrection is indirectly just that. I am amazed
that the problem posed by the Resurrection is not the only
historical reality that excites curiosity. I realize you find it
hard to accept the Resurrection as experience and not as
illusion. You will doubtlessly say once again, 'Is the admission
of a dead man into a glorified life an ascertainable phenomenon?' As I see it, once you have admitted this, then you have
no choice but to say that Christianity is either founded upon
a spiritualistic experience, or that belief in the Resurrection
is nothing more than a symbolical teaching device. But, it
is a question of something entirely different — the initiation
at this moment of the spiritual life when all that was

dispersed will be recreated, reunited, re-integrated into a higher unity which Saint Paul defined in simple and unaffected language: the moment *when God will be all in all.* Is there any more beautiful definition of the true life? And, at heart, have philosophers ever said anything else?"

*Excerpt from another of Olivier's
letters in which he accepts the Resurrection
as a mystery but not as a miracle*

"I believe I understand what you meant in your letter. It seems to show that the Resurrection is more mystery than event. You see the Resurrection in its essence, you shield it from history. It is not really a return to life, you say, but a passage into a new life; the chrysalis becomes a butterfly. Wings appear for it to reach out into a fourth dimension — space. I have a text from Proust which I think translates what you mean. I shall copy it out for you:

" 'Wings, a new breathing device allowing us to traverse the immensity of space, would be useless to us for, if we journey to Mars or Venus and keep our same attitudes, we would interpret everything we saw in the same light as the things of Earth. The one true journey, the only Fountain of Youth, would consist not in heading towards new horizons, but in seeing with a different optic, seeing the universe with the eyes of another man, a hundred men, seeing a hundred universes which each of them sees, which each of them is.'

"For you, then, resurrection would be this fountain of youth on a higher plane, since we shall not have a hundred other pair of eyes but we shall actually have escaped from this universe and entered into a new creation where everything in it will be transfigured. Or again, you would doubtless say (this time with Valéry) 'the body has too many properties, it resolves too many problems, it possesses too many functions or resources for it not to respond to some transcendent necessity. You know, of course, that Valéry admired the dogma of resurrection 'so contrary to pure spiritualism, which sets the Church apart from other Christian confessions in a most discernible way.' It even conceives the mode: a relationship different from the one exerted in this world between mass and attraction, between mass and the speed of light. Your calculations, proposed to some modern minds, would not falter at the edge of a vast abyss, but would instead encounter slight cavities designed to receive them.

But then my former objection swells up even more intensely within me: what relationship does the concept of the 'glorified body' have to history? If Christ's body was liberated from the earth, how can it really appear on it again, affect history and be observable? I realize that Christ's glorified life is, like the Trinity, something revealed. But I do not understand how it can be an object of experience, let alone of touch. Nor do I understand how it is linked to this almost detective-story incident of the volatilization of a cadaver. So, I oppose you. I do not deny the mystery, but I state that the *mystery*, if there is one, is *revealed*, and that it is un-related to *miracles*. To interpret the Old Testament well, 'the pure religious teaching' contained in it was rightly ex-tracted from the marvels that the faith of our fathers took as historical fact and in which a figurative language, an idiom, is seen. No well-educated believer today would dare maintain that man was formed *in fact* from the slime of the earth, or that woman *was historically* fashioned from a man's rib. So! I look forward to the epoch when the mystery, this teaching of God about God, will be set apart from the mirac-ulous quite as much from the marvelous. I will go with you so far as to admit that, in the early stages of humanity, prodigies were actually necessary. I will not deny that it was fitting for the sun to come to a standstill in order to move the stiff-necked Jewish people. Nor do I say that a certain amount of miracles was not necessary to move the fearful hearts of the first Christians and initiate them into the divine mysteries. But these embellishments are useless to the well-informed. I would accept your remarks on the spiritual body, instrument of the mind, provided you do not base them on those experiences people had of a phantom."

Response to Olivier's letter:
Idea and fact;
the meaning of history

"Olivier, you have approached the very essence of our discussions from a different aspect. And I can, I am sorry, only repeat the essence of my reply which I believe is the essence of Christianity. But on every level of our dialogue, this difficulty and this response appear in ever sharper relief accentuated by the effort each of us makes, whether to establish closer agreement or to define our terms more precisely.

"To begin with, let me say that your quotations of certain modern authors fall short of the mark. Valéry and Proust still keep to the carnal order. They multiply, they refine the functions of the body, but their body never gains entry into the sphere of the *Pneuma,* which is the sphere of the spirit. Now, the resurrection, if I understand it, is a change that differs in nature from anything the mind can conceive. The risen body no longer has any function. It is no longer artist or artisan. It is indeed impossible to imagine such a spiritual conclusion from our seed. One can at least reject all the images which distort it.

"You oppose *mystery* and *miracle,* as though (historical) *miracle* were only a parable for expressing a *mystery* (extraneous to history). And you say you will accept the mystery stripped of its miracle clothing because you have passed from the state of childhood. Or at least you no longer need the *milk* they give you which, in its day, might have been 'rational.' I will tell you what I think about this primary and difficult point:

"That the Old Testament contains 'wonder' narratives wrongfully represented as historical, that the faithful for a long time believed them to be historical and that they were presented as such by the common teaching of that religious society, does not concern me directly and I am not disputing them. It is difficult for me, however, (and in itself) to distinguish between the prodigy account and the improbable original event. I am scarcely led to believe that everything in legends is invented. I merely say that my personal faith would not be shaken if it were demonstrated to me that the fabricative function was exerted here accidentally in some few and peripheral instances, provided that it be to illustrate a religious truth. The difference between the canonical Gospels and the apocryphal ones is precisely that in the case of the apocryphal, besides being more probable and nearly twenty times as numerous, this fabrication was exercised without restraint and was applied not upon the accidents, but upon the very essence of the narrative. Footnotes are not the text, fringes are not the cloak, the penumbra enveloping a light is not the light. And we cannot apply to what is fundamental in the Christian event that which could have affected its contours.

"Let us go on to more important matters. I come to what you assert about *mystery* and what you would deny as *miracles*.

"If the essence of Christianity is the Incarnation, that is to say the Eternal temporalized, then *mystery* is also *miracle*. Not only is mystery actually present within the given subject, but it must be transmitted to minds made of flesh that are hurled into temporal evolution and submitted to the conditions of indirect knowledge through testimony. Then, an intimate relationship exists between *idea* and *fact*, between revelation and testimony and, to use your terms, between *mystery* and *miracle*.

"If you want me to, I could say that resurrection, as a unique sign, has two aspects: the one by which it is a

Christian mystery known through revelation, the other by which it is an historical miracle known from witnessed evidence. I know that what Rudolf Bultmann calls 'existential' and the 'historical' interest are mutually exclusive; this disjunction of his does not surprise me, for I see the natural process of the Western mind and *gnosis* in its very essence.

"I agree that, in these last few centuries, perhaps since the close of the Patristic age, certainly since the sixteenth century, there has been a desire to prove Christianity by an almost mechanical process that stresses the historical character of the events which have given us salvation. But, by stressing this historical aspect, they forgot the actual character of salvation which is the presence of Jesus Christ right here and now. They turned Christianity into a beautiful ancient narrative which must be learned, whereas Christianity is really the preaching of an *actual* mystery renewed in each of us.

"Saint Paul shows us that death and resurrection are not simply finished-and-done-with events, but that they are reiterated in some way in each human destiny united to Christ by faith. But does that mean we have to reject the essential historical element in the fable? Actual salvation is only salvation because Christ died historically *once for all*. And faith, as the sacraments, effects us by causing us to leap backwards through time, by making us coeval with the times Christ lived in, especially with the short and complete time of the historical Christ that has passed forever.

"It is remarkable that these two aspects are seen to be indissociable in the Resurrection: it is a divine mystery which, as a miracle, gives proof in an historical context.

"The Jews saw mystery and miracle as bound together. What was history for them if not the act of divine Presence, implying that an eternal mystery is hidden in every event and that every mystery is expressed by an episode?

"To cast some more light on our subject, I would ask you to distinguish between *Resurrection-in-itself* and *Resurrection-for-us*. I would ask you to note that these two notions are

not necessarily linked together, that the first could have
occurred without the second, that the Resurrection could have
existed and that the apostles could have been informed of
it ecstatically or prophetically and also through what the
Acts of the Apostles calls *manifestations,* that is, by testifiable
facts. The Jews thought that some divine events, some sacred
episodes which had no witnesses to them, nevertheless were
real. They were, so to speak, in history without being historical
in the social sense, in the sense of testimonial, as are most of
the causes behind events in this world, as is the interior life
of each man, and as are the truly decisive acts of liberty.
'The history' of Adam was such a one, and so was the Gospel's
account of Jesus temptation.

"The Jews looked upon the Resurrection in itself as this
higher type of reality. The Gospels specify neither its mode
nor moment (whereas these points would have been central
in a fabrication). The act of returning from among the dead
is a mystery hidden in the night, enclosed in the profundity
of God's secret. It belongs to the intimacy of God. The
Resurrection is Christ's entry, now that he is totally humbled
and emptied of himself out of obedience, into his former
original glory enhanced by his merits. Read the passage in
Paul's letter to the Philippians and you will see the expression
of this faith: 'God has exalted Jesus and has given him a
name above every name.' He made Christ pass from death
into life: God made him sit 'at his right hand'. These expressions, though necessarily imperfect since they are drawn
from human things, make us aware of the *mystery.* I think
that the Resurrection could have been brought to man's
knowledge through another economy, that is, by revelation.
It seems that the apostles thought these 'manifestations' of
the Risen One (which could and should give rise to testimony
accounts) were condescensions of Christ *who wanted to
show himself.* These manifestations are indeed the signs
which permit the Risen Christ to offer himself to the belief
of men more intimately, more discreetly, more pedagogically,

more in keeping with the methods of God who respects freedom and favors those quiet increases of certitude enkindled by experience.

"From this perspective, there is a difference between the methods which revelation showed before Christ and those which he initiates.

"Before the coming of Christ, God communicated his secrets to men through the mediation of Seers, *nabis*, inspired prophets who wrote the Jewish Scriptures or caused them to be written. But, after having spoken through the prophets, as the *Epistles to the Hebrews* says, God through his Son: this word is the historical Incarnation which comprises life, death and life after death.

"The apparitions are not the Resurrection, which had no witness, which surely could not have had witnesses, but rather they are the observable *signs* of the new existence of a being victorious over nothingness.

"You see that I do not fall into the error of burying mystery in history and yet I do not take mystery out of history and testimony. You are correct to say that history *by itself* cannot substantiate a supernatural fact. I shall take a further step than you by stating that the historian as *historian* does not have to substantiate a miracle. It is not required of him. He is restricted to say that certain attestations were made by someone or other and that the witnesses had some psychical or moral character. But the historian *as historian* cannot tell us whether some event is possible, where it does or does not surpass the limits of nature. The philosopher alone, or rather the whole man who has knowledge of science and human nature, can speak through his knowledge and define what transcends and what does not transcend the potential of things.

"In the case of the Resurrection, history places me before the data. The witnesses have interpreted them ahead of me. From the presence of their teacher, whose death they verified, they concluded that he passed into a new state of life. It is my job to reflect on this point.

"That is why I shall say that in the beginning the Resurrection is a mysterious and divine fact known only to the Son and the Father and to whomever he wishes to reveal it. But it is also a human and miraculous fact seized by the witnesses who have the mission to transmit it.

"Note that the distinction I propose appears in the symbols: in them 'he is risen' is distinguished from 'he has appeared'. The one is fundamentally necessary; the other is the contingent and favorable consequence. Imagine that other beings belonging to the moral order lived somewhere in the cosmos, and that they were redeemed, saved or raised up by an irradiation of the Incarnation that took place solely on earth: then, the Passion and Resurrection would be made known to them through a divine testimony and not a human testimony.

"Let me sketch out one final consideration that touches upon the definition of what is *historical*. We are deeply interested in this aspect today.

"If one denies what is *historical* by saying that what is universally ascertainable is alone the object of history, then the apparitions do not belong to history. For, although their object is a man known to many people before his death, the Risen One is not publicly presented to all men as he was at the time of his trial. History in the strict sense of the word can only know events ascertainable by a normal man.

"The preceding definition excludes in advance from the historical zone all *real* events that are not perceived by any observer. Certainly, in most cases (in all cases but one, perhaps) this definition is sufficient. *But the whole problem posed by the Resurrection is precisely whether there are not some temporal realities of a higher order that are only perceptible by special witnesses.* That is my question. And if I do not want to solve the problem before examining it, I must rely on a definition of history that is large enough to include any solution. I am led, then, to say that history appertains to *any event whatever, as long as it is certified.* In short, the ascertation of an event by one or several witnesses — this is my definition of the *historical.* In this sense the Resurrection would be the most perfect type of an historical event because the event was of unparalleled singularity and could not possibly be reproduced — because it took place in front of some very exceptional witnesses — because, finally, these witnesses, transformed by the event, consecrated their lives to give testimony to it. These same elements are found in the most ordinary cases of testimony, but to a lesser degree.

"Here again is one of those points at which religious reality better understood can aid in the understanding of an ordinary problem. Whatever one many think about it, the study of the Resurrection sheds a great deal of light upon the act of testifying, also upon what we call historical knowledge.

If we are to solve this extremely difficult question of the relationship of *mystery* and *miracle*, we must not only make a thorough study of the Resurrection, but we must also examine this second point which is called 'the divinity of Jesus,' although it is more constant, less marvelous, but more mysterious and interior. We should actually look at Divinity and Resurrection *together* and never separate them, though they are logically and essentially separable since the idea of one does not permit us to conclude to the idea of the other. Indeed, the two beliefs are intimately related.

"What I am telling you about miracles is imperfect because I am not so to speak bringing up the subject of miracles in the context of mystery. I would think that since the problem posed by divinity has not been settled and since no one has hit upon an approach through history (or revelation) by which the mind can attain this 'divinity' of an historical man, we are still in the penumbra and on the threshold of the most profound problems."

CHAPTER X

The Mystery of Jesus

"**I** NEVER questioned," said Simone Weil, "whether Jesus was or was not the incarnation of God; and actually, I have never been able to think of Him except as God." That indeed is the most disturbing paradox of Christianity. It is, to use religious terminology, the Christian *scandal*. And this scandal is perpetrated: it existed for the "Gentiles and the Jews" in Saint Paul's day. It still exists for the rational and the religious minds of our own times. Yet, it is upon this original, lasting, unobscured affirmation that the religion of Jesus continues.

One could say that it is easier to think of Jesus as God than as man. We are hurled into the divinity of Jesus before we have fully accepted his humanity.

How can we prove that Jesus is God? How can we avoid building our faith upon faith? What are some reasons we can give to one who asks for them?

I am faced with an immensely difficult problem that touches the bounds of the possible.

To begin with, I find that, of every man known to us through history, Jesus is the only one about whom it is not ridiculous to ask whether there has been at least once a real superman, a real supercreature, in the human species. A mind as trained, as alert and present as Bergson's came to this minimal conclusion: Jesus is the supermystic.

Is it enough to say that Jesus is the "greatest of mystics," "more than a man," a man unequalled up to the present time in the realm of our experience? Bergson set this question aside, but he was brave enough to ask it.

Did the control over the human on the part of the divine which marks certain privileged souls develop in Christ to an unimaginable but still human degree? — Or, must we leap every boundary and say in a way that is simple enough for grammar but inconceivable to the intellect: "Jesus of Nazareth *is* God"?

The Mind's Wavering between Two Types of Explanation

Once again I encounter the mind's eternal rebounding, but this time it is brought to its ultimate conclusions.

Either we say that belief in the divinity is a product of enthusiasm quickened by an extraordinary man. Jesus could have made such a strong impression on his contemporaries that they heaped upon him every possible honor. After some undefinable event, every distance between Jesus and God was wiped away for the faith in somewhat the same manner that a circle is constructed from an inscribed polygon.

But one can also reason in another way by saying that the Idea of God-made-man pre-existed in the realm of myths, that this Idea which thrust itself upon the mind as a greatly-to-be-desired and perhaps necessary impossibility was directed by chance to the real or imaginary person of Jesus of Nazareth and that it found the perfect atmosphere in this historical moment and milieu to become transformed into a dogma that was preserved from then on by a Church and protected against questioning.

In my opinion the historical explanation is the least probable of the two. Jesus, by a kind of self-exaltation declared himself God in much the same way that a madman insists he is Napoleon. But, besides the fact that the Gospels give no grounds for such an hypothesis, it simply would not work: the idea of a man-God still would have to be accepted into the society in which Jesus spoke and worked, and would have to correspond to its expectations and concepts. We are left with the mythical explanation: the pre-existing idea of a God-man might have been imposed upon Jesus. The theme of man's divinity crops up time and again in mythologies that depict a god or goddess assuming human form. The mind comes to look upon Jesus as a myth of the same sort. Naturally, it is difficult to picture the Jews consenting to the myth of a God-man when one considers how uncompromising they were to such mythical conceptions. It is highly improbable that they would accept a myth that developed in their own times. It is also unlikely that the earliest Christians could have succeeded in presenting this myth to the Jewish world as a real history by using false testimonies and false details. But if one wants to badly enough, one may find certains avenues of approach between "Jesus of Nazareth prophet" and Jesus-God: take for example the unreal and superhuman personage heralded by the Jewish Apocalypses. Or, one may consider a cultual rite such as the immolated Passover Lamb and contend that it virtually contains the belief in a divine being who becomes a victim. These are just some of the not altogether inconceivable links between the Jewish belief and the idea of a God made man. Their advantage is enormous.

Through them Jesus is brought into the cycle of the creations of the human mind: he becomes what Kant called a *category* of the mind. And the Christian religion falls into line with those which preceded it, with those which will perhaps follow it — except for Islam, since Islam represents a protest against the humanization of the divine principle.

But this deeply alluring, advantageous and simple explanation needs further qualification. I said many times that Christianity does not behave as a myth should. Myth is projected into a timeless era and bears the stamp of the unrefined mind that conceived it. Now, if my efforts at reflection have resulted in anything, it is that I am convinced that Jesus does have historical consistency, that he did live as one of us, and that to strip Jesus of historical existence is to become involved with considerable difficulties bordering on the edge of the absurd. Indeed, the simplest solution is to say that Jesus is a man who was divinized. I grant it provisionally; but what does it mean? When did this transformation take place? What brought it about? My mind is an exacting one; I cannot satisfy it with so vague a proposition. What is overly clear is also captious. What you think you understand at first glance remains forever unexplored by you.

To avoid this mental rebounding, I would like once again to look for a starting position, a runway. And I begin wholeheartedly from a fact most observers will admit. Now I shall try to get to the bottom of this fact.

The Immediate Fact of Faith

It is not difficult to show that Christian belief in the divinity of Jesus has remained constant. It was established right in the beginning without one being able to discern, at least after the death and resurrection of Jesus, any genesis and growth except in the way of expression. Athanasius illustrated this fact in his opposition to Arius. But in the last few years a much more thorough and technical analysis guided by scientific concern alone has confirmed this view. The *Formgeschichtliche Methode* school has established that the worship rendered to Jesus is the first fact, the first positive element which the historical method finds, with the result that for certain intrepid members of the school who push their method to the extreme, the Gospels are merely a justification of the liturgy. Without delving into this hypothesis, I can study Saint Paul's Epistles which contain these cultual elements, these primitive expressions of faith in the assemblies of Christian worship.

The first articles of faith, the first hymns to Christ in a just-beginning liturgy, the words of Saint Paul and the other writers of the New Testament Epistles, the deeds of the apostles as recorded in the book of *Acts*, the observations of the Roman magistrates — these all assure us of the fact that the first followers worshipped Jesus, adored him and that, in these often divided communities comprised of Jews and pagans, there was no argument at all on this point.

If Jesus was not considered a god from the very outset, we do not see how a fellah crucified by Pilate could have become God for the same reason as the Roman emperors, but above all how he could have been conceived *as being God before his birth* — which not even the most fanatical Roman would have attributed to their emperors who, like the evil Caligula, indeed became gods, but only after an apotheosis and not *a fortiori* before their birth. To be legally declared "god" is simply the final action of a policy.

The earliest propagators and adherents of the faith never once considered Jesus to be a supercreature, nor did they conceive him as a singular human being having relationships to God of the same nature as our own relationships, nor even as having the relationships we ourselves have to God but infinitely extended. No, it is something entirely different.

From the very outset without our being able to perceive any beginning, Jesus was held if not always explicitly, at least he was implicitly, *equivalently,* held as equal and co-eternal to God. Later they would use the term *consubstantial*: at first it seemed shocking and improper because of its almost material concreteness, but it added nothing to the faith shared by everyone. It was a criterion for defining. Jesus was believed to be the Son, and this seems to imply inequality. But to those who believe it, such an expression by no means lessens this equality, this assimilation to God. The formula which finally prevailed "God of God" with its explanatory metaphore "Light of Light" transmitted the original underlying idea. If some passages found in several of the Fathers before the Council of Nicea suggested a subordination of the Son to the Father, it is because these Fathers were fascinated by certain texts of Saint Paul, Saint John or the Jewish Scriptures which they had taken out of context. It was difficult to speak of *generation* without insinuating the anteriority and superiority of the engendering principle. The faith asserts the equality and unity of the Father and the Son. The renowned texts of Saint Paul did not shock the communities he intended them for:

He is the image of the invisible God, the firstborn of every creature. For in him were created all things in the heavens and on earth, things visible and things invisible, whether Thrones or Dominations, or Principalities, or Powers. All things have been created through and unto him, and he is before all creatures, and in him all things hold together.

Again, he is the head of his body, the Church; he who is the beginning, the firstborn from the dead, that in all things he may have the first place. For it has pleased God the Father that in him all his fullness should dwell, and that through him he should reconcile to himself all things, whether on the earth or in the heavens, making peace through the blood of his cross.

For in him dwells corporeally all the fullness of divinity.

To examine this question from another angle, I shall consider the virtual significance of one essential rite in the new cult of Jesus: the breaking of bread.

To believe that the bread broken at the Last Supper is the true body of the Lord is to imply that the faithful ascribe to Jesus a certain power (it is not our concern here whether this power is genuine or not) over his body and blood as over the bread and wine, a power conceived as analogous to the power of the creator. This power was inseparable from God in the Jewish mentality: they ascribed to God alone the power to make something out of nothing, to make each essence to be what it is. How could the act by which a human being turned bread into his body and wine into his blood in the real and almost physical sense understood by the first Christian (as we see in Saint Paul and Saint John) be considered for very long as distinct from that power which the Jews attributed only to God? Belief in the Eucharist, so characteristic of the infant Christianity, implied to the Jews either sham or the mysterious divinity of its author.

And this, moreover, is what the pagan observers thought of the eucharistic cult. The words *god* and *divine* did not have the metaphysical meaning for the Romans which they have for us, but a Roman administrator was certainly able to discern an act of worship and adoration. And a persecutor even more so. Now, when Pliny the Younger, proconsul in Bithynia, wrote to the emperor Trajan for advise on what he should do with his new people, he gave an impartial description of what he observed: "They sing to Christ as to a god." That is how Christianity struck him then and would have appeared to every investigator from the beginning: people in other respects honest, gentle, moderate, taking part in certain harmless ceremonies and who adored *Chrestus*, an obscure individual, with the same feeling of total dependence which the pagans felt toward their own gods.

Impression Produced by a First Reading

Now I would like to begin with another primary datum — one more flexible than the last and more dependent upon personal sentiment. This sentiment is a universal one experienced by the average man who reads the Gospels. Some find it delightful, others irritating and exasperating. I read over the four Gospels to get an over-all cursive impression, paying no attention to the details. Sometimes this is a good way to read. When I finish I closed the text as though it were a novel, and then ask myself what impression I had of the chief character. How do I feel about him even now? Is he contradictory, vague, or is he definable?

I felt that I stood in the presence of a being whose identity was not clearly defined and who puzzled those close to him: "What kind of man is this?" You never ask this question of one whose life you share, whose origins you know. It is not that Jesus was unknown, that he suddenly appeared as an adult with no origin, no father or mother; or that he lived differently from other people as certain prophets did, such as Elias and John the Baptist. According to the Gospels he lived among other people. It is impossible to lead a secluded life in the Eastern world where everything occurs in public, where everything you do is seen, where people mill about constantly and there is no sanctuary of private life. The Gospel is detailed enough to please anyone concerned about Jesus' geneology. It even gives more than one could ask for: the names of his parents; information about his "brothers" and "sister," the name of the village he was born in.

Here I could raise an objection. Is this semblance of *incognito,* of being *unidentifiable* and, so to speak, hidden beneath a disguise not one of the marks of mythical fabrication? Do not Ovid and Virgil describe the gods this way when they assume a human form? I recall the apparition of Venus to Aeneas recounted by Virgil in Book One of the *Aeneid*: Aeneas is walking along with a maiden who has gone hunting, and he does not seem to know who she really is. He asks her *who she is....* Is not this similar to evangelical fabrication? Did the authors not place an artificial halo over the chief character's head and give the impression that he was not an ordinary man?

Certainly if the Gospel contained one single episode of one apparition of Jesus inserted into a foreign history, as a dream in life, the objection might stand. But the Gospel is a network of episodes forming a body. All the evidence we

have points to the fact the impression produced by the
historical Jesus is the primary reason behind his influence.
He was one of those few individuals who exude mystery.

The general impression of Jesus retained by the un-
impressionable reader I wish to be is that of an individual
who keeps distant, who communicates but as a king in
hiding, a man among children, an exceptional poet, a man
gifted with a certain superiority he wants to disguise and
cannot suddenly hide because it is diffused like a perfume,
like the air of nobility and genius.

We possess no information about the human appearance
of Jesus. At the end of the second century Irenaeus said that
there was no description of him, though he could go back
through Polycarp and John the Elder to the Apostle John.
The Gospels and especially Mark's which is the most primitive of them insinuate that Jesus penetrated those who
came into contact with him, with that dread men feel in
the presence of things sacred. He had an authority that the
witnesses could compare to no other.

He did not act like a messenger, a teacher, an instructor
or a doctor. He acted and spoke as though he were the
source of what he did and said in the same way as the one
to whom he was intimately linked, the one whom he called
Father, my Father (I shall return to this deeply mysterious
point shortly). We never see him wavering. He is reliable. He
shows no signs of regret and repentance. All this has been
said before and said so many times that I am almost ashamed
to repeat it once again. But the most immediate characteristic
of the Gospel is the conduct of Jesus (whether it is historical
or fabricated ... but then how?). Pascal left us a passing
thought about this: "The rich speak well of riches. The
king speaks calmly about a huge gift he has just bestowed.
And God speaks well of God."

At any rate, the problem of ultimately defining *who he IS*
increases. The time comes when all the other problems that
the life of Jesus have posed fade away to nothingness before

this: to know what is his nature, his *identity* in the juridical, detective and the psychical sense of the word. Exegetes will argue in the attempt to establish whether Jesus was condemned for claiming — he so poor and humbled — the title of messiah which the Jews associated with the idea of triumph, or whether it was his intention to portray his divinity before Caiphas by comparing himself to Daniel's transcendent being. I am content to say that according to the Gospels, Jesus declares *who he is* and that his assertion was immediately condemned as blasphemy. I say that Jesus died for claiming to be something intolerable.

Jesus and Time

What is just as remarkable about Jesus is that, although situated in his own particular time and environment, the Gospel is contemporary to all ages, whereas very similar writings (the Dead Sea Scrolls for one) are dated. Universality bound up with what Helena called intellectual beauty — how can you explain it?

There is too much insistence these days on the *eschatological* aspect of Jesus' doctrine. It is said that Jesus lived in the expectation of the last days, that his teaching proclaimed the end of time. Actually the duration of the future, however long it might be, did not interest Jesus as duration. The faith was established so that should the world continue even for a great many centuries the work would be carried on: Jesus would still be on earth throughout this time. He would be present in the world in the form of community. But, having taken the measures necessary to install himself in time, *if there was to be time*, Jesus had his eyes fixed upon the end of time. To read the discourse on "the end of time," to see the first activity of the apostles, it is clear that the hypothesis of a short span of time was the most probable one to the educated minds of the age.

The arrogance with which Jesus looks at time, the contraction he caused it to undergo beneath his gaze, his way of respecting the slow substance of time, though he always refers to the moment when the flux of time will be annihilated — these are indeed noteworthy. They hint at a sort of underlying presence in time, at least an intimate knowledge of the essence of the mystery of time. I do not know that this knowledge is also a control over time. But everything points to the feeling that Jesus was in something more than simply a human position with regard to time.

*Improbable Character
of the Divinization
of Jesus in the Jewish Milieu*

Here is another point for meditation: from what history tells me, just how probable is it that Jesus could have been divinized in that original milieu? It would not have shocked the leaders of the people to see one god more or less in the Roman Pantheon. But, from the point of view of Jewish tradition, it was an inconceivable thing.

It must be kept in mind that the notion of a man's divinity had all the anterior tradition of the Jewish religious leaders against it.

If there were one certainty in Israel it was that of the *divine unity*. A thoroughly inbred and racial truth handed down by faith and blood. The Moslem religion may be understood as a revolt of this same Semitic blood against any attempt to attribute plurality to the simple Being. The gap between Mohammed and Allah cannot be crossed. Mohammed never once dreamed of calling himself God. The muezzins still protest five times a day against the scandal of this Christian leap across the gap. The ancient Jews saw the unity of the sanctuary in Jerusalem as the symbol of this fierce monotheism. It is well to note that such a strong monolithic faith, protected by institutions, could permit the exaltation of a human person,

9 *Jesus*

king, sage or messiah, even an angel, without the least fear
of superstition and blasphemy. This is evident also in
Catholicism: the exclusive divinity of Christ permits Catholics
to exalt the Virgin without fear of idolatry. So too, as far
as Jewish speculation about the Messiah went, the postulate
of God's incommunicable unity errected an unscalable wall
between Messiah and Yahweh. The God of Israel could not
be depicted in any form. The prophets labored long and
hard to cleanse the belief in the One, from the material symbols
such as the golden calf by which they formerly adored him.
The Decalogue forbade images of God as emphatically as
it demanded exclusive adoration. And the sacred name, those
four vowelless consonants, an early vocal image of God, in
later times were not pronounced.

A God in the form of a man was doubly unthinkable,
doubly abominable. It is sometimes said that certain Scripture
passages virtually contained the notion of the Messiah's
divinity. But these scarce texts were by themselves obscure
— *before the event.* It does appear, however, that Jewish
"Sages" had a vague presentiment of a kind of plurality in
the Divine Being. Though it is not easy to know to what
extent the *Logos* and the *Pneuma* (mentioned in the Book
of *Wisdom*) were *really* distinct in the mind of whoever
wrote this book. In any case, if critical theology could tag
some beginning onto the idea of divine duality, it would
make most difficult any approach to the knowledge of an
historical incarnation of Yahweh from a birth. Daniel's
"Son of Man" to whom Jesus so vividly related himself is a
quasi-celestial being *appearing on the clouds* on the Day
of Judgment. Nowhere is it said that he would reveal himself
in the form of a human nature before this final judgment.

Did this Belief have a Genesis?

The Jewish horizon did not include the "divinity" of Jesus.
Now then, without my being able to perceive any link to

warrant a connection, transition or development in the concepts, states of mind or ideas of these people, here, *all of
a sudden*, the sect of Jesus is seen to spring up rapidly across
Asia and Europe immediately after the death of Jesus. And
history betrays no sign of any conflict or misunderstanding
on this point among the Christian Jews who were so divided
on other matters as precedence, rite, discipline and pastoral
technique. The cult of the Christ-God simply appears, and
that is all. Moreover, the word "god," which could have led
to confusion, was never pronounced.

The question of duration is extremely important here.
There is no interval, neither progress nor transition, nor
change. *It was not. It was*: there is a real origin, a pure
emergence.

I cannot discount the explanation by cause, and by a
cause proportionate to the effect. But how is the cause to
be conceived here?

Proclaiming the Resurrection cannot be adduced as the
total and adequate cause. Surely this preaching did support,
spread and illustrate, but of itself it could not possibly have
induced the assertion inconceivable to the Jewish mind: the
divinity of Jesus, understood as identity with God. We see in
Peter's first discourse in the *Acts of the Apostles* that he does
not directly associate "Resurrection" and "Divinity": he
speaks of Christ as "a man approved by God," as "a man
whom God has risen." The Jews believed God could communicate his power to men, and also that the devil could,
with divine permission, produce "wonders capable of leading
astray even the elect." They did not conclude from a miracle
made in the name of God to the identity of God with whoever performed this miracle.

The rabbi healed the incurable, made the dead speak,
calmed storms, brought the dead to life. No one dreamed of
attributing divinity to them. Even outstanding wonder workers
Rabbi Hanina ben Dosa are to be found among them.

Furthemore, some men in the Greek world equaled the gods in their power to perform miracles — men like Pythagoras or Apollonius of Tyana: they were not confused with the gods. Elias, Elisha, Moses performed marvels: they did not equate these men to Yahweh.

Nor does the fact that the Messiah was called *Son of God* imply his divinity to the Jews; the Angels are sons of God, men also; Israel is a son of God. Princes, judges are sons of the Most High, the king of Israel is a son.

I would like to repeat this once more:

Even if we grant that Jesus performed many miracles besides those mentioned in the Gospel, could the belief in his divinity be accounted for by the awe induced? I recognize that a miracle can engender a holy and *numinous* dread. But dread has never engendered a distinct thought, a continuous and ascendent faith, a well-defined cult. Miracles excite; they impress; they do not teach. Miracles by themselves cannot be considered an origin.

The same goes for this kind of natural miracle that is the unlikely survival of a powerful personality. It communicates enthusiasm, momentum. It bewitches. But, in the second generation this impetus begins to vanish and demythicization takes place. Consider the history of Gandhi, not to mention Lenin, which has continued on its own power.

If a religion is to come into existence and continue there has got to be some element that is greater than awe or the actions of a renowned individual: it must have an *Idea* that can grow. For Christianity this Idea is the Christ-God.

The Extreme Difficulty of the Problem

I see a belief held by every Christian group and I do not see its source. In general, as one work of art proceeds from another, so too belief springs from an anterior belief. However, I see no antecedent belief where the divinity of Jesus is concerned.

There is nothing similar to the Resurrection. To find out whether Jesus has truly risen is to suppose an examination similar to that which the judge, the historian and investigator make in their special fields. After his death has been established it must then be determined whether Jesus appeared to certain people with the same body he had in the tomb. It ought to be proven that the witnesses were not predisposed, that their expectations ran counter to what they saw, that they found it difficult to let themselves be convinced of a seemingly impossible fictitious event; their mental health must be ascertained; it must be shown that the many testimonies bear each other out. This is exactly what comes to light in the Gospel narratives, the seed of Christian apology directed even then against doubters. It was, in advance, the method of the historian as the moderns understand it. It is also that of the psychiatrist when he establishes his patient's sanity.

But divinity is something else. No miracle however great can be taken as proof of divinity. Of course, a power and certainly a facility with this power cause one to think of a superhuman creature, of a person acting as God would act. And the miracles of Jesus that refer to his person verify the truth of the testimony he gives of himself. But divinity cannot be proven by a fact, no matter how spectacular it might be. The proof, the human motive for believing, cannot consist in anything other than in the attestation of this being concerning his person, his intimate self. When it is a question of knowing what a being is in his most hidden recesses, WHO he is, then he alone is witness. His word is supported only by his word. This is the purest state of testimony.

Here I am confronted once again with simple propositions that show a subject and a predicate linked by the verb TO BE.

I met with similar relationships when I studied testimony earlier. I said that testimony centers on the connecting link between a *normal* subject and a *preternatural* predicate, as in the sentence "Jesus *is* the multiplier of loaves." We see Jesus, we see the loaves; but the testimony points to *the fact that* Jesus has multiplied those loaves. I would think that it is at once the heart of the miracle and the essential point of the testimony.

I am confronted with a proposition that unites a subject and predicate that are not of the same order of grandeur, which do not belong to the same order of reality. The word "Jesus" designates an historical character, a human being. But the predicate is not historical or human. It is infinite. When I say that Jesus IS God, I affirm a mysterious and — for a finite mind — unknowable bond. I cannot perceive it the way witnesses perceives a miracle — the healing of a sick man, for example. And only he who is the subject of this relationship between the finite and the infinite in himself can bear witness to it.

Without a doubt the supreme testimony is that which one gives on the substance of his own being, the testimony in which the *I* does not distinguish itself and into which no error can enter except that of pride or folly.

But then I face another difficulty — the written documents. Nothing is simpler than counterfeiting. What could be easier than to invent a text in which one character declares he is God? A papyrus and a reed are all it takes. I meet with a paradox: the highest conceivable affirmation corresponds to the weakest kind of proof; a few black letters scrawled upon a fragile surface that a child could draw.

And all these difficulties are compounded one upon the other. What I demand as necessary — the knowledge whether Jesus revealed himself to be God — seems impossible to me, even if Jesus insisted upon it, because of its nature. If he revealed himself by word, how could his contemporaries understand it, for their whole mentality was directly opposed to the notion that a man-God was conceivable? If he revealed himself through written documents (this is practically indispensable for those who are not contemporaries with him), how could one help but doubt? How can one help suspecting a commingling of faith and fabrication? It is so easy to mix the two together.

New Method of Inquiry

Nonetheless, the oldest and least suspect evangelical tradition does beyond question contain several declarations whereby Jesus defines himself in relation to beings known to the Jews in this world and in the other. The Gospel, for the most part, is an attempt to situate Jesus with regard to all the anterior beliefs and the types of existence admitted by the religious men of his day. Just as the sailor measures the angle from which he sees several constellations to get an accurate siting, so too the reader of the Gospel, as those who heard Jesus, is eager to locate Jesus in relation to the historical or divine figures portrayed by the Jews. Thanks to our knowledge of what the Jews believed and their frame of mind, we can determine the meaning, actual or virtual, conscious or unconscious, that the words of Jesus had for those Israelites.

Seen from afar the method I propose resembles the *Formgeschichte*. I try to determine only the mental contents of a given text and not its literary form. I am especially trying to gauge *between what is conformable to the mentality of the group and which is opposed to it*. This gap between mental expectation and the object of perception or of narrative indirectly defines reality. The real, in this perspective, is what we do not expect and only reflect upon with certain retouchings and transformations, with the mental cliché we project upon it.

We must make the following studies by confining our-selves to the first three Gospels in order to find the content of tradition as near in time as possible to its source before any development:

1. The situation of Jesus in relation to the eminent personages of Jewish religious history, in relation to the prophets — in relation to the concept of a "Son of Man" conceived as pre-existent.

2. The situtation of Jesus in relation to the angels and devils.

3. The situation of Jesus in relation to Yahweh.

4. The power Jesus possessed through which he accomplished certain actions or said certain things which in the Jewish mentality belonged exclusively to the transcendent and incommunicable being: Jesus' supremacy over the law promulgated by God, the power to forgive sins, the power to judge, the power to be the condition of salvation for men accordingly as they received or rejected his person and work.[1]

Types of Jesus in the Jewish World

It is rather strange to hear Jesus claiming to be greater than Solomon, David, Elias or Moses when he did not even look like a prophet, sage or king. He quietly lifted himself far above all those whom the Jews rightly or wrongly esteemed beyond all other men. Let us assume that Jesus actually said these things. They are in direct contrast to the Jewish prophets who never exalted themselves and only claimed to be men sent by Yahweh. They were content to reveal the word of Yahweh — never once did they present themselves as this very word. It is difficult to find an equivalent in our times, but perhaps we can find it in a French prophet proclaiming that he is greater than Napoleon or Pascal, when in fact he bears no similarity at all to them.

1. For exegesis and commentary on these passages I refer to my book La Problème de Jésus, II (Aubier), pp. 64-80.

Such pretentions, difficult to reconcile with sanity, make
the Gospel disconcerting and irritating to the unbeliever.

These pretentions crop up everywhere in the synoptic
Gospel, if not openly they at least are suggested.

When the Gospel is considered in the light of the age
it was written in, then the most striking thing is not the
somewhat vague title *Son of God,* but the very precise
Son of Man, for the *Son of Man* mentioned in the Gospel is
obviously Daniel's Son of Man who, coming on the clouds of
heaven, approaches the "Ancient of Days" to receive domina-
tion and glory, to rule the peoples forever. He is the
eschatological leader of the Chosen People, different from
the Davidical King, a temporal *triumphator.* The Parables
of Henoch tell us that he is "The Chosen One hidden before
the face of the Lord before the creation of Moses and for
eternity." Jesus places himself in this transcendent perspective by very often calling himself the Son of Man. One
cannot say that Jesus revealed himself to be God by this,
but rather that he chose the highest approximation which
the Jewish mind had made of a creature to God, so that he
could tell others who he was.

I will not go into whether the angels and devils do exist:
they were, at least, beliefs. It is clear that Jesus assumed
these antecedent qualities irregardless of how noble they
were. And he did so without defending his position, by
right, I daresay.

Could we still be able to overlook these passages if they
were but isolated incidents and imagine them perhaps as
the product of an early legend germinated by the Parables
of Henoch? What Jesus says about the relationship he realizes
he has to the Supreme Source are, in my opinion, very much
more profound and unyielding to explanation: they are his
religion, his message, his definition.

The Relationship of Jesus to the Source

For each of us the relationship of our being with Being
— extremely intimate and hushed over often by modesty or
cautiousness — is linked to our awareness of our existence.
Unbelievers possibly are not different than believers where
the awareness of the relationship one has to one's source is
concerned, although they lack the means to express it.

Though Jesus remains the most impenetrable of all real,
imagined or possible beings, yet we have intimate knowledge
of his prayer life and his rapport with the Source.

In so many ways Jesus remains unknown and obscure to
us. We cannot tell what he looked like, how he talked, and
we scarcely know anything about his daily life (apart from
the day of his death). Yet, we have an intense knowledge
of his prayer. Moreover, the only thing we really and distinctly know about him is that which ought to have been
the most deeply hidden secret: the union of his SELF with
the divine SELF.

There is one striking aspect found only in this one case
of spiritual and mystical history. Considered in the light
of his declarations, Jesus' relationship to his principle is
not a function, a quality, an aspect of his being: it is the
definition of what he is, it becomes identical to his essence.
He communicates the secret of this essence to men. He is
THE SON. His consciousness is inseparably linked to his
relationship to the Source who is "his Father." This prevents
him from praying like men or with men because this would
be to falsely represent his being. He does not act as a "son
of God," for all the Chosen People were "sons of God" as
the Jews saw it. Rather, he acts like THE SON. His doctrine,
his mystique, his solitude, his way, and his truth are to be
precisely this Son in an incommunicable degree.

That, at least, translated into a somewhat abstract language is the most primitive sense of the Gospel — a sense

which the Johannine Gospel would only make more explicit later on.

Jesus sets himself absolutely apart.

In particular he never puts himself on the same plane with his apostles when he defines his relationship to the Father. He says "My Father" when he wants to teach that he is the Son. He says "Your Father" when it is his intention to impart to the disciples and the apostles the knowledge that God, while truly being his Father, is also their Father. Since there seems to be a common paternity, one would expect Jesus to complete the equation by saying "Our Father" in speaking to the apostles about God. But never does the Jesus of the Gospels descend into their communion to pray the Our Father with them when he instructs them to say "Our Father," nor does he say, "Forgive me my sins." In the necessarily numerous passages in which Jesus speaks of his Father or of the Father of men he does not situate the two relationships of himself to his Father and of men to his Father (who, however, is also their Father) on the same plane.

I wonder how much this constant, real and insistent, but nearly imperceptible distinction can be explained by the influence of myth.

The Supreme Judgeship

The anecdote of the paralytic's healing and the remission of his sins is to be found in the very oldest strata of evangelical tradition. Jesus said to the paralytic: "Your sins are forgiven you." He then heals the paralytic "so that you know that the Son of man has the power to forgive sins." The Jews believed that sin affects God and God alone. And if the gift of penetrating consciences was granted the Messiah, the power of absolving from sin was thought to be God's alone. The scribes called Jesus' claim to forgive sins blasphemy.

Let us go back now to the very well known scene of the
Last Judgment in Saint Matthew's Gospel.

The Son of Man will come in his Father's glory, accompanied by his angels, and he will judge each man according
to his deeds. It is then, before his Father, that he will be
ashamed of those who were ashamed of him before men,
that he will disown those who disowned him, that he will
acknowledge those who acknowledged him before men.

To fully understand all that the text conveys, it is necessary
once more to keep in mind the Jewish idea of the Messiah's
role as judge.

Without admitting the Messiah's divinity, the Jews regarded
the sanctioning of men's conduct as one of his duties. He it
is who would judge the living and sometimes the dead.

"Here we still have the same viewpoint, but the *spirit*
is different. The judgment in question is certainly a judgment
of the nations, solemnly decreed in the presence of all conscious beings. As in the popular apocalypses, the Messiah
makes his appearance 'booted and armed', a warrior chief
surrounded with his bodyguard. Yet in spite of these re-
semblances it is something quite different from a political
restoration of Israel, or even their spiritual restoration. No
privilege counts, no social advantage; neither does membership
of the chosen people, nor even services to God's cause, if
these have been rendered from interested motives. On the
other hand the friends of God, even if unknown to the world,
are to be found among strangers, unbelievers and enemies,
whereas some who have proved unfaithful servants will
find themselves cast out. Therefore the judgment of Jesus
reaches 'the very division between joints and marrow' (namely
to thought itself) and with no possible appeal. He has no
regard for the decrees of any anterior racial predestination
but only for the moral life of the individual; this he scrutinizes
in the light of charity, this being the very plenitude of justice.
Jesus behaves as if he were Judge-in-himself. What is more,
he judges according to the strictest moral law but also accord-

ing to men's attitude to his message, in fact their attitude — the attitude of each — to his own person, considered as anyone who is poor, anyone who is a prisoner ... He identifies himself with the moral law. Man's adherence to Jesus, his impulse of love for *him*, is the necessary condition of his eternal salvation.

"Consider, now, what this claim implied for the Jewish mind. In order to pass such a sentence, which would determine the destiny of each human being, it was necessary to have access to that which was secret. Such knowledge, according to the Jews was peculiar to Yahweh, the direct source of all that concerned the moral law. God, as I have said, might reveal the state of an individual conscience to a supreme judge of men, who would be a man like others. But it was an established tradition for the Jews of that day that judgment was reserved to God; the Messiah never appears as judge except in the parables of Henoch, and even there his judgment is not a universal judgment. The day of judgment is 'the Lord's Day' *par excellence;* and as the coming of the Son of Man coincides with the day of the Lord, so the Son's act of judgment coincides with God's. This identifying of time and manner and function makes it hard to distinguish the Messiah's role from the Father's.

"To do justice to both aspects of what we are given, of what I would call the 'structure', one would have to say something like this: everything suggests that Christ is not only acting as supreme judge but identifying himself with the Person offended by sin: *you did it to me ... you refused it to me....*" [2]

In much the same vein one could also analyze the content of the equally numerous passages where Jesus is represented as a control of the Sabbath Law. The Jews considered this law established by God himself. It was

---

2. Problème de Jésus, II, pp. 75-76. Problem of Jesus, pp. 80-82 — Tr.

a divine law, a law that God also obeyed by resting on the seventh day, a figure of this first holiday by which he ceased the act of creation. The Gospel texts show Jesus entirely at ease with himself when he put this primordial law quite naturally at his disposal. It makes no difference whether this anecdote is genuine or not for the analysis I am making here and now. It merely implies that the oldest tradition attributes words to the Nazarene which imply his "madness" of self-identification to the supreme authority.

I would like once more to point out other passages like those solemn verses in which Jesus refers to his *authority*. But we must always study these expressions in connection with Jewish and Hellenic conceptions.

The Messiah possesses the authority (*exousia*) which has been "given" him in "heaven and on earth," an authority which, as we see in Saint John's Gospel, extends over his own life and death. This authority has already been clearly shown in the synoptic accounts of the Passion where we see Jesus dying, so it appears, all of a sudden to the utter astonishment of those used to watching this kind of execution.

According to Jewish concepts this *exousia* belongs to God alone. It was thought of as an absolute juridical power that permitted no opposition. It is true that this power could be communicated, since we see that Jesus conferred it to the apostles and that Satan possessed it, but the Gospel represents Jesus using this *exousia* in the same manner as Yahweh. Once more it looks as though Jesus and his Source are one, although their relationships are different.[3]

---

3. The reader will note that in this examination, because I have tried to be extremely cautious and prudent (like the chess player who begins the game by losing certain pieces to his opponent in order to show that he can win without them) I have by-passed even in the synoptic accounts, certain very explicit texts such as the renowned passage of Matthew and Luke:

"I praise you, Father, Lord of heaven and earth, that you hid these things from the wise and prudent, and revealed them to little ones. Yes, Father, for such was your good pleasure. All things have been

The Implicit Content of these Passages

These assertions are scattered throughout the earliest Gospel tradition and, as they form a unity, are inseparable from this tradition.

They do not actually constitute a distinct *bloc* with sharply defined contours, nor a monolith that shows signs of being added at a later date (like an obelisk is superimposed onto a temple) in the development of the faith. These passages are not superimposed, daubed here and there like buckles and rings to enliven some early obscure text. They depend on the context and are of the same fiber and stuff as this context, being interwoven with the narratives, and an attempt at separation can only do them violence.

These texts are written in a very simple language. They lack that Greek or Hellenistic terminology borrowed from imperial paganism and used in so many theological texts of the New Testament — words like "Lord" (*kurios*) "Savior" (*Soter*), "Son of God" (*Theou Uios*). Nor do they contain such expressions as "Word" (*Logos*), *or* "Son" (*Uios*) which John would adopt from the Greek translations of the Scriptures. It goes without saying, of course, that the more abstract, precise and metaphysical terminology used later by the Christians in the confession of their faith are not to be found. This would include such terms as *consubstantiality, co-eternity, generation,* — *nature, person*. Here it is, the ordinary and concrete language of everyday usage. There is no display of coined expressions so necessary for protection against philosophical errors, but having the disadvantage of bearing the marks of human fabrication in addition to the fact that they are meaningless to the people in general.

---

delivered to me by my Father; and no one knows the Son except the Father; nor does anyone know the Father except the Son, and him to whom the Son chooses to reveal him."

It is said that this text was a later addition, but from where I stand it contains nothing not already implicitly contained in those texts that no one questions.

I call attention to the accidental, episodic nature of many of these texts which crop up in some passages where generally the line of thought is pointing to something else.

The Gospel often shows clear-cut affirmations. The difference between the Old Law and the New Law in the *Sermon on the Mount;* the proclamation of the divine paternity; the condemnation of pharisaism. Here Jesus is bringing home a point; he insists and reiterates. He uses formulas like "Amen, amen I say to you" to lend solemnity to what he is about to say. But in most of the *sayings* I have examined, the emphasis points very often to something entirely different than the being of Christ. Christ sometimes speaks of *his* angels. What did the original people concerned — and later the first readers of the incident — bear in mind when Jesus forgave the paralytic his sins? Certainly the unique character of this prophet, perhaps his power over sin: no one then dared admit what we call divinity. It might be asked whether those involved really understood that the "Son of Man" forgave him his sin. For in what follows there is no sign that the Jews came up to Jesus to be healed of their sins and to confess them, which they did in going to see John the Baptist.

What a curious thing! Grant for a moment that these texts are genuine. Try to go back into the state of mind of those who heard those propositions which shocked them so deeply and were so difficult to interpret in the light of their religious culture, and were so contrary to the undying tradition of their nation, their race and their worship. Did they have the *ability* to imagine Jesus as God? Was it *possible* for them to think that?

Yet this almost unspeakable and unthinkable notion alone could fully express what they understood in the words spoken by this man whom many knew and everyone knew about.

But did they have to think such revolutionary thoughts? After all, the traditional idea, the official notion of *Messiah* apparently seemed to account for all that Jesus said about himself: Messiah, one set apart, predestined to come as the "Son of God."

Still, this middle-ground could only be held with difficulty. They were led further beyond that. The Gospel intimates that the presence of Jesus excited in them the same kind of dread, love, trembling, acquiescence and adoration as the presence of God.

But in other respects it was impossible to liken Jesus to God, as though the two were one. Since Jesus always showed himself to be dependent on God, the Jews would have seen this as idolatry.

These two conflicting exigencies should have disturbed them no end. They should have excited the Jews to overcome them and thereby avoid any mental anxiety stemming from the necessity of admitting two self-exclusive thoughts.

How many questions might be raised that could shatter ancient boundaries and necessitate a whole new language and state of mind that had not until then "entered the heart of man"? If Jesus is God, must not the divine unity then be destroyed? He calls himself the Son: therefore, he is not God!

To translate the appearances exactly and write out the equation of the difficulty one would have to make a proposition similar to this: *Jesus is equal to a being who can have no equal, although he is distinct from him by what he terms sonship.*

Problem Posed to the Human Intellect by those Virtual Assertions Jesus Makes about Himself

What a great mystery it is which first Jewish thought, then Greek speculation and finally every thinking must tackle to the very end! This is no dialectical problem rising out of ideas such as one meets in ancient and modern philosophies. It is a higher fact come to us through experience and yet it seems inadmissible. In such cases the problem can only be solved in heaven. We must yield to a new dimension, a higher order. If we are to fully understand, we must accept the fact we cannot understand. We must create a new and apparently absurd vocabulary through which inferences can be made. It is on a very different and lower plane, a problem somewhat like the one a physicist-mathematician encounters today when he desires to unite opposing aspects of experience, for example the emission and undulation of light rays.

We cannot understand everything all at once. Nor shall we ever. We must have time for the seeds of our thoughts to unfold in. Certainly this is true when we are confronted with incompatible and yet inseparable information. We must ascend to the point of their union and assert that which is incomprehensible for us but which is not incomprehensible in itself. Through prior tradition, or by uniting several traditions, we must find a language that is adequate, perhaps even shocking at times, which, as Karl Barth says about the word "consubstantial," is truer in its folly than all the wisdom combined to attack it. This all requires time, possibly the whole span of time allotted the human species on earth from Jesus down to the consummation of the world.

We cannot take two positions at once: we must, I say, try to see how the two ends fit together, and if we cannot see it, at least we must try to conceive of it.

From this point of view I have a clearer understanding of what might be called the *origin* of dogma. The formulation is not primary. First come the exigencies imposed on the faith in a certain kind of experience, and so imperiously that one exigency cannot be sacrificed for the other. Both demands must be maintained and protected. That is the true *origin*. Later on this clashing of the appearances of experience is formulated and becomes enforced as an article of faith in the Church. This moment in which the belief, until then latent, is defined as a dogma is not its origin, but merely what I call its *emergence*. Dogma is not born in this second moment of development any more than a man begins to live the day he leaves his mother's womb. Dogma emerges under the species of a formula drawn from human language in a certain state of culture. Proposed by a council, this formula protects against error, serves as a model and points out the axis where one will find thoughts which do not corrupt the essence of what was believed from the beginning. But the formula does not solve the mystery by fencing it in with guide rails (to *define* means to "set boundaries around"). It is for me to think and ponder over this dogma. The task of coming to grips with it is one meant for the whole Church and every thinker.

●●●●●●●●●●

What I have found out in my reflection has often been set forth and propounded in the Churches. It is basis for the traditional argument.

Because I am being cautious and am trying to follow the principles of my method, I have set aside the texts of St. John's Gospel written at the close of the first century. These texts are often very explicit. Strictly speaking, because of the time-gap they do not testify to the first state of Christian consciousness at the moment of Jesus' death, but only to its second state, its early development as it could be formulated at the end of the first century in the Johannine milieux: a half-century of testing and reflecting elapsed between these two states of consciousness.

But Are These Texts Authentic?

Now I am ready to pose the famous *preliminary question* our critical age wants settled first of all — a question that the faith would not have considered had it not been for some merciless critics. Are these texts authentic?

I have taken great pains to reduce as far as possible, after the manner of the learned who seek out the incontrovertible

minimum, the given I began with. I took into account the
age-old beliefs of the Jews, their historical remembrances
and their religious mentality. Then I sought to define not
what Jesus said, but rather *how the sayings of Jesus which
are contained in the first evangelical tradition impressed the
Jewish mind.* If I had to, I could say, like Bergson in the *Two
Sources of Morality and Religion,* that I am not questioning
the existence of Jesus or even the Jews. Even if the Gospel were
an *Iliad* that came from the hand of a single Homer, one could
examine the differences of value, authority and dignity that
the author introduced among the fictitious characters. One
could, for example, establish whether Hector's bravery is shown
to be lesser than that of Achilles.

But I must from here on out abandon these cautious
methods akin to those withholdings of judgment, those putting
between brackets dear in the lineage from Husserl to the
phenomenologists. I must ask the ultimate and most important question: Did it or did it not happen?

My first task will be to formulate the judgment of an
unbeliever confronted with this collection of texts and observations. I expect his answer would be something like this:

"What Jesus said about himself and his position in exitence
which you recently referred to are not the *cause* of the faith
of those who believe in Jesus' divinity. On the contrary they
are the first written traces, the first *effects.*

"In other words these things are not what the historical
Jesus really said. They are but sayings spontaneously or subtly
attributed to him by the first groups of his followers who,
after whatever the paschal event may have been, augmented
their faith in keeping with the law of every living belief which
decrees that a belief, being founded only upon itself, needs
to be continually supplemented in order to prove its consistency. In this case the expansion went immediately to the
farthest degree possible. It is easy to see why. The notion of
'superman' is unstable, as is also that of 'demigod.' It is more

enticing and safer to go all the way at once, to turn Jesus into
a god, to assimilate him to God.

"Let me be more precise. If people remembered something
of what was said by the Jesus of history about whom we
know so little and who is so unknowable for us, these words
would have been almost immediately modified, codified and
sublimated by faith.

"Now if you ask me where these first communities got
their belief in the divinity of a crucified prophet, I would
have to answer you through what I find in the history of
religions. The idea that a god can take on a human form and
tell men his divine name goes hand-in-hand with the pagan
world, as mythology shows."

Here once again I come up against the most current
objection which is based on the new concept which today's
historians have of history.

Because there is no history outside the historian it is
impossible to discern the good grain of wheat, the authentic
kernel, from its shell. From this point of view the Gospels are
but the indirect testimony to the faith of the communities and
Jesus cannot be known in himself, but only his image and
legend.

Like every sophism, this sophism (more complicated than
Zeno's) is the combination of a self-evident proposition and
a false one. One who listens to a sophist rivets his mind on the
obvious: he feels certitude and peace and quiet. But while he
acquiesces, a paradox is insinuated into his certitude and it
is mingled so well with the obvious that it is camouflaged.

Of course Jesus cannot be known directly — neither can
any historical figure. True, we know him through accounts,
images and reflections. But must one immediately conclude
from this that there is no way, by a criticism of these images,
to discern what they contain of the true Jesus and what is
added to them by the narrator or by the milieu that denounces
or receives his story?

A New Examination of the Mythical Hypothesis

I have said that to define religious understanding as the power of imagination would be to distort its description. Indeed this power does exist, and if one is not on his guard it will always tend to embellish the initial kernel with a proliferation of detail, supplement and other additions. But no one will deny that the normal man has the faculty of attestation by which he is able to discern and express what he "saw and heard," what he picked up from reality, from what is positive and undeniable.

Because attestation and fabrication act together and become confused in many complex ways it is difficult to say in a given case what belongs to fabrication and what relates to attestation.

I have been trying to establish certain criteria which would help us distinguish between the two.

Fabrication and Its Seeds

Fabrication projects outside the present state of the *beliefs* of a community. But it does much more: it tends to make them more explicit, to schematize them. Fabrication stresses these beliefs and brings them out into the open; it shapes them, paints them with as much outline and color as possible. The inventive function of a community tries to build bastions around beliefs that are unverifiable by giving them the same kind of existence as the realities perceived through the senses.

Balzac wrote a penetrating text on the vigor of this inventive function which is so closely bound up with the epic, poetic or romantic function. In *The Country Doctor* he shows us veterans of Napoleon's army in 1830 reviving the legend of the Emperor. Those peasant-soldiers were not interested in making or reproducing a critical history of Bonaparte as emperor, nor were they concerned with telling of his little-known childhood at Ajaccio, Brienne and Valence. Theirs is the Emperor in his majesty, journeying through ice and snow, a rugged, invincible man. There is no saying that we shall not see these legends rise up again.

But fabrication cannot produce texts where the beliefs of the communities exist *implicitly*. Why should it? If I wanted to tell the story of a god who appeared on earth, I would not start off by getting caught up in pointless difficulties. I would not depict him as weak or ignorant. Nor would I conceal my proofs of his divinity with narratives that do not at first glance support them, that occasionally seem directly contrary to what I want to demonstrate. What fabrication desires to make known it does not project in the form of seeds which are necessarily minute, obscure, enveloped, disguised. Whether it takes place in a mental world or in texts — in a "tradition" or a "Scripture" — fabrication presents perfectly delineated realities that are alive and vibrant. There is no approximation. The realities it conceives are those highly expressive realities found present in religious rites, in the ecstasies of the mystics, in the dogmatic formulas of the creeds.

Fabrication does not restrict or tone down. It tends to exceed the actual content of a belief rather than to obscure it, to cover it up or limit it.

This is generally the case especially in the East and particularly for the Jews living in the time of Jesus. Historians once lacked a clear idea of the difference between the past and the present and they did not find it hard to transfer what they believed into an imaginary past. That is how the Jews represented the divine worship of their people in the time of Moses (thirteen centuries before our era), and the same holds true in the time of Esdras in the fifth century B.C. They projected their increasingly complex rites and the temple service into a primitive past.

There can be no question that when those documents serving as the source of the synoptic Gospels were written the Christian communities "adored Christ as a god." The people would have rejected them at that time had the Gospel texts been tampered with so as to despict a Christ clearly pro-claiming his divinity. As I have mentioned earlier, the source-documents of the Gospels said very little about their master's divinity. If, in spite of the power of fabrication and the most praise-worthy motives, the redactors of what was remembered about Jesus did not refashion the Lord to suit their purposes, it is because they must have been conscious of a solid and refractory element, something given them that simply had to be respected.

The faithful were convinced that Jesus was as much as a god as God. And had they given vent to the power of imagination — being spurred on by the belief that the end of time and Jesus' "return upon the clouds" were close at hand and that they were going to see Jesus with their own eyes making an economy of death — they would have induced or sanctioned other kinds of narratives besides the synoptic Gospels. The *Apocalypse* is an excellent example. Also Saint Paul's first letters in which he speaks of Antichrist, the last days and the avenging heavenly Christ.[4]

To examine this question from another angle I would say that the strangest aspect of the first three Gospels (called "synoptic" to set them apart from and prefer them to Saint John's Gospel) is not so much what Bergson calls "the divine humility" as what I would call the *divine incognito*. In Mark Christ rebukes somebody who called him *"Good Master"* by saying that "no one is good except God." In another place he says that he, Jesus, son of the Father, does not know when the end of time will be. He asks his Father to spare him the cup of his passion. He does not, generally speaking, reveal his essence. How could an ingenious myth-maker who had invented a God that actually became a speaking and acting man resist the temptation to put on his lips certain explicit

4. For further development of these aspects I refer you to **Problème de Jésus**, II, pp. 82-89 and 253-255.

declarations of his divinity? How could he resist concocting splendid scenes of triumph or passion? The frenzied and paradoxical human imagination might be tempted to reconstruct the suffering of a God. But then it would be inserted into some vague place and undetermined epoch. The ancients invented the agony of Prometheus. The Jews could have divinized Job's sufferings. But I think this sublime mythmaker would have to be more than a genius to paint the picture of a suffering God with the control, the verisimilitude and the simplicity of the Passion narratives in the four Gospels. These narratives, moreover are consonant with the intricate practices of the Jews and Romans at that time. They are in accord with so many other scenes of human life.

There are not very many possible explanations. I have given the reasons for saying that on this plane there are two solutions and two only. This forces the mind to adopt one of them, not because it sounds true or probable, but simply because the mind recognizes the impossibility of the others.

To anyone who is really thinking, this necessity applies right here at this stage of our investigation.

If you are certain that the answer of faith is in itself unthinkable, then you must accept the hyothesis of fabrication regardless of its difficulties, or there is no other way out.

But if you are certain that the explanation by fabrication renders the real development of the original Christianity unintelligible, you have no way out except the one that leads to the threshold of faith.

And you will say, "All things considered, it is impossible to give a mythical explanation of the implicit statements of Jesus in the synoptic writings. So (as the only possible and truly residual solution) we are left with the conviction that the Nazarene actually spoke those things and that he (a man much as any other man) was conscious of existence and attributed to himself the characteristics which the long religious tradition of his people had given to God."

Or better still:

"Everything suggests that Jesus, aware of his identity to God, instructed his witnesses with certain declarations put in a way they could understand so as to make this revelation gradually assimilable."[5]

The Divine Education

This is not all extraordinary if one grants the hypothesis of divine humility. Each mind that is on a high plane of existence and must impart itself to a mind on a lesser plane (a mind that cannot grasp knowledge all at once without a necessarily slow and tortuous thought process) has to make allowances for this weakness. Wisdom advises him to proceed by gradual stages. The Greek Fathers called it "economy." We call it more simply yet "education." Now, if I accept the idea of a divine revelation in the history of the Jewish people that is staggered out over more than fifteen centuries, I realize that God used the same patience and gradual process of illumination. He parceled out his legislative teaching by using untechnical expressions and by permitting great periods of silence upon certain doctrinal issues which were nevertheless of prime importance to the life of the soul, such as the doctrine of the separation of good and evil people in the afterlife.

Consequently, I am not at all surprised to find in the Gospel, which is Israel summed up, that the Revealer worked with the same method of respect for freedom and discretion, letting the task of developing the seeds be done in time. The hidden and implicit larva character of Jesus' statements on his own mystery are like a teacher's approach. Before there can be revelation there must first of all be an initiation, stages,

---

5. The reader will find further developments of these views in **Problème de Jésus**, II, pp. 82-95.

progress, development. Jesus' methods on a small scale are like God's approach throughout the history of his people.

This gradual approach is similar to nature's methods when it inserts a ferment into a lesser order of existence which has to lift this order up to a higher level it could not have attained by itself, that is when nature plants by this infinitely small particle which is called a germ, a particle, a point of matter charged with the future. "With respect to any order whatever, an order which is superior and thus infinitely higher can be represented in the first only by an infinitely small one. The mustard seed — the instant, image of eternity — moderation. The infinitesimal expression of pure good." [6]

Jesus and the Teacher of Righteousness

Once again we shall make a comparison with the Dead Sea Community and the "teacher of righteousness" — I have often found this comparison helpful, at least indirectly. Here we have a prophet, the leader of a new covenant, preaching repentance and truth, distinguishing two races of light and darkness, raised up from the earth, with a view to returning, referring himself to the Mosaic Law which he perfects. We get the impression that a man once lived when rightly or wrongly gathered over his memory the ordinary themes of the Jewish mentality. He is never called the Messiah. There is no record that he called himself the Messiah or that he suffered a violent death. He is unaware that he has any special authority over the Mosaic Law — on the contrary, he wants to return to that law. The many elements which make up this individual do not let us see him living his day-to-day life. They are not inter-related so as to form a system of thought.

---

6. These highly compact formulations are Simone Weil's. Confer with my philosophical works in which similar views are developed at greater length: **La philosophie de Newman; L'existence temporelle; Pascal et Leibniz.**

They did not become a theology. The sect was a short-lived one. The seed kept closed in upon itself. We face one of those aborted developments found in all levels of biology, in aesthetics and every spiritual history. Above all, we do not see a living person depicted and marked out through human concepts, but transcending them utterly as the poetical idea and poet's personality transcend the sounds of words and their meanings. There is no gradual progression, no almost imperceptible growth from a seed. The criteria we have defined have an application here. Fabrication concocts or colors a hero or god, but it is beyond it to create a living person, especially this God-man who gradually awakens the minds of men to the awareness of who he is.

CHAPTER XI

Insights into the Divinity of Jesus

IT is easier to believe in God than in Jesus.

Jesus-God is God engaged in history, living for us, God become a word spoken to me. Because of this fact, instead of being in that distant and abstract relationship to the source of being which occurs when we think of the transcendent God stripped of any resemblance to man, here we are precipitated into the very presence of our source. We encounter, as if he were our other self, this infinite being who pre-exists us, envelops us and calls us. We realize that man's mind and freedom steel him against this fact and demand proofs that are proportionate to the outrageousness of this assertion.

A proof will always be inferior to the infinity of its object. The Gospel so clearly points this out by stating that to believe in the divinity of Jesus one must also have the light of grace. But it is the mind's job to reduce this disproportion as far as it can. And it does so when it shows that the problem of Jesus' divinity is raised by the facts themselves. I believe I have determined as far as the human mind is able the principle of a positive method which can lead the impartial observer to raise the question whether Jesus is God, and then to gradually approach a solution — a mysterious one I grant you, but a rational one. Here again I do not think that the future holds any new perspectives or methods in store for us. I believe, as Karl Barth believes also, that the *eternal dilemma*

will be with us always: either a man divinized out of
enthusiasm, or a mythical idea clothed in the garments of
history, OR ELSE an ultra-real and superhistorical fact, a
human nature possessed with a divine person, as the Council
of Chalcedon defines it.

Advantages of the Method:
Outlining the Development of Thought

I want to emphasize the advantage of the method I have
proposed. This method examines how the belief in one
man's divinity develops from its very earliest assertions which
were written down without being fully understood by those
who first heard them. These primitive assertions were not
grasped in their entirety because they were discreet, virtual,
veiled and they required a great amount of time and reflection before they could be fathomed. From this point of view
the two New Testament theologians, Saints Paul and John,
added nothing essentially new. They simply developed what
was there to begin with. In this way one can follow for about
a half century the development of these first assertions. This
development is like every thorough speculation which un-
folds from a real fact that is minutely examined to find concepts and terms equivalent to its content that describe this
content without deforming it.

If the idea of the divinity of a man is not ruled out from the
outset as altogether impossible, then from the plane of facts,
of historical knowledge to which I limit myself, I find nothing
to contradict the divinity of the man-Jesus. But I repeat that
these problems of possibility belong to the realm of the
theoretical and not to that of acceptance.

In this case and this one alone everything suggests the
divinity of a man as being the answer to the problem raised
by the facts themselves. I do not think an open mind can go
any further than I have gone, but I think it has to come at
least this far.

The Discovery of the Original Likeness

I will say further that the moderns have developed a new means for convincing themselves of the divine existence. Through their critical methods they have developed a new approach that is reflexive, positive and acceptable to many exacting minds. It even permits of a retransmission of Jesus' very words.

This method would also have the added advantage of not requiring what the modern man considers to be an uncalled for preliminary effort, as is the effort of believing in many miracles.

We desire a more direct approach, one which, without suppressing the interposition of a narrative, even a written one will reduce it in some way so as to permit each man to arrive at a conviction and almost enable us to hear the very words chosen by Christ in front of his first companions. In short, it should bring back the impression and the savor of the beginnings. Then perhaps the critical approach which has been so fiercely attacked because it has been seen so far only in its first phase which is necessarily negative, might bring about a renewal of the sense of presence impaired by the passing of time and the overabundance of commentaries.

I do not know what to make of the Shroud of Turin upon which it is said the face of Christ is imprinted like a negative. I believe its questionable truth from the historical, exegetical and chemical point of view. Proof of the authenticity of this linen cloth would be tremendously profitable: then, the people of this century would be able to see the face of Jesus during the Passion without the intervention of verified reports, accounts and human testimonies that serve as indirect and imperfect signs only. We would possess the imprint of his agony. Photography made it possible to print the negative of the man of sorrows, and this photograph surpasses the Gospels of the Passion in precision and in suggestion. This was scientifically impossible before the nineteenth century.

We must leave to a future investigation the task of deciding how valuable this photograph is. The approach I have used, although more difficult than the simple inspection of a "negative" or the technical decomposition of a piece of cloth, nevertheless is more important. For the analysis of a piece of linen and a picture taken of the Passion, were it possible in the year 33, would reveal nothing about the divinity of Jesus — and it is precisely this divinity which is more necessary for belief than the Passion because faith gives the Passion its whole meaning.

Here, above all, we do not stand at the mercy of a chemical analysis of aromatic substances or of an historian's remarks about cloth and burial customs. Here, the texts are within easy reach of every reader, and it is not difficult to study or compare them.

The Gospel Illumined by the Idea of Divinity

I would like to return for the last time to the impression the Gospel produces upon the reader — by assuming the hypothesis of divinity. It seems to me that it sheds light on the Gospel's details after the manner of a genuine *mystery*. This approach renders the Gospel more human, more intelligible and, I daresay, more probable.

Renan mistakenly believed he could make the Gospel more accessible by likening Jesus to a superman.

The more one exalts Jesus as a man, the more difficult it becomes to imagine him as God. To assert that Jesus is the finest of the sons of men, like Renan, or the supermystic, *par excellence*, like Bergson, does not prepare the intellect to conceive him as God. The superlative expression *"the greatest . . .of"* makes us think we are filling up the vast abyss — but these words are deceiving. These words have engendered a pagan attitude in the midst of the Christian faith, and I would call them "Arian" since Arius only saw Christ as a superman. It is tantamount to telling an ignoramus that flowers are the finest of sapphires, which would lead him to believe that vegetable life is simply the consistency of crystal or matter carried out to infinity. The more one seeks to depict Christ as a genius, the further off he is, if Christ indeed is God. Likewise, to study the higher forms of apes is to widen the gap between them and man who is not a more complex pithecanthropus.

As Pascal would have said, you do not make a book by adding lines onto a line, nor by adding flesh to flesh that you obtain the spirit, nor by enhancing your intelligence that you love.

If, contrary to every possibility, God "became man" he would economize those excesses we credit to "heroes" and "saints." He would be so evident that he would be able to do things in such a way that people could not require these excesses of him any more than they could demand a line from Ingres or a stroke from Delacroix. They would not ask him to display through virtue or wisdom that type of excellence sought in men before unconditionally admiring them. On the other hand they would ask him to *be* truth and to *be* wisdom in an inimitable manner. Some critic once said that Beethoven was the greatest musician, but that Bach was music itself.

It is difficult to describe a profound impression, but I think I am correct in saying that the Gospels depict Jesus as being humanity itself and not as being the most perfect of men. We are not faced with a superman or one who fasts or a stigmatic. John the Baptist, who is pictured in the Gospel context as an ascetic of the Elias type so popular among the Jews of that period, emphasizes in Jesus' case the absence of all specialization in the doing of good. Jesus bears no resemblance either to the wisest of the Greeks, the most devout of the Jews, the most detached of Hindus, to Pythagoras, Solomon or Gandhi. Each petition in the *Our Father*, the prayer Jesus taught as *his* prayer, already existed in rabbinical tradition before his time.

Another impression taken from the Gospel is Jesus' indifference to events, his readiness to accept what each moment might bring. This indifference is directly contrary to what we see in those *lives* wherein the hero acts upon history, like Hercules, by his labors. Throughout his exceedingly brief career which ended abruptly Jesus never seemed in a hurry. His abstruseness and slowness, his rare manifestations, his furtive passage, final downfall and hurried passion, all these events steeped in paradox that seemed to go wrong and were so contrary to what the prophets did, are justified in the God-made-man. Why should God try to use time to its fullest or perform great deeds in time? It is enough that he exist in time, that he endure it, that he spend it, that he appear before several privileged ones and say: I AM.

His life hardly seemed extraordinary. His active life was very short. And, except for the miracles, it was a simple life. The passion itself was brief and not hideous. Even in this very passion there was some uncertainty: the angel, the cross-bearer, his mother, the vinegar, his death which was a speedy one when you consider that the crucified usually writhed on the cross for several days before relief in death.

If for a moment we think of Jesus as God (an incomprehensible thing, *mysterium fidei*), we begin to see that, being eternally able to choose from many modes of temporal existence, he wanted neither an heroic life nor a visibly ascetical or solitary one, nor a dramatic one like Jeremiah's, nor a long life, nor a life filled with accomplishments or one consummated in extreme old age, like John the Evangelist's. He desired only an ordinary human life, one that would be quickly terminated as soon as the essential act had been accomplished, his testimony given. Time was an unimportant factor in the manifestation of this divine essence. It was simply the dignity and fullness of suffering, not its length and agony. Had Leonardo da Vinci painted a hundred canvases, would he be any the greater? It was enough for him, and also Pascal, to prove to himself that he could solve some very difficult problems. What is original does not have to be multiple. Does number add to oneness?

When I make a thorough effort to think of the divine essence becoming one of us without ceasing to be itself, I can sound out and justify certain peculiarities I perceive in the Gospel.

I would go so far as to say, without being paradoxical, that divinity unites Jesus to man. An exceptional man alienates himself from others because of his very greatness which makes other people realize that they are incapable of rising to such heights.

If a great man stoops to our level (for example when Napoleon tweaked someone's ear or when Louis XIV spoke with perfect politeness to a commoner) one has the impression that he is playing the intimate. But we are continually on more than intimate terms with divinity. By divinity I mean the utterly holy and independent source of every existence, the creator of this being contemplated as possible from eternity. This relationship, though obscure, is enveloped in our impression of our existence. The Gospel brings out this very coexistence of two unique beings. The infinite remains an unknown source, a boundless center without countenance in the ordinary life of each of us. But thanks to the evangelical Incarnation, God has a form, a voice, a presence, so that assenting to the divinity of Jesus, which is a complexity (as putting an infinite quantity in certain calculations), becomes a way to simplify it all.

Divinity and Miracle

I wish to return once more to that embarrassment of the mind in view of the abundance of the miracles and the lack of a control apparatus in each particular case.

Now let us talk the problem from another angle and suppose for an instant, by the right every mind has to suppose incomprehensibility as a principle of explanation, that Jesus is God. Being God, he is the creator of natures. As John says, he is the *Logos* through whom everything has been created; he is, as the *Epistle to the Hebrews* proclaims, the one by whom the ages (*aeons*) have been made. What difference is it whether he does or does not exercise the power he possesses? It is a question of opportunity, of convenience, of "economy" as the Greek Fathers insisted.

If Christ possesses this divine nature, unless we suppose him bound to regularity or to the simplicity of his ways by those elegant conventions so dear to Malebranche, it is probable that Jesus-God will exercise this power by an outpouring of love or by pity for the apathy in the face of this too constant mirror of the law, of nature, which hides God,

If God exists, and if Jesus of Nazareth is God, it is clear that the possibility of some miracle or other can no longer be questioned. Everything is possible, except the ridiculous, if it is measured by the wisdom whose tranquil, slow and discreet, humble but irradiant work we see in the cosmos. It is likely that God may manifest himself in this second complete universe that is the humanity of Jesus in the same way he manifests himself in the cosmos — usually by concealing himself in inverse appearances and revealing himself only to those, says Pascal, whom he wishes to call into his service.

A Reversal of the Perspectives

If Jesus is God, then everything changes direction, not only in the Gospel but in human history, in our attitude towards the universe and the situation of this isolated planet. For he who before was but a point in history now becomes the center of history. He was a passer-through, an episode, and now he is immobile and the fixed axis around whom all else revolves. This is what Saint Paul thought, and his theology might be

said to consist in drawing out every consequence of Christ's
equality to God.

This is a revolution of thought that changes the direction
of the rotation of things. It is much more intimate than what
Kant took pride in when he compared himself to Copernicus.
From here on out we must call the creature-Jesus Creator —
we must call the mutable and historical Jesus improbable
and eternal. He was only a privileged point in history and
now we must call him the center of history. Actually, this
is the only overturning of appearances which really deserves
to be called "dialectic of history." Perhaps Hegel transposed
into his universal history and logic what he had learned of
the mystery of Jesus during his theological youth. Perhaps
the dialectic which the Marxists have placed at the center of
everything in perception and in being is the ultimate
laicization.

The Relationship Between Event and Mystery

Now I am ready to ask what the connection is between
the event of the Resurrection and the mystery of divinity.
The two sustain each other.

We have largely reduced the number of difficulties
stemming from the Resurrection though our reflection on
divinity and the reasons for positing it. How is a body united
to divinity to be thought of as touched by death? The probability arises that he may have been preserved from corruption
and even that he may have shown himself to his followers
in a way we cannot imagine. I would even state that the
idea of a man being equal to God includes confusedly the
concept of glorified body. On the other hand if the Resurrection did actually occur, we can see that it would dispose the
human intellect to think the unthinkable about a man seen
living after his death, living a sublime life. We can also see
how this event, actually experienced, might cause people to

suddenly recall those veiled statements in which Jesus proclaimed that he was God.

The event has not led to the mystery, but it has thrown some light on, and given some force to, the virtual revelation of the mystery.

We begin to suspect that the two problems of *event* and *mystery* can never be separated. To suffuse the event in its fullest sense into the mystery of God is in turn to shed light upon the event. In this way we avoid giving Christianity the appearance of a cult founded upon a marvel isolated in a nature and history.

One of the most significant passages in Saint John's Gospel is his narration of Jesus' apparition to Thomas. It shows how the first reflective Christians understood this substantial connection between event and mystery. Thomas represents doubt — a twofold doubt: doubt about the Resurrection, doubt about the divinity. Had Thomas believed in the Resurrection would he have admitted the divinity? If he had believed in the divinity, he surely would have believed those who saw the Risen Jesus. But Jesus showed himself so that Thomas could experience him, and at that very moment Thomas called him "his Lord and his God."

Also, if we are not to become slaves to a particular order and if we are to show this reciprocity, we must, in accordance with the expositions we use, choose one or the other of these two courses and vary the other in which the two unknowns of historical algebra are presented.

In an earlier work I began with the *Divinity* and proceeded to the *Resurrection*.[1] Now I am following the most common order, one that is also most in keeping with the actual development of faith among the apostles and the first witnesses. It seems that they only began to equate Jesus and God after the Resurrection.

---

1. Le Problème de Jésus, II, pp. 47-54.

Possible Plurality of the Incarnation
Excerpt from One of Olivier's Letters

"If the Incarnation exists in the sense faith understands it, you are right to say that it is in itself more important than creation. There is more in God's taking on a human form than in the unfolding of matter and life we call the Universe, even more than in the "rational plant." Here I agree with you: if one were to reflect upon what the idea of Incarnation implies, one would be led to *reverse* the order of all the problems. One could no longer say "The world was created so that God might become incarnate." But rather, "God, wanting to unite himself to his work in the most intimate way possible, made the universe and the ascending order of species and the development of religion in mankind so that this Incarnation could at a certain moment be possible." Actually this amounts to saying that the Universe is a machine for turning out gods, as Bergson wrote in his last published work, if by *gods* one means the saints united to Christ.

"Let me tell you what bothers me immensely. I am astounded that, from all possible places and moments, God selected this universe, this humanity for, when all is said and done, so short a time. What are two thousand years in relation to those millions of years which measure the duration of living species? That is my chief difficulty. It amounts to saying what the judges in Galilee thought (with good reason): that the idea of a God-man presupposes that this place and this moment are privileged. Now everything suggests that this privileged place did not exist. That is too nice. That is too easy to invent.

Because of what the sciences show us, people today refuse to believe that man is the center of the universe, the focal point of evolution. They see it as unworthy of God's wisdom that he would expend so much wasted energy to obtain practically by statistical chance what is taking place on one satellite of the Sun. Besides, it is easy to explain that man

thought himself the center of the universe and imagined that
God had pre--------him. . . ."

Excerpt from a Reply

"...and I also think that if the physical universe is as
vast as modern astronomy contends, if there are millions of
galaxies, billions of suns (in spite of the extreme improbability
of our planetary system and the persistency in it of some
highly unstable conditions for life), I find it hard to imagine
that this very improbability might not have occurred other
times.

I realize very keenly that there is always a great splendor
in the workings of God. And I know also that there is more
in one single thought or in one single love than in the infinite
mass of matter. But it seems to me as well that the idea of
absolute wisdom implies a proportionality between the power
expended and its effect, and that the physical universe is too
huge to have only this earth and this humanity for its sole
purpose of existence. The pedestal is far too grand for the
statue.

I find nothing wrong with the opinion that in the indefinite reaches of time and space there might well be other
results similar to our own — perhaps superior to our own!
In short, other "rational plants."

The Bible is remarkable in that while it is above all concerned with the earth, mankind and especially with the
Hebrew branch of the human family, *the axis by which the
Spirit passes over this planet,* it never limits God's action
to this axis.

Why could not God communicate himself elsewhere in
forms impossible for us to imagine but not to conceive? Saint
Thomas thought that each angel was an entirely different
species. Since there are many choirs of angels, why could
there not be other rational species? And to return to your
criticism, why could not God unite himself to those creatures

in a way analogous to this union we call the Incarnation? Of course, the Incarnation *can only take place once* in our history, but by what right should we limit God's action to this one history? We are entering here into an abyss. The divinity of Jesus is a depth which, to quote David, calls out to others.

It will always be a touchy problem for us to know which of the two hypotheses involves more anthropomorphism. You imply, I think, that to look upon earth as the center of the universe, to view human history as the only history, and to see Christ as the only Incarnation of the Word, is to be anthropomorphic. Is this so absolutely certain? I wonder.

If you suppose a multiplication of universes and histories, of biospheres and anthropospheres in order to render creation more worthy of infinite power, is this not still to imagine God according to our human modes, *for whom power and profusion are one and the same?* And must we perhaps think that space and time and everything contained in space and time are like landscapes, and the present moment like an identical oblation always renewed with Christ as its center?

What reality do space, time and number have for God? Can the One truly repeat himself?

I leave to you, Olivier, with these unfathomable problems, but how good it is to face them sometimes for a brief instant before imitating Job standing before the Eternal One and putting his hand over his mouth.

Part Five

Jesus – History and Existence

CHAPTER XII

Locating Jesus in History

Until now my examination has centered only upon Jesus, that is, upon Jesus abstracted. I had to weed out the rest of history and concentrate upon this instantaneous passage described by the Gospel. I have considered the marks left by some very improbable events distributed over a period of about fifteen years (as Tacitus observes, fifteen years is a long time). If you merely consider the original shock, barely two years, this passage of Jesus. . . .

Surely Jesus can be abstracted, for everything else can since it is the mind which abstracts. The mind's most familiar operation, the one by which we learn consists in focussing attention to one point to the exclusion of all else. But it is difficult to isolate Jesus; his nature is to be *before* and *after* the moment in which he was. Above, beneath, beyond, he eludes us from all sides.

Saint Paul's example is noteworthy. He was the first man *to think in terms of* Jesus, if it is true that to think is to place a part in a whole, a moment in a process of development, a being in the scheme of beings. Saint Paul knew what Jesus was according to history. He supposed that it was known, but his attention centers upon Jesus omnipresent in the continual movement of history and absorbing finally all of history into himself.

A study of Jesus will aways lead you further. It cannot
be restricted to first conclusions. Jesus (and this is why we
so readily think of him as Idea and as Myth) is not like any
ordinary historical being who cut a wake behind him. He
possesses a superexistence which makes him remain a sort of
eternal first mover for the history of spirits living in time.

He, doing practically nothing at all, in a very short space
of time toppled the unshakeable: religion.

Jesus and the Earlier Religions

He overturned the two seemingly indestructible religions
of the Romans and the Jews. Look at them. For two divergent
reasons they should have been equally eternal. The Roman
by its connection with the State, with the fabrication which
created gods in it, with sex, with the cosmos, with the basest
and most sublime elements in man wonderfully brought together in harmony, with the protection of tradition, law,
censure: combining the senses, reason, faith, hope, ceremonies
and authority, holding therefore every promise for survival.

But from the point of view of faith, the Jewish religion
rested upon even securer foundations and had more of a
chance to survive. The Creator founded this religion and
bestowed an exclusive eternal alliance upon it. It enjoyed
twenty centuries of accomplishments and improbable successes. Her thinking soared higher than the Greek philosophies.
Developing in precision and in purity it was blessed with a
communication through the prophets to the very Source of
all things.

These two religions passed away. The Roman one dis-
integrated into a superstition kept alive in the countryside and
lingered long in its senility. The Jewish religion on the other
hand was ennobled, elevated and finally dissipated in the
heights. It is sublimated in Jesus' religion which accomplishes
in him and in his followers all that the former faith proclaimed
and promised without distinctly knowing it. Judaism, its

dynamism crushed, continues to this day as a witness to
suffering and expectation.

Obviously the work of Jesus' followers alone could not
have achieved this undeniable double effect. There had to
be some Energy behind the scene — some Energy proportionate
to the results: This X we call Christ.

Breaking of Duration into an Absolute Past and Future

It is a remarkable thing that Jesus is inserted, enrooted
and incardinated into duration as no historical person has
ever been. To be sure he is not the only man from whom
everything begins or starts anew, especially with regard to
the computation of time. But he is the only one who breaks
duration into two parts around him, creating behind him an
absolute past, creating ahead of himself an indefinite future,
and filling this human duration with such force that though
he may be doubted and even reduced to nothing, it would
nevertheless be ridiculous to wait for, or even to conceive,
either a new Jesus or a Super-Jesus.

The great figures of history come and go like meteors.
Certainly they are bound up with the conditions which prepared for them, sustained them and limited them. Their
actions often have very long-lasting results, but they could
be obliterated without setting the direction of general history
off course. One can conceive that comparable figures would
arise from roughly the same set of circumstances.

Not so with Jesus. His relationship to Jewish history is
unique of its kind and will always remain so. An examination
of this history in a retrospective light shows it to be entirely
orientated around him to the extent that it ceased being a
progressive history when he appeared. Jesus took upon himself, lived, summed up and recapitulated in himself what
had been conceived, prayed for, established and suffered by
an entire religious people, *the* worshipping people *par excellence* obsessed with the idea of truth and justice.

One cannot avoid asking himself how the action of Jesus exercised contrary to the march of time can be explained in an atheistic conception. In every period of Western history I see the human mind searching for ideas to translate the unique relationship of one people to a single being, of a present to a past. Consider what Saint Paul said in his letter to the Romans about the meaning of Israel. Look at what all the Fathers, from Saint Irenaeus to Saint Augustine, had to say on the symbolical and preparatory aspect of the Old Testament. Recall Pascal's mathematical conception of *"Figuratifs"* and what Cournot and Newman wrote on development. Consider also Paul Claudel's wonderment over the allegorical sense of Scripture. Without accepting this last type of exegesis which has value only if you already believe, we can say that over the past fifty years the researchers have deepened the nature of this Gospel preparation and we have a more comprehensive idea of it. For the verses, characters, rites and events are not alone in vaguely symbolizing the Christ to come (accounts which the unbeliever can easily dismiss as imaginary). Rather, it is the integral and unfolding history of an entire people devoted to a moral God, a unique God closely related to the God of "Philosophers and scholars" which through very probable disasters and highly improbable solutions, always awakens man to the knowledge of the Transcendent and to all the consequences of this existence for social and individual conduct: the equality of men, equal justice for all, sanctions beyond the grave, the universality of religion. So, he who places his faith and certitude in the future, in spite of the denials by transitory experience, awaits a blessing for his race in the presence of an exceptional but not unknowable Being, one who is even more and more knowable. And the "men of God," the prophets, describe the face of this being under the (otherwise irreconcilable) aspects of glory, sorrow and humiliation.

It is not, therefore, a question here of an episodical passage such as the passage of some king, prophet, some mythological

being, or the Essene Teacher of Righteousness, or a saint, a
sage, a hero, a leader of a school or a religion. Nor is it a
question of a marvelous episode like halting the course of
the sun or bringing a dead man to life. Jesus is not accidental,
he does not act through prodigies: *he accomplishes*. His is
linked to previous human history along that spiritual axis to
which this history always returns in order to again progress
to its source and to take its flight.

But Jesus is not some point or other on this axis: he is
that towards whom this axis turns and who gives it its propul-
sion toward the future. If this is one chance in a million or an
appearance due to illusion, it must be called a well-founded
one: how can we satisfactorily explain the situation of Jesus in
relation to this force which seems to lead up to him (the
Jewish religion dries up after him as though it had borne its
fruit) in relation to the force animating all of history after him?
This development stretched out over forty centuries is contrary to the laws governing historical phenomena. It seems
we have here the action of an anti-chance which, instead of
letting coincidences happen and fail to happen according to
static laws, arranges them about a generative axis and an
historical personage who, nevertheless, occupied only a very
small part of time.

In particular, what Jesus taught about man and God
reached, without studied care or progress, such a state of
perfection that no one has been able to add to it since. We
may deny his message *en bloc*, or pick it apart or obscure it,
but if we do not deny that divinity can communicate itself
fully to man, it is on this single point about this single being
that minds for twenty centuries have been discussing to try
to find out whether this communication did actually take
place. Progress in moral and spiritual teaching (I am not
speaking of their application which is subject to the law of
great numbers and of varying effectiveness) from then on
can no longer be sought in an excess of light, in a "myth" of

superior value and dignity. Henceforth there is a fixed point
similar to a seed that grows but which never assumes a new
nature and develops nothing beyond what it first possessed.

Now and Forever

It is a curious thing that the first witnesses foresaw before
they experienced it and were deeply aware of the impossibility
of change and further addition to doctrine and example. Their
sense of this perfection realized both *now and forever* would
be akin to what we would sense in the presence of a perfect
work of art (if one existed), or, better still, a demonstrated
theorem. Though they lacked proof, they were absolutely
certain from the very beginning that they possessed something *eternally singular* given them this one time only with
no appeal to future ages, with no possibility of progression
and perfection — given them once and forever: *hapax*.

They proclaimed what actually happened: the excellence
of this way and its strange ability to benefit by contact with
what ought to have destroyed it, persecutions and obstacles
without, human weakness within. Though they were but a
mere handful of mediocre, uncultured men with no expansive
horizons or talent, they knew with an almost unwonted assurance that they already were the conquerors of everything.
And this they knew not by ecstasy or fervor, but in the same
way we know an axiom.

When a critical mind given to denying explains all these
things by the improbable encounter or several causal series,
as Epicurus explained the order of bodies by the coming
together of atoms thrown into the void, he may doubtless
give a purely logical development from the fact of Jesus to
the instant T. But he does not explain how this instant continues in other instants in the flow of time after him. I am
speaking here of *history* on its highest plane, not the history
of the masses, but of the spiritual elite.

Similar Cases

One will say without doubt that religious history presents many great events, themselves improbable, which have had an immense expansion. Take for example the cult of Mithra, the coming of Mohammed and the triumph of Islam, or the success of Lenin and his associates which was undreamed of before 1917 and which my generation bore witness to. But even if we retain these last two somewhat analogous examples we could not assimilate them to the Gospel which promised nothing material and earthly except persecution. Today a Marxist will believe he is witnessing some transformation similar to that of the Gospel, for Marxism also introduces new values, it also is going to renew the face of the earth. But we can ask whether the ancient world could have been seduced by Marx without the Christian preparation, without the idea of universal justice. This is tantamount to saying that the strength of Marxism stems in part from what it kept of diffused Judaism and Christianity. And, for what it brings of itself, the negation of eternal values, it resembles the persecuting Empires. The future will say who survives the other, Marx or Jesus.

The prolonged existence of Jesus renewed in exceptional people is an abnormal phenomenon and one not to be found in the many civilizations we know of.

This renewed and prolonged existence of Jesus is not historical in the classical sense, for it does not leave any direct, palpable, cultural and monumental traces that can be studied. On the surface one sees nothing of this hidden Christ acting in men's minds to delicately influence, vivify, modify or sublimate. As Bossuet said, Jesus is without influence, or rather his influence is only manifested by the action he inspires. I have said that the division of Western history seems to give Jesus an advantage by computing time as starting with him. In reality, however, this division of time is unfortunate. Our schools either neglect Jesus or we suppose him already known. One can be a doctor of history without ever having directly tackled the very problem of his existence. Whether in the realm of being or in the realm of knowledge, it appears that Jesus lives in history as though being absent from it. It is strange that the computation of time begins with him and that he is so hidden.

Jesus' Influence on Ideas

Yet no sooner does one look for the source of spiritual history then one realized the influence of Jesus. Every idea we live was inspired by him, not that it was created by him, but rather each one has received a certain balance and plenitude from him.

From among a great many concepts I have selected two that are the objects of heated discussion today: the concept of *love* and the concept of *history*. The question I raise is this: what would they be outside Christ and his restoring influence?

Jesus and the Idea of Human Love

This tender and noble sentiment that forever binds one man and one woman together was never absolutely unknown to mankind. But what we mean by *love* implies an equality between man and woman. Outside the current of history centered around Jesus, or by him, woman remains a servant, sometimes privileged, but essentially inferior to man. The woman of old was either part of the domestic organism, the "matron" mother of citizens who fulfilled the social role, or she was the mistress of the crossroads or the high places who filled the role of Eros. Even Plato accepted this division of functions; for him woman was only the occasion of the fire of Eros which ascends toward the beautiful: she was not the *beloved,* the one-and-only, the *dilecta* of the *Canticle of Canticles.*

It took Jesus' coming to re-establish the original unity so that woman, instead of being *dissociated* as "mother" and as mistress," becomes united to man and united to herself, so that she may become once and for all herself: at once she who gives life and she who is beloved. Wherever this synthetizing thought, resulting from the doctrine of Jesus, loses its edge, we see the essence of woman being once again dissociated into two parts. And these two incomplete types of woman reappear, the one given up to generation without being cherished, the other condemned to pleasure without being respected.

We must add that the invisible influence of Jesus has something more to contribute to the role of sex in the spiritual life: for, while honoring this new couple of father and mother who are going to found a new community, Jesus, by this example, raises above marriage (as a gold coin is higher in value than its bronze change) the virginity of those who consecrate themselves to the Kingdom. Almost without saying it, he *re-establishes* human love and *establishes* divine love without setting one in opposition to the other. He compliments the one by the other. That is difficult to do. Outside the zone where the spirit of Jesus is still alive we do not see this harmony attained.[1]

Jesus and the Idea of History

Contemporary thought, as I have depicted it often in this work, as soon as it found itself in possession of the concepts of *history* and *time,* applied them to the existence of Jesus in order to reduce this existence, to dissolve it (and it is a fact that Jesus suffers at first from the light he sheds). The nineteenth century confused Jesus in the stream of

---

1. I refer you to my book **An Essary on Human Love.**

becoming and made of him the moment of a necessary dialectic. The nineteenth century explained him entirely by the mixture of environment and chance.

But who brought to rational man the germs of the notion of a *truly* historical time, if not the Jewish people in their ascent to Jesus, if not Jesus himself, who is this singular Event? Before Jesus and in civilizations not inspired by him, history is reduced to a succession of events which begin over and over again in cycles so that, for the ancient Greeks and the Hindus the "eternal wheel," so dear to Nietzsche, brings back time and again the same destinies. But such a conception which would multiply the birth and death of Jesus to infinity, which would oblige the saints to be reincarnated, is unacceptable to anyone who believes in the Being come once and for all. It is unacceptable to whoever accepts a *singular advent* which is also a definitive *event,* prepared for by a long and progressive élan, continued by the Church's unfolding. As Culmann has shown (in the spirit of Newman, Pascal and Saint Augustine) Christ brings us, through an indirect lighting, the intellectual light which establishes history, this history that we must conceive, after him, not as a *wheel* but as an arrow, having a beginning and an end, launched into being by the Creator, creating time by its passing.

This may justify the creative conservation we call progress and which people today are correct to consider as the ideal, although they err as to man's capacity for accomplishing progress. Thus, Jesus was in fact the establisher of the idea of history conceived as a centered, continued and ascending current emphasized with events that have a posterity.[2]

We could show through other examples that Jesus is the very root of many of the great Ideas in which we contemporaries "live, move and are." Only, since people no longer believe in him who is the salt and yeast of these Ideas do they

---

2. I refer you to my book **Le Temps et l'Eternité** (Aubier).

degrade them in their hands: they contaminate or they dissociate.

Right and Fact

By *right,* mankind should have been able to respect woman as person. *In fact,* outside Christ she is not respected as such. *By right,* mankind should have been able to carry out its own history, its progress, its individual or social duration. *In fact,* outside Christ it is not fully carried out.

Everything suggests that mankind required some improbable help, not to discover the order of grace, but simply to find itself, to understand its own existence and proper nature. The experience of more than forty centuries among all peoples and historical lines clearly shows the lack of consistency between what should have happened and what actually did. Everything suggests that man was incapable of being fully man without this influence. Everything suggests that the Idea of Jesus is the element of equilibrium which is not part of the structure, or at least which does not seem to be more than the other stones and which, nonetheless, is the keystone. It is not, strictly speaking, he who makes, but he who perfects and re-shapes, he who recapitulates. People would be justified to reject relationship with Christ if he alienated, as Feuerbach and Marx said he did. But he does not *alienate,* he *constitutes.*

The Constituent Work of Jesus

He *constitutes,* but without seeming to; he harmonizes without this harmony becoming visible. When Father Lagrange compared the Gospels and showed their substantial and invisible convergence beneath the contradictions in detail, he loved to quote Heraclitus: "A secret harmony is greater than a manifest harmony."

There are actually two kinds of harmony: the first of which is the synthesis manifest in the Pantheon's architecture, in the mathematically calculated poetry of Virgil's *Eclogues* and in the forms of classical art which have always, and will aways, return after periods of decadence.

But there is also a second kind of synthesis and harmony. It can be seen in a dissymmetrical figure, in a face twisted in grief, in baroque architecture, in uneven cadences, in nearly every one of our country landscapes — in Pascal's *Pensées*, in *Hamlet*, in *Faust, or* in the works of Paul Claudel. The bond uniting the parts of these works consists in the affinity of each fragment with the mind of its creator, without there being an apparent order, but only clashes, sharp transitions, unnecessary repetitions, ellipses and gaps instead. Christ's synthesis respects each of the elements it brings together; it is a discreet synthesis proposed to every generation, to every essence, to every conscience (and rarely accepted and fulfilled), but which remains present in man as a possibility and a reproach. With the "nature of things" and "the community of persons" it is a third world where the astonishment of a Greek sage is confirmed: "How is it that things form a unity and yet each one is a distinct something and itself?" In the same spirit Pascal observed that our art fits one thing into another, whereas nature leaves each to itself, each to take its own place.

Jesus did not invent these ways of conceiving and feeling. But he has preserved their essence and so ordered them that they develop according to their nature. Before him this essence remained vulnerable. But after his coming it will never be possible to fall backwards. Henceforth, we possess the means for becoming aware of interruptions and failures and disintegration. The word *henceforth* is more deeply mysterious and beautiful in this context, I think, than anywhere else. It can always be said about Jesus: HENCEFORTH.

Kittel's German dictionary[3] is an admirable instrument for gauging precisely the interior renewal of language.

The friend of words and the ideas words evoke will not pass up this book. He will find in Kittel a tool of extraordinary precision with which to measure the imprinting of Jesus upon human thinking. The words in the New Testament were used by the Greeks and the Greek-speaking Jews; these words receive an essentially new meaning. By using them Jesus added his own little twist. Take the word *love*, the word *justice*, the words *Church, Father, apostle* and so many others like the words *spirit* and *sin*, and even simpler words like *bread, heaven*, the words meaning *law, king, true, beautiful, good, pure*, or *eternal*. You are constantly aware of new wine being poured into old wineskins, seeds being planted and leaven being mixed with dough: so many other images of the Gospel. Here again I compare what Jesus did to these words with what the poet does with words in everyday usage: he keeps them by instilling an original meaning into them. But the change, though imperceptible, has become the rule after Jesus ascended into heaven. And yet if one compares the New Testament to the Old, or to a "literature" such as Greek literature, it is but the size of an atom: in a library, in the Budé collection, it occupies the place of one tiny volume.

The Universe of Jesus

This shows once again how utterly improbable it is that Christianity was either an upsurge of mysticism or the intersecting of points of chance. How is one to suppose that the

---

3. **Theological Dictionary of the New Testament**, Gerhard Kittel (Eerdmans, 1963). This admirable work is the product of Protestant exegesis. Only some of the set is in existence. Certain key concepts have been treated in the set **Bible Key Words** of which four volumes have been issued to date — Tr.

elan or the chance can effect a simultaneous and convergent change that is at once unnoticed and replete with consequences, in the sense of so many ordinary expressions? It is like creating a universe. For I call universe a mass of related elements forming a whole, having a center, an axis, an invisible and main threshold. A language is a universe because, in languages as in works of art, the meaning of the words are maintained and corroborated and are realized. Many sub-universes can exist within this one universe: the works of Homer, Shakespeare, Balzac, Proust — these have their own gravitation bound to the gravitation of the whole. Such is the language of Paul or John. But in contradistinction to all other languages, for they are transitory, I believe that the language of the spirit which unites spirits of the highest order, even the adversaries of the name Christian (Spinoza, Hegel, for example) will never perish. And it will save from oblivion every language that speaks it, as we see it saved Aramaic and Coptic as it has already saved Latin.

CHAPTER XIII

Accord with Existence

THERE is another and more secret reference by which we can situate Jesus into the order of being. It is the way in which the Gospel relates to life. Now, by the vague word *life* I mean the experience each one of us has of his own destiny.

Let us try to discover what is involved in the hypothesis that *God is present among men*. How are we to understand his attributes, for example attributes such as wisdom and power (since the moderation and proportionality of wisdom stand in opposition to God's capacity to do all things), transcendence by which God is above everything that is conceivable and desirable, and immanence by which he is more profound and more intimate than all of creation? Or, to take some divine qualities and values which are more accessible to our human modes of thinking, how are we to conceive that strength and gentleness can be portrayed; or the firmness of justice and the condescendence of love, or the joy of existing and of bringing into existence and a kind of melancholy rising from the fatal frailty of everything that is not Himself? Once again let us endeavor to present what might be conceivable inventions by which love — that which is most essential in God — could be known to us or lived among us. Without going into detail, I think that a mind which had no knowledge of history or the details of history, but which on the other hand knew of God and had refined the idea of God in itself and which (to give a limited, absurd but not impossible case) had tried to define the characteristics of an eventual presence of God among men would arrive at a schema and an outline of the Gospel.

The Gospel attributes to God those characteristics which an absolute being ought to possess if he were ever to become personally visible. It is a fact that the relationships between Creator and created, such as reason conceives them, are found in the relationships between Christ and souls which have their life and subsistence in him. Newman put it this way: "He is a second creator of the world, condescending to repeat in human form for our contemplation this personal world which makes the morning stars to sing in chorus and the children of God to leap with joy." The Gospel does not advance this resemblance, but it assumes it: "He who sees me, sees also my Father," summarizes the Gospel of Saint John — a Gospel filled with the idea that nature is the figure of grace, that beyond creation there is an invisible super-creation in Jesus.

Criterion for Souls

All this could certainly be explained by assuming that some unknown genius had made himself the personal rule to represent a human being thinking, feeling and acting like the Creator is supposed to.

Perhaps any Gospel scene could be explained in this fashion, for example when Jesus defies the elements and appears himself as the creator or multiplier. But this type of explanation would fail miserably if the Gospel were viewed in its entirety, in its context, in its rhythm and atmosphere, in its normal human and ordinary aspect. In the Gospel, as in creation, God seems to manifest himself through the lowly. As Saint Paul said, many years before the redaction of the

Gospels, speaking of the impression these accounts left with those who read them, he who was "by nature God" took on "the nature of a slave." Furthermore, not even the boldest man has dared to venture the impossible hypothesis that an author could have fashioned the Gospel by making it a rule to transpose the manner, tone and attitude of God into human history.

But then how is one to satisfactorily explain the Gospel's correlation with the authentic experience of existence? How is one to explain that the Gospel is verified on the spiritual plane by uneducated people who possess a profound interior life, as has been the case for twenty centuries in all strata of society and in every civilization? Why does the Gospel not correspond only to one idea, that of a man who would also be God — but also to existence as we know it with its great interplay of situations?

More than any rational argument, it is this which is the central nerve of the faith. If the average believer were questioned he would say something to this effect, "No man has spoken like this man." The believer's reaction shows that in this text, in this story (and in this story alone) he experiences a quality which cannot be attributed to man's creative capacity, neither does it correspond with what we expect of God if even against all possibility he was or became man. That is the criterion for simple souls who are neither bedimmed not materialized. It preserves them from doubt when they see a learned man doubting alongside them. By making a comparison of what men vaguely expect, what the "Unknown God" writes secretly in their heart, with what they explicitly find in the Gospel, they sense an inexplicable harmony, a harmony which is for them a word uttered in silence.

The awareness of the moral beauty which the Gospel offers each new reader was even then a preliminary proof, for beauty dwells in all things as a precursory sign.

The Gospel Conceived as Justification of Existence

One may go even further and say that the Gospel justifies existence. Our age, more than any other in the past, has become conscious of the absurdity of being hurled into existence, to be obliged to undergo accidental changes, to have an existence limited to one place in a mutable and shifting setting, to be doomed to death. The idea of a creator of existence cannot justify all the *accidental* forms of our existence because there is an infinite and ironical distance between this transcendent God and his work in man. To put it another way: for many minds weighted down by existence and by evil, the idea of God cannot of itself justify existence as they know it. Now, one can say that human existence with all its faults and failures is justified by the Incarnation described in the Gospels.

If God had not taken charge of *all* the aspects of this existence, if the supreme obligations (especially death) had not been taken on by the Being who has given us being, if the difficult *law* had not become the easy *faith*, if history had no axis, then human existence would have been possible but hard-going, for the sin in it would not have been redressed.

I have thought also that without the Incarnation the beseiging problem of evil would vastly increase. Had there been no Incarnation, then anyone who suffers and who accepts this suffering in which the Creator has no share is morally more beautiful than God. Atheistic humanists express this opinion in our times for, as they see it, the man of sorrows is greater than God since he gives himself up to absolute evil, whereas God created evil without taking a share in it. In a world so unaffected by good, the Infinite's contact with the harshness, the burdens and the cruelty of the human condition, the fact that he took upon himself all possible evil, justifies creation and removes from "the existence of God" all stigma of scandal inherent in it to a mind infatuated by perfection.

The Sublime Surprise

Thus the Gospel confirms the experience of life, at the same time as this experience finds itself confirmed by the Gospel. It responds to the problem we ask ourselves: Is God present in his work? Is he present in history? And we must add that the Gospel answers it in a way that is at once satisfying and surprising.

In the Gospel there is always some excess, for it surpasses what would seem necessary. And if the word *sublime* translates this "going beyond what is expected," then it can truly be said that the Gospel's atmosphere is sublime.

The Gospel surpasses the bounds of the expected, yet at first sight it is less than what one would expect and it seems unworthy of our concept of the "divine." But we perceive something deeper in the Gospel and we cannot help but say that it surpasses our wildest fancies of the Almighty. We experience something analogous to this phenomena when we encounter new art forms which scandalize us in the beginning, but when we have accepted them they open up a whole new world of beauty. The astonishing thing here is the disconcerting manner in which God reveals himself so indistinctly. Bergson placed the discovery of the "divine humility" at the very apex of the mystical life, above and beyond ecstasy. And Pascal said that God always hides himself in nature, then in the humanity of Jesus and finally in the eucharistic bread. One might be tempted to say that God's greatest glory, his personal delight, would be to show and reveal himself through a kind of absent, enigmatic and compassionate presence.

In my opinion then, along with critical reflection, the most authentic motive for the common man's belief in Jesus, his constant, discreet and progressive confirmation which grows in him throughout his lifetime to the degree that it is calming, and is in accord with our nature. Sometimes I think Mallarmé's definition of poetry might be applied to the

Gospel: "Poetry is the expression of the mysterious meaning of the aspects of existence written in human language reduced to its essential rhythm. Thus it endows our sojourn with authenticity and constitutes the sole spiritual task."

If there were no accord with our nature, Jesus would long ago have gone the way of Apollo, Osiris or Mithra, and his ashes would have joined the dust of creeds outworn. But those who think they have buried him are still quite apprehensive. If the person, the teaching of Jesus, the events of his life had not corresponded with what every man desires in the best and most hidden recess of himself, people long ago would have stopped talking about him. If the finest souls in their greatest efforts and their loftiest states of thought, of love, of acquiescence to love, had not found a norm for growth in what they knew of Jesus, then Jesus would have the same kind of reputation today as Diotima of Mantinea or Apollonius of Tyana, as Mohammed or Buddha. He would at best be numbered among the mystics. He would not be their model, their measuring rod, their master. If the Gospels did not correspond to what every poor man experiences, either in the duties it imposes or in its understanding of misery, failure and grief (even before it is a question of recompense and hope), the name of Jesus would have ceased being uttered a long time ago.

I am fully aware that the subtle mind will balk and say that this fiction succeeded precisely because of Jesus's correspondence to our instinct of the boundless and our need for consolation. Jesus was dreamed up in accordance with human nature. The key fits the lock so well because the lock was fashioned first and the key was shaped after it. But what makes us think that this is how it happened. What genius, what group of geniuses, what combination of chance occurances could have produced this intimate and multiple correpondence universally felt, in spite of the wide differences among men, and becoming more profound with moral experience? What I have developed in this work concerning the limitations of the fabricative faculty can apply here: the reader could easily draft another quite different work.

Man's intuitions bear out the conclusions of criticism, and criticism in turn lends support to these intuitions. And perhaps the day will come when this difficult problem, the highly desirable agreement between the elite and the masses, between intelligence and common sense, will be realized. I am far-removed from Spinoza, Voltaire, Kant, Renan or Brunschvicg, who saw especially about Jesus, an immense interior difference between the attitude of the simple man and the competent man: the difference black and white — the *inferior* being protected only by "good will" and sincerity, not by the intellect. I have always considered the aristocratic conception that reserves salvation to critical knowledge or to innocent error a difficult one to defend.

We have had to wait until the twentieth century for the Gospel's accord with experience to have its full impact.

Actual State of the Problems

Until recently the world of documents was as unexplored as the globe was before the Conquistadors. One could always hope that the wisdom of the East — Egypt, China, India — would introduce a higher wisdom into the West. One could always hope that the rationalist influence on science, or a new secular and desperate godliness would be imposed on mankind, giving the Gospel either a finished, outmoded character, or simply the characteristics of an incomprehensible adventure, an inassimilable rule, an Eastern Jewish or Hellenic dream that has become meaningless, a believing humanity no longer in tune with our own.

It required three generations to catalog the best texts of the other religions. It was also necessary for secular wisdom, the rationalist ideal and humanitarian atheism to have the time and opportunity to show us the characteristics of a humanity finally delivered from superstition. Time has past. The impartial observer cannot say that this wisdom is anywhere nearer, nor that conditions are ripe for the advent of a superman or a new humanity.

CHAPTER XIV

Jesus and the Saints

LASTLY, we must pursue another path from experience and consider the mystics and religious connected with Jesus. Here again it should be plain that Jesus is extremely singular. He has always been present in thousands of consciences. Throughout every generation he has risen up people more attached to him than to themselves and who found in him the principle of their lives. Let us call these people by the traditional word *saints*. Going by appearances, I believe it can be said that Jesus is the only being in history who has had the privilege of engendering saints.

It is essential to define what is understood by *sanctity*, especially because sanctity is even less ascertainable than genius. Sanctity is something different from moral perfection which is a prerequisite for sanctity. But the saint is neither sage nor hero, for the sage and the hero are consciousnesses that depend upon themselves. Like the Jewish prophet, "the man of God," the saint is a man who not only has realized his eternal type in spite of his fall, but who also has effaced himself so as not to be anything but an instrument of divine causality. Hence, it is not surprising that every saint is so outstanding, as if each were an entirely new species without lineage.

It is possible to study, although the subject has hardly tempted critics and philosophers, what makes these Originals similar. This study would gradually lead us to define the relationship between the saint and Jesus. It is an immediate one. Saints do not beget other saints. Of course they, like great artists, sometimes have followers, but they are imitators. The saints teach them how to ascend, as they themselves have, towards the unique source who is Jesus, at first contemplated thanks to the Church's tradition, and then seized individually within themselves. This is how the saints form a body. Although each one is solitary and often, as I have said, without a genealogy, they are actually a city, a society, a communion. They respond to each other, they complement each other, and we must consider them as a totality. Then it can be seen vividly that they are rays and prolongations of Jesus. They do not imitate him in his mode as an historical being (as the disciple of Saint Francis of Assisi imitates his style of preaching and dress), but they imitate his interior life. For Jesus had a hidden existence in which he was alone with the Father, and this was the type of the relationship we could have with him. In a sense this relationship marks the Christian and the concrete man and, as Louis Lavelle wrote in his admirable study on sanctity: "In each man round about us there is a saint in potency.... The sanctity of the beggar and the king is not easily seen under the aspects of beggar and king, for sanctity is inseparable from a completely interior attitude which we attribute to it and which finds in us a mysterious echo: then the beggar and king resemble the unknown saint whom we daily rub shoulders with and do not realize it because there are no identification marks."

The saints are not content with this secret resemblance. Each saint reproduces, or rather radiates, one aspect of his model like a painter who can only capture his subject from one angle with few colors and according to the technique he was first taught.

That is why if the saints resemble Jesus, Jesus does not resemble them. In him there was no limitation or speciality.

To page through the lives of the saints, those partial imitations of his being, is to see that in his short lifetime on earth Jesus was at once everything which was reflected in so many ways: laborer, master, prophet, worshipper, slave, king, priest, contemplative, apostle, martyr, victim. Analyzing Jesus by the prism of the saints helps us to understand his proper and inimitable self. The saints are like the colors of the spectrum in relation to the light.

One cannot separate Jesus from saints of Jesus. They are, round about him, like latter-day witnesses and, in a sense, more than witnesses, since they revive him in silence in other times and in other circumstances, thereby making up for the absence of those few first-generation witnesses. The saints stretch this instant of the Incarnation throughout time.

Nothing like this is to be found anywhere else, even where history shows us founders, heroes, teachers, yogis. It is a question of something entirely different from the tradition of a school or a memory: it is a kind of continued existence through other beings.

When one thinks of humanity and its relationship to the infinite, one cannot help wishing that all the possible relationships between the consciousness and God be realized, that every kind of human perfection be projected into history — so that every possible form of action and patience can be justified by the models. This is most certainly the significance behind the invisible community of the saints.

In this invisible community there is, as it were, a new universe of spirits who belong to Jesus alone. And this universe is, above all others, knowable: for it is common to observe in Christian lands the life of these often humble and untutored consciousnesses who live only the Gospel. Then it seems that time contracts and the interval of twenty centuries is wiped away.

Naturally, the believer could insist that the Idea of Jesus is the source of these perfections and not the real Jesus. He could say that Jesus exists in these people as their principle, because man estranging himself through the influence of the Churches, concentrated everything in himself of goodness onto the image of Jesus. The unbeliever might say that the saint is actually adoring himself. Really, there is no other conceivable explanation if the negative position is taken. But does it correspond to actual moral experience? Can one suspend for Jesus alone the law of reason which dictates that the reality of the effect is to be found entirely in its cause?

CHAPTER XV

The Choice

I HAVE completed my examination to the best of my ability. I resolved to pass over non-essentials because excessive attention to minor details is detrimental to problems of this nature where nothing must veer one away from the *single necessary goal*. I wanted to avoid the obsession over details that is so peculiar to our times which are at once erudite and distressed. Knowledge and distress deflect one to little things and cause the important matters to be neglected.

This dogged research along the essential lines was within my range of competency which centers on the most general aspects of thought. I did not put myself above others, my work reflects the thought of a modest man no different from anyone else. I wanted to use common sense in areas until now reserved either to the technical, or to the assertions of the faith.

To my way of thinking, in this study and in many others as well, it seems that when all the avenues of approach have been diligently pursued and all the intersections have been crossed, we realize that there are only two directions to take.

One more crossroad lies ahead of me. It is a question whether the Jesus of faith is a product of the mind or a reality of history, whether Jesus is an Idea or whether he has an Existence, whether he is a myth or whether he has a history.

I have been deeply aware throughout this examination that at its completion I would have to make some such decision. This realization has followed me every step of the way. The time has come to describe this definitive choice, to see how much light enters in here and how much the will influences this decision, and how much I make use of it in one or the other determination. The human mind generally makes its decisions in a muddled light, in the torpor of habit or under the influence of enthusiasm. To choose is often simply to approve a choice you already have made within yourself by your body, your desire, your preferences for some thing or other. I do not scorn this. But since I have been using my reason, I find some enjoyment in defining the ultimate motive for my choice without condemning those who have chosen differently or who hesitate, but neither do I forget that my choice is alone fully reasonable.

Few would question that the idea of Jesus produced the effects I have described. This is a great fact of civilization. Undoubtedly some would say it is necessary to view the whole picture, including the effects of tyranny caused by credulousness, and also the increase of evil resulting from the increase of the ideal, men being incapable of such progress. But they could not doubt that the effect-Jesus was great and they would say with the dying Valery (these were the last lines in his notebook) that "the word love is only found associated with the name of God ... since the time of Christ." Yet they would immediately say that Jesus is a pure Idea. Regardless whether there was an exceptional historical personage in the beginning, religious thinking — that creator of dogmas — evolved very shortly thereafter to cover up the traces of this first highly doubtful experience. At least one can say that this religion, far and above every other known religion, has been the best representation of man's highest aspirations. And just as we call the geometry that accepts the three dimensions of space Euclidian geometry, without bothering to find out who Euclid was, so too we shall call the civilization that accepts the evangelical morality a Christian civilization without asking *who* Jesus *was* and we shall suspend judgment on this point.

But other minds will not accept this suspension of judgment. *They want to go from the Idea to the Existence* and take up the profound question, the only one worthy of the intellect: does this Idea of Jesus which has been so influential correspond to a personal reality? *To believe* means to accept this passage from the *idea* to the historical *reality* of this idea actually incarnate in time.

Are There Intermediate Solutions Between Affirmation and Denial?

Faced with the two solutions described above, one is tempted to look for, if not compromises, at least some intermediate options. I came across several during the course of these investigations, and they are indeed tempting, but I do not think they are very supportable. I notice that those who hold them are either tormented like people who accept two contraries at the same time, or I recognize their longing to adopt one of the two extremes.

1. One may revive the old Nestorian and Docetan division of the two Jesuses by insisting there are really two Christs, the first of which is the *Jesus of history* — a common man who never performed any miracles no matter what astounding things he did, and who died and never rose from the dead. The other Christ, the *Jesus of the faith,* is what the faith makes him out to be and whom it worships: the *Jesus of the faith* rose from the dead. Such was the heart of the thesis of liberal Protestants, of modernist Catholics, in brief of those who wished to associate without sacrifice what they thought to be the demand of science with the essence of the faith. Right now, this tendency might be represented in Bultmann's

posterity, if not in Bultmann himself, by the faithful who consider the Gospel a "true discourse," a kind of myth about
Jesus revealed by God — a myth that does not have to be
accepted so long as this history is historical in the realist
sense of the word.

2. At the opposite extreme, some people admit, prolonging
and improving Renan, that Jesus was an exceptional mystic,
a great inspired man, the chief of mystics and source of
mysticism, united to the fount of love more than any other
man. Bergson's *Two Sources of Morality and Religion* reflects
this thinking.

Such, today, are what I call the intermediary solutions
that try to preserve Jesus' Christianity while denying its
truth as the common faith understands it.

What I have said in this work sufficiently indicates that
to my way of thinking the solution of the two *Jesuses* amounts
to negation. Since the essence of faith and testimony is to
uphold the unity of Jesus Christ "true God and true man,"
it goes without saying that every expressed or implied division
of this unity takes the heart out of the Christian mystery:
whether one lives for it or dies for it.

I said this division is not a modern one. Actually it was
the first of many subsequent attempts to define Christianity
against which the genuine faith had to struggle and had to
be defined. The Johannine Gospel affirms this unity and
hence it is the first to refute this dichotomy. There are many
more deeply religious souls today than in the past who try
to hold both extremes at once. The resulting mental confusion
and indecision spawns their distress.

Now I shall examine the approach that studies Jesus as
a great and inspired man. I see in it a twofold tendency.

On one hand, like Bergson, the mind that sees Jesus as
the great inspired man, the *pneumatophore*, tends towards

the faith. And it is easy to see why. The more one ponders the *gap* separating Jesus from other inspired men, and the more the work of Jesus in the Church and in humanity is attributed to Jesus, the further one moves beyond the initial point of view. If anyone admits that Jesus had a unique influence, then it becomes easier for him to go all the way and grant him the fullness, for he is already walking upon the path that leads to the act formulated by: *I believe in you.*

On the other hand, if Jesus is viewed as a new emergence of the vague spiritual impulse that produced Buddha, Socrates, Mohammed, Francis of Assisi, Luther and others ... only a nebulous sort of religion will result. So, the work of the churches which cling to Jesus, that especially of the Catholic Church, seem like corruptions of Jesus' thought because of their refinements and anathemas. The authentic teaching of Jesus is reduced to highly imprecise assertions, and we are stepping to the very brink of pantheism, of becoming, of the thought of Hegel or Renan.

One will always see the intermediaries slip to one or the other tendency. And in a century like ours that, unlike the preceding one, condemns caution, compromises, contrived solutions, the mind will cut across the intermediaries and go the full limit. *Attestation* or *fabrication*: these will be the two terms lined up facing each other.[1]

Ultimately, *to believe in Jesus* and *to admit the historicity of Jesus* is one and the same act. And that is the drama. Only the solution that elevates you above history can fully respect history. To believe is to think that "it happened." Not to believe is to reject what is real and to trap within men's minds what only has the appearance of having happened. Between

---

1. One may admit attestation for the essentials and concede fabrication for the non-essentials, and it will be no less an attestation — conversely, one may admit fabrication for the essentials and concede attestation for some of the details, for most of the facts even, and it will be no less a fabrication.

these two attitudes which ultimately are related (the unbeliever can look upon the faith with admiration, regret and
desire; the believer can respect the unbeliever's doubt) there
looms up an abyss. Yet this great abyss can be leaped across
in life or at the end of life in a split second by an act of
thought.

It remains for me to say what from a critical standpoint
compels me to unceasingly make this act at every moment of
my life.

It is not Pascal's *Wager*.

I am convinced that when one goes down to a certain
depth the two theses are not opposed to each other with
equal force and appearance. One thesis glows increasingly
brighter as it is examined from many angles, though it is
overcast with shadow, enveloped in a net of difficulties whose
mesh-work can be described. Newman clearly showed this
aspect of certitude in religious or moral matters. Conviction
may be riddled throughout by swarms of doubts, but these
swarms do not form a part of the conviction just as dust par-
ticles are not part of light rays. Also, like grains of dust, these
difficulties do not form a body: they are not coherent. They
flutter about like shadows around a steady light.

Certitude is based on the ever more perceptible convergence of diverse lines of facts we are learning more about,
and of diverse experiences that are penetrated in the course
of a lifetime. And it is this convergence going on in time that
the deepest part of the intellect grasps in us: the spirit. The
intellect cannot avoid seeing the mark of the Spirit within
this convergence.

Hence, on another plane the solution of the problem posed
by Jesus resembles all other solutions of intellectual and
scientific research. At the conclusion of most researches the
intellect encounters a corpus of fact which seems to falsify
the conclusion because this conclusion appears contrary to
its laws and what it is accustomed to. Then a choice must be

made. Either we fall back on the mental constructions called axiom, reason, necessity, and reduce what would seem to be given, bending it to fit within the capacity of our intellects, or we fall back on this datum judged more certain, more durable, more real than the habitudes of the mind. The intellect is not made to surrender, but rather it is expanded and deepened. It is inseminated with a seed that is ultimately closely related to it.

The Eternal in Time

At the beginning of this study I said that our age preferred a Christ-History to an historical Jesus, God's evolution in mankind, God's shaping each man into a virtual Christ, rather than a divine insertion into a single privileged human nature situated at a particular point in time. We understand this desire to see the divine unfold and develop in humanity throughout the on-coming ages of civilization. It might be described today as the unformulated religion of disbelief when this disbelief is mystical.

The day may come when Marxism and Christianity will be combined. One cannot know what Arius, what Pelagius, will give it its name, style and color. But we can conceive how the elements will be proportioned. This future heresy would declare that Christ is similar to the dialectic, the immanent progression which urges mankind onward to surmount itself. It will say Jesus is the mythical and symbolical name for the longing to recapitulate the whole into unity. The Nazarene was perhaps the occasional cause of it all. But he *will* only truly be its real and final cause when the humanity he symbolized is unified. Such a combination of ideas should have its followers and win over many, even the masses, to its die like Arianism in the ensuing confusion. It will not be Christianity.

In other works I have tried to analyze pairs of minds of the highest order as they confront the problem of time in its relationship to salvation: in the contrast between Plotinus and Saint Augustine at the threshold of our civilization, between Leibnitz and Pascal at the beginning of modern times and, more recently, between Renan and Newman at the dawn of the awareness of history. I have long been aware of two kinds of intellectual attitudes in people: on one hand those who cannot accept a privileged history, a moment of incarnation, a supernatural person, who can accept the insertion of the divine provided that the divine be always and everywhere disseminated, diluted, dynamic. On the other hand, those who, affected by the special virtue of Christianity and without ceasing to admit the irradiation of the divine in history, fixed the point of origin of these rays in the historical Incarnation. Leibnitz would be inclined towards a progress, Pascal thought in terms of a singular Christ, the Christ of history who shed his blood for him. This is indeed the tragic wall of separation that has divided men's minds.[2]

Upon examining the facts, the believer professes that the Infinite has entered into the history of this sickly species, that he began with the smallest possible beginning (until his death which he did not want to linger on and on), that he knew all the stages of time uninterruptedly, that he took the form of time entirely upon himself and crossed every interval of that time. He adjusted himself to this gradual history beginning with a long prior history which, as all history, came to be summed up in the womb of a woman where all human history begins and begins again. This is how he wanted his first sojourn. This is how he wanted *to be born*, as we say. *To be born* is to sum up and to begin anew. It is to be oneself, individually, and to separate oneself from the phylum in order to work out an individual destiny.

The universal Christ contemporal with mankind, the mystical Christ growing in humanity, would be without roots

---

2. See **Plotin et Saint Augustin; Pascal et Leibniz; Renan et Newman** (Aubier Editeur).

and truth if he had not *existed* in the most normal sense from the womb of his mother to the womb of the earth where every human form takes its final repose. History can only be human by means of a knowledge of the past.

Such is the idea which emerges from my meditation: to study the concepts it presupposes and the consequences it includes would surely require many lifetimes of thinking. Man in his brief sojourn on earth can only scratch away at the surface of this work. But the thinking humanity can try it. Mankind must devote all its time to this task. Might it not be that leisure time and hours for thought have been given to mankind for just that purpose?

Kierkegaard's valid question — whether historical truths can form the foundation for an eternal life — would carry much weight indeed if Jesus were without roots in a past, without a subsistance and posterity in history, if he were like a sudden upheaval without any time-period either before it or after it. Because one cannot say it any better in so few words, let it suffice to quote Pascal as preserved by Filleau de la Chaise: "Most certainly all truths are eternal, are related to, and dependent upon, each other; and this chain holds not only for natural truths and morality, but even for the truths of fact, which one may say are in some way eternal since, being assigned to certain points of eternity and space, they form a body subsisting all at once for God."

Problem of Jesus and
Problem of God

The problem I have raised is largely of no concern to many people today because it is resolved in advance.

This is not the first time while studying the genesis of convictions that I have run across the power of IN ADVANCE, that is, of prior assent. How we must be ever on our guard to protect the accused from being found guilty *in advance,* to keep the auditors from being convinced and predisposed! Freedom is barely introduced into these spheres where, when it seems to appear, the games are judged *in advance.*

The axe-blow of doubt is falling much lower yet these days, for today it is not Jesus who is being discussed, but rather the very existence, the very possibility, of God. How could anyone who is certain that the problem of God is a meaningless one find any sense at all in the problem of Jesus?

In the age of philosophical deism one could believe in God without admitting the existence of Jesus, and secular education during that period of bourgeois compromise marking the nineteenth century was programed with that in mind. They then sought a middle-ground for respectable agreement between materialism and the Christian faith — vague "spiritualism" clothed in biblical wrappings that nearly became the official religion of Europe and, especially of the New World.

Furthermore, the existence of Islam and some of the greatest names in Greek philosophy show us that belief in God is distinct from faith in Jesus. It is clear to those who philosophize that belief in God may be justified without any preliminary religious faith — the Church teaches this when she stresses what Saint Paul thought when he held the pagans inexcusable because they did not conclude to the invisibilities of God from the things he had created.

But if we step off the plane of right and onto the plane of fact, contemporary fact, we are not far from seeing the time appear when there will be not distinction between those who admit God exists and those who believe in the divine person of Jesus. For many, the two problems are interdependent. M. Couchoud correctly observed that the Eternal One is in fact no longer adored alone in the Western World, but in and through Jesus. In England the unitarian is little different from the agnostic; in France the deist is practically equivalent to an atheist. In short, here and there people pray only to the God of Jesus.

Possibly the time will come when this division of minds into two universes according to two gravitations will have achieved its ultimate extreme: the pole of militant atheism becomes a religion, a worldly mystical doctrine, the pole of the Church which will gather together once more into itself all who believe in the existence of God. The unstable intermediate positions will disappear or will gravitate towards one or the other of these poles.

This real connection of the belief in God and of the belief in Jesus is explained through two profound reasons. I have heard it said that when Claudel's sister, Camille, got him to read Renan's *Life of Jesus,* he did not hesitate and immediately concluded, "If Renant is right, there is no God." And he drew the consequences out of that. If God does exist, he must be defined by perfection, and if Jesus is a myth, one must attribute to the absolute being who is conceived as trustworthy, fully respectful of his creatures, the sovereign educator of consciences and master over chance — a morose and cruel irony. Sadism then would define the ultimate secret of the divine moral law. God has made sport of this so-called privileged species by leading it through so many appearances and verisimilitudes to take for the revealer and even more so, for a divine person, this ambiguous scarcely existing being called Jesus, around whom have gathered, like jackals encircling a corpse, all the infirmities of the mind and soul. And this misunderstanding is not limited to merely the Jews in a single moment of history: it strikes the finest and wisest and most noble of natures. Irony, finally, carried this time to the third power, common error, divine "false witness" have had more fortunate effects on man than the knowledge of real results and real causes. The misinterpretation of Jesus has become the ferment for man's highest achievements: it has been the motive and regenerative element of history in the West.

Reflections of this kind are not long tenable. It is better
to proceed immediately the consequence and say: *If there is
no Jesus, it is because God does not exist.* This non-existence
of God, which has some vague support in the silence of nature
and in the reality of evil, is masterfully confirmed in the
criticism of the Christian origins. For we can almost verify
through positive methods on this point the non-existence of
a divine love. It is clear that along with the burden of suffering, the continued and ever renewed existence of the Christian
illusion, especially under this exceedingly precise, categorical
and insolent form which Roman Catholicism gives to it, is
the most valuable and most palpable argument one can find
against the existence of an infinite being and perfection
ultimately defined by love. And contemporary atheism has at
its disposal an unceasing easy to understand and effective
confirmation.

But can one who sees only this way of feeling, reasoning
and concluding be reversed in his decision? I believe that
the reflections presented in this work will help such a one
to reverse the *con* for the *pro*.

If, having left the existence of God in doubt, one takes
the question by the other end, that is if one starts with the
given subject of Jesus: if one does not look to deny this in
advance by the postulate that there is no God, if one admits
the convergence of many lines of experience in favor of the
fact of Jesus — then one can rationally ask himself how,
apart from a Providence amicable to man, one could explain
the insertion of this Inprobability into the context of history.
If God is related to Jesus (in the sense that to deny God is
to nullify all meaning in the very problem of Jesus) one can
say that to make a real being and not a myth out of the
Gospel Jesus is equivalent to give back to God his chance for
existence in the eyes of many people.

I would say that it is even to give to God's existence a
density, a presence, an intimacy reconciled to the exigencies

of modern minds, for the fact of Jesus is like a new plane of existence. It is a basic given more accessible to man that the domain of the universe or even the realm of the moral life. "Existence by itself," said Hamelin, "in the absolute sense, the universe with its so desperately vast and profound organization, are prodigious burdens. But the load is not too much for God to bear." But humanity, taken up with its work or sorrows, absorbed in its techniques or concepts, dazed and, so to speak, materialized by its conquests over matter, has not acquired the thinking ability to ascend to God either from the world itself or from consciousness. One must either have a rare metaphysical aptitude or be in a state of innocence before he can attempt a meditation on the universe, on its admirable order seen at all levels, on its well-proportioned chance events, its advantages for the improbable thing life is, for the still more improbable thing which is the human species and the evolution of this species in spite of so many obstacles, and everything which inclines the reason to believe that there exists a creating, regulating, concerned cause sovereignly ruling over man.

Now if we take the examination of the interior life as a starting point, particularly in the experience of man's incapacity to abandon himself to the infinite being who fashioned him, then one finds himself before a second given subject distinct from the first, which is like a second world present within the world and which, by thought, envelops it. This second world is more easy to explore because one merely has to reflect upon the experience of existence. It speaks to human minds more distinctly, and every man carries this world within himself. Those who, like Pascal or Maurice Blondel, have explored it have had more of a hearing.

Perhaps these two planes still lack something, for if one begins with the universe, then the God that one attains by the cosmos is an Infinite Planner. If one beings with consciousness one finds himself at the feet of an unrepresentable Law or Infinity. Yet the inability to see what is conceived does not divert one who thinks; but it is difficult for one enamoured with experience who will always falter before a faceless infinite being. Now, the fact of Jesus, when examined in itself and then situated into integral history, become a third plane of the given subject. This third plane is in accord with the other two, but it is more meaningful and better proportioned to that light for which man begs, to guide him in his existence.

The Final Dialogue — The Unbeliever:

But why then do you compel me to make a choice? I realize that an argument from fact will never confound the faith, as it was thought in the nineteenth century, particularly in the realm of exegesis. It is already evident around 1910, after the promising beginning of this century, that the faith had not suffered from the fact of historical knowledge. The two adversaries stood their ground. Those who had science working for them and those who had it apparently against them no longer are seen in conflict as in the preceding century. At first sight some ambivalent facts could be interpreted in the sense of faith and also of doubt and negation. In the last few years the ideal of the coherent and the rational (in the ancient sense of the word which has been that of the sciences since their Greek origin) lost its absolute value. Today science develops by assuming the impossible in advance: science makes its discoveries through paradox, through the apparently absurd, through the unrepresentable and nearly inconceivable. Why then should it censure the faith for being mysterious? It is evident now by what atheists declare, that atheism involves more absurdity than the belief in God involves mystery. But since there is no verification possible in the domain of faith, I find that I lack the illumination and energy to make a choice.

"The stakes are high because this is a choice involving existence. We need an almost invincible probability to make

this choice an intelligent one. How can you ask me to ex-
change anything for the practically unchangeable element
that is the habit of my life and thought — by taking a stand
on some strange phenomena whose only witnesses were a
few Orientals twenty centuries ago who had no critical background?

"I shall go further. Even though these events were real,
and you were correct to believe them, how can you condemn
me if I remain in the attitude of expectancy and declare with
the rest of mankind, 'I am unable to know, I am reluctant to
believe.' Because, in spite of everything, it seems more reasonable to assume that these phenomena, though highly improbable, are natural, I find it more prudent to stay in the
non-hostile state of ignorance.

"And if later on I am to be judged culpable for my indifference, I shall use the solid argument of the disproportion
of proof for my defense. I shall tell the Judge that he is
responsible for my uncertainty and that I do not possess
the additional strength called faith which he alone can give
me if he exists. Without faith I cannot bridge the final
gap."[3]

---

3. The deceased master of historical studies, Lucien Febvre, wrote
the following moving lines about my past examinations: "It is clear that
the exegetes of the Christian origins have been spending an immense
effort for the past century, working from a few documents picked up
time and again and analyzed, dissected, put back together and compared
— only to confuse a bit more what they thought they knew. It is obvious
helplessness certified by the fact that each exegete ends up with his
own kind of Jesus who, different from the Jesus the next exegete will
construct, but all noteworthy if the exegete does not write in the form
of a novel (as Renan did throughout his book of 1863), his great book
or books are always only 'written around Jesus': a peripheral assemblage
of inconsistent data circumscribing a void just-inhabited by a barely
tangible shadow — it is certain that the futility of this work will lead
only to two conclusions. Either to an acknowledgment of impotency:
'It is useless to go on.' Or to a recourse to the faith which carries the
believer beyond the limitations of positive reason and into the mystery
accepted as such. — But this is easy to say and quickly said. Does M.

The Believer:

"If you have read the account of how my thinking developed, you will see that I studied the plausible motives for not believing. I took sides with them and submitted them to a trial by fire. I was influenced by the failure of the opposite explanation carried out to its final conclusions when all its postulates and consequences were unravelled. I have grown inflexibly against them. My voice has been neither one of pure affirmation nor refutation, but it has been a much deeper one, being the voice of obligation born of reflection, and it does not impinge on my freedom. As for me, without judging anyone, I am happy to have lived in the twentieth century where this path is clearer and more intimate than it was before the development of positive knowledge, for I have a greater opportunity 'to give reasons to whomever asks me to justify the hope that is in me.' Being what I am, it would be impossible for me to remain in your state of uncertainty without debasing the noble part of my being which desires to advance always at whatever cost toward the point where there is more reason and light. When death comes to you and me, sooner or later (but however far off death may be, it is absolutely negligible), then we shall see which of us was right. Your eternal experience then will be the only confirmation I aim at in these reflections made in the time of shadows and responsibilities. There is nothing more to be said. Let us keep quiet. Let us not disturb."

Guitton's attempt ultimately add very much to this short conclusion? And how many men formed, as he says, 'in the school of Goethe' consent to run straightway onto the path of the mystery when they have read it, instead of simply concluding: 'We do not know'? How are we to determine they are on equal footing? I mean by what appeal to reason?"

My book has attempted to answer this question.

CHAPTER XVI

On the Road to Emmaus

If I had to sum up the whole Gospel in one scene, I would not hesitate to choose that of the disciples on the road to Emmaus.

It may well have been Saint Luke's intention to write it as a transition between the interval when the visible history of Jesus ended and his invisible presence began. It may have been his intention to depict the progress of the faith in people's minds through decreasing difficulties. This book is but an explanatory note written in the margins of that ancient text, for in each educated man, perphaps especially in our times, there are always two beings who secretly argue about Jesus.

Two persons are exchanging words as they walk along the road. They talk about what is always so evident in this world: the downfall of founders, conflicting appearances, deception, unkept promises. And in particular, the absurdity of the movement of Jesus which did not materialize and which is proof that there is no more basis for hope. There is no end to solid reasons for doubting, and each disciple adds his personal doubts to those of the other disciple. And while they are speaking, the Problem they are talking about is walking with them. He places himself in the center of their being in the guise of a zeal to learn. They listen to him, like some who have just read this book, without finding anything to

cling to, but with a condescending air and to convince themselves once again by the failure of my reasons that this question is eternally insoluble. But Luke lets us see the rekindling
of light in the darkness of shadow. Just when the material
day is waning, the spiritual day begins to dawn. The unexpected mystery at hand, incomprehensible but not unthinkable, reveals himself in many ways: through the sense
of presence, through illumination from the past and what
was written of this past, through his act of bearing witness
to himself, a community created in their consciousness by
the sharing of bread, through an enigmatical and tender
intimacy, a mysterious rite. Then the Eternal One disappears
just when they need him most.

After which there is nothing left in time but traces, that
is the memories to revive, accounts to repreat, creeds to
formulate, absences to support, witness to give, foundations
that must be made because there is duration to fill, because
time continues — this time which one indeed realizes from
having tested it in a moment of plenitude is already inseminated by an eternal being.

While refining my reflections about Jesus I have often
had the same kind of experience. At first I handled the abstract
ideas according to very strict rules of reasoning. Then by
the obligation born of thinking, I was put in the presence of
something or other that defied analysis and was sketched in
these outlines by my attempt to question them, like a hand
in the night gropingly explores an object and defines it by
the sense of touch. Then, armed with questionings which
were my tools for learning the opposite hypothesis of mine,
and giving them as much credit as I could, then, in spite of
that, perhaps because of it, I became aware of an element at
once deep-seated and refractory: an X source of light, provided it is not reduced in advance. By what word in our
language could I designate this presence, this resistance that

is at the same time opaque and transparent? Only the purest term, the one seemingly most void of suggestions, the commonest would do. Let us say that this X is closely related to that which in us and outside us and above us we call BEING. One can experience BEING in things and persons on condition that one lives with them every day, and one exercises all one's powers. But there is perhaps no more passionate reason to experience Being by using today's knowledge than the problem raised by Jesus. IT IS: this profound and simple word through which everything begins and ends, how long it takes to learn it! The research we have just completed shines a bit of light on it, if it is true that the lesser forms of being exist in the greater in a nobler way than in themselves.

Every time one analyzes a real subject to find out what it is, one experiences an intimacy. How much more in this case! As one penetrates the folds of this extraordinary problem, the marvelous aspect, that of strangeness and the incredible that it assumes which frustrates so many minds and makes them see Christianity as something like a very nice legend — the side which blinds one — is effaced. Insecurity, dread, the feeling of an inassimilable impossibility (these first states of consciousness in the encounter with the mystery) vanish and give way to a feeling of human verisimilitude, if one at least does not believe it unthinkable that the absolute could take on a human form.

This metamorphosis of the attitude of the mind is similar to what one observes when he encounters a work of art which he was quite incapable of conceiving possible, but which, once it is proposed to him, and especially once he has lived with it, appears given to him at the same time as he is given to it, admitted into existence forever.

That by no means prevents the obscurities from subsisting. The difficulties remain because the solutions do not absorb them any more than the light can suppress the shadow cast by the object. The night is never more than the shadow of the earth illuminated from the invisible side.

But the obscurity which then subsists is similar to that of the union of soul and body, or again to the obscurity of the mind's knowledge of the world. It is of the same nature as this turbid transparency in which we move, live and are, but which is so favorable, which perhaps is necessary after the human manner of knowing, loving, and obtaining.

*   *   *

Now, what will the future have in store for the human race? Perhaps man has not yet reached his maturity and that this instant of twenty centuries since Jesus simply represents man's pre-infancy period. *Perhaps the experience has lasted long enough* and is on the verge of completion. But, as I have often said, time is of no importance. We are witnessing a kind of regrouping of nations, an attempt at recapitulation into unity. But around what principle, what center and by what source? Is there a BEING, an IDEA, an EXISTENCE who really in our days would permit men to unite, to progress whatever their level, to redress their losses in an instant? It seems to me that the history of Jesus, illuminated by the history of the ages preceding it and the twenty centuries following it, permits me to answer that quention. We have performed nearly all the experiments, we have exhausted all the negations, and there is no other name that can be spoken which gives the man of the twentieth century hope and joy.